The Poetry of Ernest Jones
Myth, Song, and the 'Mighty Mind'

LEGENDA

LEGENDA, founded in 1995 by the European Humanities Research Centre of the University of Oxford, is now a joint imprint of the Modern Humanities Research Association and Routledge. Titles range from medieval texts to contemporary cinema and form a widely comparative view of the modern humanities, including works on Arabic, Catalan, English, French, German, Greek, Italian, Portuguese, Russian, Spanish, and Yiddish literature. An Editorial Board of distinguished academic specialists works in collaboration with leading scholarly bodies such as the Society for French Studies, the British Comparative Literature Association and the Association of Hispanists of Great Britain & Ireland.

MHRA

The Modern Humanities Research Association (MHRA) encourages and promotes advanced study and research in the field of the modern humanities, especially modern European languages and literature, including English, and also cinema. It aims to break down the barriers between scholars working in different disciplines and to maintain the unity of humanistic scholarship in the face of increasing specialization. The Association fulfils this purpose through the publication of journals, bibliographies, monographs, critical editions, and the *MHRA Style Guide*, and by making grants in support of research.

www.mhra.org.uk

LONDON AND NEW YORK

Routledge is a global publisher of academic books, journals and online resources in the humanities and social sciences. Founded in 1836, it has published many of the greatest thinkers and scholars of the last hundred years, including Adorno, Einstein, Russell, Popper, Wittgenstein, Jung, Bohm, Hayek, McLuhan, Marcuse and Sartre. Today Routledge is one of the world's leading academic publishers in the Humanities and Social Sciences. It publishes thousands of books and journals each year, serving scholars, instructors, and professional communities worldwide.

www.routledge.com

EDITORIAL BOARD

Chairman
Professor Colin Davis, Royal Holloway, University of London

Professor Malcolm Cook, University of Exeter (French)
Professor Robin Fiddian, Wadham College, Oxford (Spanish)
Professor Anne Fuchs, University of Warwick (German)
Professor Paul Garner, University of Leeds (Spanish)
Professor Andrew Hadfield, University of Sussex (English)
Professor Marian Hobson Jeanneret,
Queen Mary University of London (French)
Professor Catriona Kelly, New College, Oxford (Russian)
Professor Martin McLaughlin, Magdalen College, Oxford (Italian)
Professor Martin Maiden, Trinity College, Oxford (Linguistics)
Professor Peter Matthews, St John's College, Cambridge (Linguistics)
Dr Stephen Parkinson, Linacre College, Oxford (Portuguese)
Professor Suzanne Raitt, William and Mary College, Virginia (English)
Professor Ritchie Robertson, The Queen's College, Oxford (German)
Professor David Shepherd, Keele University (Russian)
Professor Michael Sheringham, All Souls College, Oxford (French)
Professor Alison Sinclair, Clare College, Cambridge (Spanish)
Professor David Treece, King's College London (Portuguese)

Managing Editor
Dr Graham Nelson
41 Wellington Square, Oxford OX1 2JF, UK

www.legendabooks.com

Ceramic jug commemorating Ernest Jones — patriot, poet, politician.
Reproduced by kind permission of the Working Class Movement Library, Salford.

The Poetry of Ernest Jones

Myth, Song, and the 'Mighty Mind'

Simon Rennie

Modern Humanities Research Association and Routledge
2016

Published by the
Modern Humanities Research Association
Salisbury House, Station Road, Cambridge CB1 2LA
and
Routledge
2 Park Square, Milton Park, Abingdon, Oxon OX14 4RN
and 711 Third Avenue, New York, NY 10017

LEGENDA is an imprint of the
Modern Humanities Research Association and Routledge

Routledge is an imprint of the Taylor & Francis Group, an informa business

ISBN 978-1-909662-90-2 (hbk)
ISBN 978-1-315-56054-0 (ebk)

First published 2016

All rights reserved. No part of this publication may be reproduced or disseminated or transmitted in any form or by any means, electronic, mechanical, photocopying, recording or otherwise, or stored in any retrieval system, or otherwise used in any manner whatsoever without the express permission of the copyright owner

Disclaimer: Statements of fact and opinion contained in this book are those of the author and not of the editors, Routledge, or the Modern Humanities Research Association. The publisher makes no representation, express or implied, in respect of the accuracy of the material in this book and cannot accept any legal responsibility or liability for any errors or omissions that may be made.

Trademark notice: Product or corporate names may be trademarks or registered trademarks, and are used only for identification and explanation without intent to infringe.

Library of Congress Cataloging in Publication Data
A catalog record for this book has been requested

© Modern Humanities Research Association and Routledge 2016

Printed in Great Britain

Cover: 875 Design

Copy-Editor: Charlotte Brown

CONTENTS

	Acknowledgements	ix
	Abbreviations	x
	Preface	xi
	Introduction	1
1	Influences and Early Poetry (1840–45)	11
2	Jones and Myth (1846–48)	44
3	The 'Mighty Mind' (1846–48)	66
4	Lyrical Prison Poetry (1848–50)	90
5	'The New World, a Democratic Poem' (1851)	126
6	Pseudonymity, Revision, Songs of the Low and High (1851–60)	167
	Conclusion	200
	Bibliography	204
	Index	210

*To Libby, whose love has been the prime mover
in this project, and in my life*

ACKNOWLEDGEMENTS

I am profoundly grateful to Professor Francis O'Gorman of the University of Leeds, whose support, engagement, and erudition have been invaluable to the composition of this study.

A vital contributor in terms of critical discussions on the subject of the poetry of Ernest Jones and Chartist poetry in general has been Dr Mike Sanders (University of Manchester) who, along with Professor Malcom Chase (University of Leeds), encouraged my initial interest in Chartist poetics.

I am grateful for the intellectual stimulation provided by discussions (however brief) with the following people: Owen Ashton, Ian Heywood, Brian Maidment, Alec Newman, Michael O'Neill, Stephen Roberts, Mark Sandy, Miles Taylor, Herbert Tucker, and Roy Vickers. If I have omitted anybody from this list I apologize.

I also wish to thank Adrian Knapp for his assistance in translating Jones's German-language poetry from the *Deutsche Londoner Zeitung*.

Finally, I am indebted to my partner, Libby Tempest, for allowing a long-dead Chartist to become the third person in our relationship.

S.R., Exeter, July 2015

ABBREVIATIONS

BD	*The Battle-Day: and Other Poems*
CJ	*Court Journal*
CTFC	*Corayda: A Tale of Faith and Chivalry and Other Poems*
EJMP	Ernest Jones Manuscript Poetry
MCRO	Manchester County Record Office
MP	*Morning Post*
NP	*Notes to the People*
NS	*Northern Star*
PT	*Poetic Thoughts of E. C. J.*
RT	*Rhymes on the Times*

PREFACE

This book studies the poetry of Ernest Charles Jones (1819–69) from 1840 to 1860. One of its aims is to cast further light on the critically neglected area of Chartist poetry, and to investigate the social, political, and aesthetic implications of poetry whose explicit function is that of propaganda or polemic. As well as offering close analysis of many poems which have not been studied before, this work presents previously unrecorded poems by Jones and, most importantly, a complete collection of his pseudonymous poetry. A study of original manuscripts has provided significant insight into Jones's process of poetic revision, and some of his German-language poetry has been translated for the first time.

My research covers Jones's first publications in conservative newspapers shortly after his arrival in Great Britain from the German Duchy of Holstein, his early Chartist period, his imprisonment, and his years as the effective leader of Chartism. Although the six chapters are in broadly chronological order, each addresses a conceptual or contextual theme. These are, consecutively: poetic influence; mythopoeia; poet/reader relationships; prison writing; epic poetry; and poetic revision.

Themes recurring throughout the study include the political and literary implications of republication and revision; the relationship between poetry and politics in the early Victorian period; the figure of the 'gentleman radical' and his relationship with his readership; the influence of Romantic legacies on mid-nineteenth-century radical poetics; links between Chartist and Irish nationalist poetry; and intersections between radical and conservative imaginative conceptions of the past. Close analysis of the poetry is consistently related to its historical, political, and cultural circumstances — the declarative and socially-engaged nature of Chartist poetry demands it be studied alongside its extra-literary contexts. What emerges from this study is a new version of Ernest Jones, a political poet whose exceptional complexity is here fully mapped for the first time.

INTRODUCTION

This study of the poetry of Ernest Charles Jones (1819–69) reveals important aspects of the cultural intersections between Victorian social classes, between the conservative and radical imaginations, and between German and British literary cultures. The poetry that Jones produced as a Chartist 'gentleman radical' straddles the formal boundaries between poetry and song, poetry and polemic, poetry and propaganda. More than a century and a half after their composition, Jones's most popular short pieces, 'The Song of the Low' (sometimes known as 'The Song of the Lower Classes') and 'The Blackstone Edge Gathering', are still occasionally sung, and beyond any evocation of radical nostalgia, they still possess the power to stir the singer and listener with sentiments which appear perennially relevant.[1] Bearing in mind this continued emotional agency, the thematic triumvirate providing the subtitle to this study — myth, song, and the 'mighty mind' — represents culturally generated, imagined futures or histories; poetry as a communal experience or as a means of mass communication; and the nature of the relationship between writers and their readerships.[2] The study of Ernest Jones's poetry, and what that poetry can reveal about the cultures from which it emerged, and which it aimed to shape, leads to exploration of each element of this triumvirate, and their interdependent relationships.

It is a critical commonplace that canonical mid-nineteenth-century poetry inherited and adapted the Romantic lyrical voice, but it is less widely appreciated that the radical poetry of the same period embraced and modified Romanticism's political legacy. The Chartists, through widely-read newspapers including the *Northern Star and National Trades' Journal* (hereafter referred to as the *Northern Star* or abbreviated to *NS*), brought to political poetry an unprecedented immediacy, redefining the nature of radical poetics for a working-class generation undergoing the social upheaval brought about by rapid industrialization and urbanization. Perhaps because there is no real modern equivalent to this kind of politico-poetic discourse, the study of politically declarative mid-nineteenth-century poetry has been critically neglected. Successive artistic movements subsequent to this period, including aestheticism and modernism, tended to create distance between poetry and politics by the construction of walls with variable degrees of permeability, and our understanding of the nature of the relationship between poetry and politics in the early Victorian period is skewed by our absorption of this attitude. This work, through the study of Jones's poetry, aims to enhance our understanding of the radical poetry of his time, to look beneath its polemical surface, and to explore its purpose and properties in greater depth.

2 INTRODUCTION

The Critical Field and a Chapter Overview

Critical material that deals directly with Chartist poetics is growing but much remains to be studied and written. In many ways, the only comparable precedent to this work is Mike Sanders's *The Poetry of Chartism: Aesthetics, Politics, History*.[3] Sanders's book was the first serious critical work to deal exclusively with Chartist poetry and provided a valuable critical survey of the *Northern Star* poetry pages through the crucial years of the Chartist struggle. Needless to say, Ernest Jones featured in that work and this study attempts to narrow the critical focus to that particular writer, but also to broaden the critical field into his pre- and what might be termed extra-Chartist poetry. I have also made use of two notable journal articles on the specific subject of Ernest Jones's poetry which are Ronald Paul's '"In Louring Hindostan": Chartism and Empire in Ernest Jones's 'The New World, a Democratic Poem',[4] and Roy Vickers's 'Christian Election, Holy Communion and Psalmic Language in Ernest Jones's Chartist Poetry'.[5] Works which deal more broadly with radical or working-class Victorian literary production but include critical material on Jones include Isobel Armstrong's *Victorian Poetry: Poetry, Poetics and Politics* (1993),[6] and Anne Janowitz's *Lyric and Labour in the Romantic Tradition* (1998).[7] The latter in particular contains an invaluable sustained engagement with Jones's writings. In common with the present study, these works are indebted to the pioneering work of Mary Ashraf in *Political Verse and Song from Britain and Ireland* (1975)[8] and Brian Maidment in *The Poorhouse Fugitives: Self-taught Poets and Poetry in Victorian Britain* (1987).[9]

The biographical material on which this study relies so heavily has been collated from contemporary sources (including Jones's diary material stored at the Manchester County Record Office) and accounts from the twentieth century, including the introduction to John Saville's *Ernest Jones: Chartist* (1952).[10] But by far the greatest debt of gratitude in this regard is due to Miles Taylor's *Ernest Jones, Chartism, and the Romance of Politics 1819–1869* (2003).[11] There may be points at which different conclusions or interpretations are reached by this study, but Taylor's accuracy and depth of research is largely unassailable, and his work will provide a central basis for Jones scholars for many years to come. While Taylor's work contains a useful bibliography of Jones's writings, my own research for this study has uncovered previously critically unknown, published poems, and even, most importantly, a complete, though pseudonymous, poetry collection. Other primary sources have been Jones's own manuscripts, and newspapers and collections held at the British Library. An invaluable resource has been the digitization of the *Northern Star*, along with many other nineteenth-century newspapers, accessible through Gale online. Needless to say, the ease of accessibility and collation made possible by the on-going digitization of historical texts has been of great benefit to this work. However, a measure of British critical neglect of the peculiarly British cultural phenomenon of Chartist poetics is that the most useful collection of Chartist poetry remains Y. V. Kovalev's excellent *An Anthology of Chartist Literature* (1956).[12] Volumes consulted which are more broadly concerned with Chartist history include Malcolm Chase's *Chartism: A New History* (2007),[13] Dorothy Thompson's *The Chartists: Popular Politics* in the Industrial Revolution (1984),[14] and works exploring the cultural implications of Chartism including *The Chartist Legacy* (1999), edited by Owen Ashton, Robert Fryson, and Stephen Roberts.[15] In this last volume, Timothy Randall's essay, 'Chartist Poetry and Song', has been of particular use.[16]

Jones's habit of re-using poetic material, with or without revising or renaming, has led to some critical confusion in the past, but also poses a challenge to the chronological approach with regards to the question of when to discuss poetry which has been published twice, or sometimes even three times, many years apart, and in different political contexts. The fact that Jones increased this practice toward the end of his poetic career has led to the first and final chapters of this study being closely linked in theme and content, even as the same or similar poetry is encountered by sometimes very different readerships. Chapter One discusses Jones's early, pre-Chartist poetry, but also assesses the influences on his work which carry through to his radical phase. As one might expect, British Romantic figures including Byron, Wordsworth, and especially Shelley, feature heavily in this discussion, but Jones, uniquely, also brought to Chartist poetics the influence of German writers including Ernst Moritz Arndt (1769–1860), Friedrich Leopold von Stolberg (1750–1819), Friedrich Rückert (1788–1866), Ludwig Ühland (1787–1862), and Friedrich Schiller (1755–1805). Jones translated the poetry of each of these writers but his work also displays their influence, particularly in its mythic representations of youth, war, and rural idealism. The interaction between Jones's Germanic approach to these themes and British Chartist political concerns including the physical/moral force argument or the Land Plan contributes largely to his early Chartist poetry's distinctiveness and its undoubted popularity with working-class readers.

Chapter Two focuses on the poetry that Jones published in the *Northern Star* between 1846 and 1848, and approaches this work through a mythopoeic critical perspective. The links between poetry and myth have been discussed by critics from Horace onwards, but the reliance of political poetry on mythic formations and tropes has largely gone unstudied. Jones's Chartist poetry provides numerous examples of mythopoeic adaptations of narratives of deliverance and fertility, and also exemplifies how the seemingly conservative Victorian preoccupation with all things medieval can be filtered through a radical re-reading of history. There is also discussion of the barely-studied links between the Chartist and Irish nationalist poetic traditions. Chapter Three analyzes poetry from the same period, but uses it to assess the nature of the evolving relationship between Jones and his predominantly working-class audience, exploring how Jones used his poetry to negotiate this relationship, and incorporating discussion of phenomenology and reader response theory. There is also broader discussion of the response to Jones's poetry in the mainstream and conservative press. Because of its contemporary popularity and the multiple issues it raises with regard to Chartist culture and the nature and function of poetry itself, the poetry that Jones produced in the first two years of his Chartist involvement justifies the attention of two separate chapters approaching it from different critical perspectives.

Similarly, the poetry that Jones produced during his time in prison between 1848 and 1850 provides material for two chapters. Chapter Four concentrates on the

4 INTRODUCTION

lyrical poetry that Jones wrote while in prison which was published on his release in the *Notes to the People* newspaper in 1851.[17] These twenty-four poems, which are presented almost as a discrete collection in Jones's own newspaper, represent a retreat into the writer's own consciousness but serve as evidence of his suffering for the Chartist cause, and of his intellectual fitness to lead the Chartist movement. They also provide the basis for a discussion of the nature of prison writing by political detainees throughout the nineteenth century and beyond. Chapter Five is devoted to 'The New World', the visionary epic that Jones conceived in prison, which also appeared in the pages of *Notes to the People* in 1851 but was republished in 1857 as *The Revolt of Hindostan* to capitalize on its apparent prediction of the Indian Uprising of that year. Because of its length and status as Jones's magnum opus, the contemporary and modern reception of 'The New World' is discussed before a canto-by-canto analysis explores the themes and arguments of the poem.

The sixth and final chapter provides a survey of Jones's poetry 1852–60, from the post-prison *Notes to the People* material to the *Corayda* collection, which was his last published poetry. This period sees a diffusion of Jones's poetic styles but also an increase in the amount of republished material. There is also discussion of two pseudonymous collections, *Rhymes on the Times* (1852), which appears to be an attempt to attack the Whigs by supporting the Tories, and *Poetic Thoughts of E. C. J.* (1856), which is a largely apolitical volume containing Romantic and 'light' material. Neither of these collections has been critically discussed to any degree; indeed the latter has never been critically identified as the work of Jones. Jones's poetic shift toward the mainstream in the mid-1850s, with collections dealing either ostensibly or explicitly with issues raised by the Crimean War (1853–56) from a relatively patriotic perspective, forms the basis of an exploration into the nature of Jones's politico-poetic response to the decline of Chartism. As some republished material is directly or contextually depoliticized, the question of Jones's indeterminate social status as a gentleman radical is raised once more, as his poetic identity enters into something of a rapprochement with his pre-Chartist self, and his political identity shifts towards the centre ground.

A Brief Biography and Historical Survey

As a historical figure, Ernest Charles Jones has attracted controversy. The first major history of Chartism, R. G. Gammage's *History of the Chartist Movement 1837–54* (first published in 1854), was consistently critical of Jones both personally and as a political leader, as evinced by one entry in the index: 'Jones, Ernest, [...] dishonourable conduct of'.[18] Jones's modern biographer, Taylor, concludes his work, *Ernest Jones, Chartism and the Romance of Politics 1819–1869*, with a paragraph that contains the following assessment of his subject's character:

> Even if the conventions of romanticism required Jones to blur fact and fiction, he still emerges at times as duplicitous and unpleasant: in short, a liar, a cheat, an anti-Semite, a racist bigot, an absent father, and a neglectful husband.[19]

If a more sympathetic observer were to note that the last two character flaws might be attributed to Jones's unstinting dedication to the cause of Chartism and the plight of the early Victorian working class, then an even more recent historical survey could be cited to render the Jones family's personal sacrifice politically worthless. In Chase's *Chartism: A New History*, Jones is characterized as a major contributor to Chartism's post-1850 decline: 'Jones's second coming as a Chartist leader [...] split an already fractious movement further rather than helped heal it'.[20] However, the century-and-a-half span of this kind of criticism should be considered alongside more positive opinions of Jones's contributions to mid-nineteenth-century radical politics contained in the biographical introduction to Saville's *Ernest Jones: Chartist*, and in Dorothy Thompson's *The Chartists: Popular Politics in the Industrial Revolution*. Indeed, Jones was widely celebrated as a Chartist hero and martyr during his lifetime and subsequently, mainly due to the incontrovertible fact that he was imprisoned for two years for his activism in 1848 and immediately returned to the cause on his release.

But what of Jones the poet? It is part of this study's ambition to engage with Jones's poetry without entering too much into the debate about the man, but in the case of this body of work any attempt to separate the text from its surrounding social, historical, political, and even biographical context would be counterproductive. A significant proportion of Jones's poetry was directly engaged with the political and social questions of the day, and altered its form and content in direct response to events in his life. For this reason, though the text is always the primary concern, its relevance to the outside world, and the outside world's relevance to it, is almost always part of the discussion. Jones lived an extraordinary life in extraordinary times, and as the title of Taylor's biography suggests, poetry was a large part of that life's social and political development.

Ernest Charles Jones was born into the royal court of Berlin on 25 January 1819, the year of the Peterloo Massacre, a long way, geographically and socially, from the struggles of the British working class. He was in part named after his father, Captain Charles Jones, and the man to whom his father was equerry and aide-de-camp, Ernst Augustus, the Duke of Cumberland (1771–1851), uncle to the future Queen Victoria, fifth son of George III, and the future King Ernst of Hanover (1837–51). Young Ernest was something of a child prodigy; when he was eleven his family had a volume of his poetry published entitled *Infantine Effusions* (Hamburg: F. H. Nestler, 1830), which contained several lyric efforts and a section of Voltaire's *Henriade* translated from the French. In the same year he also had a short story entitled 'The Invalid's Pipe' included in *Ackermann's Juvenile Forget Me Not*, a London-published anthology of writing for children. Although primarily anglophone, Jones grew up absorbing the cultural influences of his family's adopted country, being taught at home by German scholars before being formally educated at a German language school, St Michael's College in Lower Saxony, from 1835. He did not live in Great Britain until his family returned there in 1838, and the influence of Germanic culture on his poetry was considerable; indeed, he composed poetry in that language and translated several works from it.

Once settled in London, Jones's young adulthood progressed for a time much as one would expect for a man of his social class and status. He was presented at the court of the young Queen Victoria, studied law and was called to the bar, and

6   INTRODUCTION

made a good marriage with Jane Atherley, who came from a Cumbrian family with extensive legal and political connections. Between 1840 and 1845 Jones published original and translated poetry in the *Court Journal* and *Morning Post* newspapers, and German poetry in the London-based *Deutsche Londoner Zeitung*. He also produced prose fiction in the shape of a novel called *The Wood-Spirit* (London: Boone & Co., 1841) and a serialized story in the *Court Journal* called 'Confessions of a King' (1843). In 1845 he published a long poem in the form of a dramatic monologue called *My Life* (London: T. C. Newby, 1845) under the pseudonym Percy Vere.

It was the encouraging reviews of *My Life* that Jones used as proof of his poetic credentials when in 1846 he presented himself at the London offices of the *Northern Star*, the official organ of the radical Chartist movement. Over the next two years Jones published forty poems in the pages of the *Northern Star*, co-edited with Feargus O'Connor (1794–1855), the Chartist movement's then leader, a magazine companion to the *Northern Star* called *The Labourer: A Monthly Magazine of Politics, Literature, Poetry, &c* (hereafter referred to as the *Labourer*), and forged ever closer links with the mass movement which sought the franchise for the working man. He was a tireless orator and travelled the country attending meetings and conventions.

There has been speculation over what might have driven Jones, at the age of twenty-seven, to become a class renegade, a gentleman radical whose life would be subsequently dominated by the cause of democracy. It may have suited Chartists to have imagined that he was drawn to their cause organically, purely through a sense of moral obligation. But they were not privy to the fact that Jones was in considerable financial difficulties, having speculated badly in the housing market the year before. Another factor may have been that Jones began to take an interest in Baptist and Presbyterian denominations of Christianity at this time, shifting away from the Anglicanism of his family. Nonconformist Christianity had strong links with political radicalism in the mid-nineteenth century, and Jones's Chartist poetry was to become frequently critical of the Church of England. But aside from religious or financial drivers of Jones's political and social apostasy, perhaps the most persuasive factor is that encapsulated by Taylor's chosen subtitle for his biography — 'Chartism and the Romance of Politics'. Financial desperation may have driven Jones into the arms of Chartism, and his attraction to the moral absolutes that characterized his faith may have kept him there, but his affinity with Romanticism, both in the emotional and literary senses of the term, informed his reactions to the many challenges he faced during his association with Chartism. In this he shared a character trait with arguably his chief literary influence (whose writings almost certainly precipitated Jones's interest in social justice), Percy Bysshe Shelley (1792–1822).

On 4 June 1848 Jones gave an inflammatory speech to a crowd of several thousand Chartists at Bishop Bonner's Field in East London that led to his imprisonment for two years on a charge of seditious speech-making. He served his term in Tothill Fields Prison in Westminster, enduring solitary confinement and periods of enforced silence. He emerged from prison in July 1850 with several poems in complete or draft form, including the epic 'The New World', and launched himself back into the Chartist movement, eventually taking over as de facto leader from the ailing Feargus O'Connor. He spent the next ten years editing a sequence of Chartist newspapers and attempting to revitalize the declining Chartist movement, producing several poetry collections which increasingly relied upon re-published material or work which had been composed some years before.

By 1860 Jones had published, and as far as we know written, his last poems, and had abandoned active politics to return to the legal profession. He worked out of offices near Albert Square in Manchester, occasionally defending cases of political sensitivity, including the famous 1867 trial of the Fenians accused of the murder of a police officer who became known as the 'Manchester Martyrs'. In 1865 he returned to political agitation with the Manchester Manhood Suffrage League, and lectured for the Reform League in 1866. Since the mid-1850s, Jones had softened his stance on courting middle-class attempts at partial franchise reform, which he had once denounced as undermining the cause of Chartist 'full' suffrage. It was largely the influence of the predominantly middle-class Reform League which led to the substantial concessions to democracy encapsulated in the 1867 Representation of the People Act (known informally as the Second Reform Act), which gave the franchise to some working-class males in England and Wales for the first time. After standing for Parliament unsuccessfully in 1868, Jones died of pneumonia in Higher Broughton, Manchester, in January 1869, just as his Conservative opponent was declared ineligible to sit in Parliament, and preliminary votes made it almost certain that Jones would become the sitting MP for Manchester. It was partly this expectation, partly his work with the Reform League, but mostly the memory of his Chartist years which encouraged many thousands of Mancunians to line the streets for his funeral cortege. He died just one day after his fiftieth birthday.

The Chartist movement had begun with a document calling for widespread enfranchisement of working-class males which was composed with the help of radical MPs by members of the London Working Man's Association in 1837. This 'People's Charter' was published in 1838 and contained six main points which were largely consistent through Chartism's history: the vote for all men over the age of twenty-one; secret ballots; the withdrawal of property qualifications for Members of Parliament; the payment of Members of Parliament; equal constituencies; and annual parliaments. Except for the last point, all of these demands are now enshrined in British constitutional law, but after several petitions to Parliament Chartism faded in the 1850s without success as a mass movement. As noted previously, its function was partially revived by the largely middle-class Reform League (with which Jones also became involved in 1865 after a political hiatus of five years), which campaigned from the mid-1860s for less fundamental reforms which were to some degree met by the 1867 Reform Act. But while Chartism existed, it was a mass working-class movement whose active national membership peaked at over 50,000, and whose petitions to Parliament were signed by British and Irish people in their millions. The movement has been defined by key events including the Newport Rising of 1839, the collection of over three million signatures for the 1842 petition and that year's attempted General Strike, and the mass demonstrations of 1848 which coincided with revolutions across Europe and led to the imprisonment of many Chartists, including Ernest Jones. However, beyond its agitational and

8   INTRODUCTION

political functions, Chartism was also an attempt to create a working-class culture — the movement had its own newspapers (of which the nationally-distributed *Northern Star* was the most prominent), songs, hymns, and, of course, poetry.

It is beginning to be recognized that Chartist poetry is a lot more than merely the formalized expression of Chartist desire. It functions as a sophisticated medium for political discourse, and it has a culturally formative and cohesive agency. Most of the leading figures in Chartist politics turned their hand to poetry at various times and with varying degrees of success. As Sanders has suggested, the ability of the Chartist movement to produce poetry, to express itself by intellectually significant and aesthetically refined means, in some sense demonstrated the capability of the working class to hold the franchise.[21] But the broader radical agenda of many in the Chartist movement — the re-alignment of British society with the needs and wishes of the majority — also triggered the mythopoeic potential of poetry. The ambition to create a new culture necessitates the creation of new myths; though, of course, myths are not created, but adapted. Jones's early Chartist poetry appropriated pre-existing conservative Golden Age myths and Victorian neo-medievalism and synthesized a radically re-imagined history which suggested the attainability of a revolutionized future. The idealization of the rural lifestyle inherent in these myths, which also chimed with Jones's bucolic German childhood, proved particularly appropriate to the promotion of the Chartist Land Plan. This subscription scheme championed by Chartism's leader at the time, Feargus O'Connor, and supported by Jones, aimed to provide viable plots for self-sufficient agriculture for working-class families drawn by lot. Several areas of land were purchased by the National Land Company, but the scheme collapsed in 1848 amid schisms within the Chartist movement, accusations of organizational mismanagement, and a parliamentary select committee deeming it financially untenable.

Beyond providing poetic support for the rustic utopianism of the Chartist Land Plan, Jones recognized poetry's significance as a formative cultural agent. In the introduction to 'The New World' and elsewhere he called for the creation of a democratic literature, insisting on the central place of literature in the formation of the moral and political definition of a people. It is in this context that Jones attacked Tennyson and Browning in the pages of the *Labourer* for their perceived dereliction of social responsibilities in their poetry (see Chapter Two), recognizing that poetry which does not challenge the status quo implicitly supports it. However, Jones could be inconsistent: as his own poetry retreated from its former radicalism in the mid to late 1850s, he increasingly began (as he had once accused Tennyson of doing) to 'do no more than troll a courtly lay'. Jones could adapt the tropes of Victorian literary medievalism to produce a radical re-reading of history, but he could also use those tropes as a gateway to a depoliticized poetry with ostensibly aesthetic ambitions and a generalized, even broadly conservative, morality.

Despite some good reviews for his pre- and what might be termed his post-Chartist poetry, it is quite possible that Jones would have been almost forgotten as a writer had it not been for the infusion of purpose that radicalism gave his work. Jones's poetry is perhaps less nuanced than that of some of his contemporaries, and if much canonical Victorian poetry appears to engage with doubt almost as a guiding principle, Jones largely appeared to lack this quality in his writing and in his life. However, what Jones's poetry does possess is a strong sense of rhythm and image, and a keen wit. The latter qualities contribute significantly to his success as a Chartist poet as his work defamiliarizes aspects of British society and attempts to re-present them from a radical perspective. This often involves a process of moral inversion, whereby the reader is invited to re-assess the prevailing wisdom in light of a radical reading of society and history. Inversions range from the commonplace characterization of the 'nobility' of the working class in 'The Blackstone Edge Gathering' (1846) and other poems, to the inventively positive embrace of hate as an emotion in 'Christian Love' (1851). Many other works by Jones depend on inversion and defamiliarization as their central functions; indeed, his ambitious epic, 'The New World', might be described as an attempt to defamiliarize the forming processes of human civilization, from feudalism through to the present and on into the future. The explicit aim of these poems is to raise the consciousness of their readers — to entertain and encourage, but also to educate. An oft-quoted diary entry from the time of Jones's first success as a Chartist poet not only provides part of the title of this study, but encapsulates the ambition of an attitude to poetics which gives primacy to poetry's social, rather than aesthetic, function: 'I am pouring the tide of my songs over England, forming the tone of the mighty mind of the people'.[22] Whatever else it may contain, the relationship between Ernest Jones and the 'mighty mind' is central to this study.

Notes to the Introduction

1. For example, 'The Song of the Low' is a regular feature of the repertoire of the Yorkshire-based a cappella group, Chorista, and 'The Blackstone Edge Gathering' is sung each year on May Day at its eponymous location to commemorate the Chartist meetings there.
2. The 'mighty mind' is a phrase Jones used to describe his readership in a diary entry of 1846 (see Chapter Three).
3. Mike Sanders, *The Poetry of Chartism: Aesthetics, Politics, History,* Cambridge Studies in Nineteenth-Century Literature and Culture (Cambridge: Cambridge University Press, 2009).
4. Ronald Paul, '"In Louring Hindostan": Chartism and Empire in Ernest Jones's *The New World, a Democratic Poem*', *Victorian Poetry*, 39.2 (Summer 2001), 189–204.
5. Roy Vickers, 'Christian Election, Holy Communion and Psalmic Language in Ernest Jones's Chartist Poetry', *Journal of Victorian Culture*, 11, 1 (Spring 2006), 59–83.
6. Isobel Armstrong, *Victorian Poetry: Poetry, Poetics and Politics* (London: Routledge, 1993).
7. Anne Janowitz, *Lyric and Labour in the Romantic Tradition* (Cambridge: Cambridge University Press, 1998).
8. Mary Ashraf (ed.), *Political Verse and Song from Britain and Ireland* (London: Lawrence & Wishart, 1975).
9. Brian Maidment, *The Poorhouse Fugitives: Self-taught Poets and Poetry in Victorian Britain* (Manchester: Carcanet, 1987).
10. Saville, John (ed.), *Ernest Jones: Chartist* (London: Lawrence & Wishart, 1952).
11. Miles Taylor, *Ernest Jones, Chartism, and the Romance of Politics 1819–1869* (Oxford: Oxford University Press, 2003).
12. Y. V. Kovalev, and A. A. Elistratova (eds.), *Antologiya Chartistskoi Literaturui (An Anthology of Chartist Literature)* (Moscow: Foreign Languages Publishing House, 1956), hereafter referred to as Kovalev.
13. Malcolm Chase, *Chartism: A New History* (Manchester: Manchester University Press, 2007).

10   INTRODUCTION

14. Dorothy Thompson, *The Chartists: Popular Politics in the Industrial Revolution* (New York: Pantheon Books, 1984).
15. Owen Ashton, Robert Fryson, and Stephen Roberts (eds.), *The Chartist Legacy* (Rendlesham: Merlin Press, 1999).
16. Timothy Randall, 'Chartist Poetry and Song', in *The Chartist Legacy*, ed. by Ashton, Fryson & Roberts, pp. 171–95.
17. Ernest Jones, *Notes to the People*, 2 vols (London: Merlin Press, 1967), hereafter referred to as *NP*. It was published between 1851 and 1852, and all further references to it will indicate in which year the poem in question appeared.
18. R. G. Gammage, *History of the Chartist Movement 1837–1854* [1854] (London: Merlin Press, 1969), p. 432.
19. Taylor, p. 258.
20. Chase, p. 338.
21. Sanders, p. 85.
22. Ernest Jones, Diary, 8 October 1846, Manchester County Record Office (hereafter MCRO), MS. f281.89 J5/30.

CHAPTER 1

Influences and Early Poetry
1840–45

Establishing influences on a writer's work is almost always a matter of balanced probabilities. Literary tropes are disseminated so widely and rapidly in modern societies that even pointing out apparent intertextual references between writers can be subject to the complications of the literary middleman, a secondary order of influence. A writer's declaration of influence should not be accepted at face value but must be cross-checked by a careful study of texts; a writer may merely *wish* that a literary idol were their main influence. Poetry would seem to have the advantage of various formal elements to trace back to a possible original text or writer, but such forms quickly become ubiquitous, and the partially unconscious and synthetic nature of the poetic creative process provides myriad paths down which the critic can travel. It is almost a literary commonplace that writers are often the least qualified people to analyze their own work; inescapable subjectivity leads to unconscious dissembling, and the tendency to place emphasis where it should not necessarily be. Prudence, therefore, encourages the critic at least to attempt to quantify the probability of a possible influence being discussed, and to present such discussion within the frame of a cautious qualification.

Ernest Jones shared with most poets of his period the influences in varying degrees of the major figures of the British Romantic period, and it is these inheritances which are first explored in the following chapter. But it is also possible to trace influences of German Romanticism in Jones's writing absorbed during a childhood and adolescence spent in the Duchy of Holstein, and these influences form the basis of the second section of the chapter. The fact that Jones translated the works of several German poets strengthens the argument that his work was influenced by these writers. Jones's tendency to re-work early material for publication in Chartist periodicals provides some hitherto unexplored links between German Romantic poetry and mid-nineteenth-century British radical poetics. In order to fully examine evidence of poetic influence, the focus of this chapter will shift between Jones's Chartist and pre-Chartist periods of production. Due to Jones's habit of republishing his early work, this will also be the case with the last section of the chapter which deals with the original poetry that Jones published before his direct involvement with radical politics in 1846. One of the contentions of this study is that, contrary to previous biographical accounts, Jones's poetic development provides examples of a growing political consciousness in the period immediately preceding his Chartist 'conversion'.

British Romantic Influences

While it has been recognized that such historical demarcations can be problematic, the complex response of canonical Victorian literature to its Romantic precursor has been widely documented. For Leon Gottfried, the Romantic movement 'stood like the Chinese Wall separating the nineteenth century from the dominant literary tradition of the eighteenth century represented by such key figures as Dryden, Pope, and Johnson'.[1] Whether one accepts the degree of historical dislocation that Gottfried's simile suggests, it can seem that early Victorian literature is interpreted by modern critics in relation to the preceding literary period. It should be noted that two Poet Laureates of the early Victorian period were the aging Robert Southey and William Wordsworth, and that the mid-nineteenth century saw posthumous cults of celebrity emerge around the figures of Keats and Shelley. The perceived sexual, political, and indeed literary radicalism of the Romantics proved troublesome issues for many Victorian commentators and writers. In *Romantic Echoes in the Victorian Era*, Andrew Radford and Mark Sandy note 'a neurotic fear that the potentially subversive, ungovernable essence of Romanticism will begin to work independently and possess the Victorian possessor'.[2] But for mid-nineteenth-century radicals, the politically subversive elements of British Romanticism provided both inspiration and important literary precedence. In Byron and Shelley, the late Romantic period produced widely-respected poets who were consistently critical of the political establishment; the early radicalism of Wordsworth, Coleridge, and even Southey served to make Romanticism appear a generation of dissent. Jones was not alone among Chartist poets in drawing on British Romanticism for inspiration and influence. The early poetry of William James Linton (1812–97) — in particular *The Dirge of the Nations* (1848) — was imitative of the work of Shelley, while the influence of Byron can be seen in the work of Jones's predecessor as unofficial Laureate of Chartism, Thomas Cooper (1805–92). At the same time as much canonical mid-nineteenth-century poetry (led by Browning and Tennyson) was becoming more insular and self-absorbed, adapting an emphasis on the consciousness of the self inherited from Romanticism, Jones and other Chartist poets were inheriting an adapted form of Romanticism's political consciousness.

Jones's rise to prominence within the pages of the *Northern Star's* poetry column in 1846 coincided with an increase in the number of Byron poems printed in the paper. In July 1845 the newspaper had begun a series called 'The Beauties of Byron'. Mike Sanders has observed that 'in 1846, Byron's poetry provided more than a tenth of the poetry column's output and only Ernest Jones — who contributed eighteen poems — came close to matching Byron's total of twenty poems'.[3] While Byron was idolized by Chartists, his influence on the majority of Chartist poets was often limited to tonal and thematic aspects of poetry. The length of much of his work, and its characteristic geographical and historical sweep, made it literally inimitable for most Chartist writers. Another element of Byron's writing that led to him being more inspirational than directly influential was what the Chartist activist Thomas Frost, in an article entitled 'Scott, Byron, and Shelley' published on 2 January 1847 in the *Northern Star,* described as 'the misanthropy which occasionally gleams forth in the writings of Byron, "the stinging of a heart the world had stung"'.[4] Byron's occasional retreats into an injured individualism, coupled with the extra-literary image of his sartorial dandyism, did not align themselves easily with Chartism's altruistic and morally upright nature, or with its essentially working-class aesthetic. Byron, as the nineteenth century's first, and arguably greatest, literary celebrity, bolstered Chartism's cause with his essential radicalism, but his manner, behaviour, and scabrous humour belonged back beyond that Chinese wall, in the pre-industrial decadence of the eighteenth century.[5]

In spite of the complications that Byron's legacy left, his name remained a touchstone for literary excellence and, for radicals, the bold expression of political truths. Jones's versatility as a writer saw him occasionally emulate Byron's poetic style. In 'The Painter of Florence: A Domestic Poem', a long poem published in 1851 in its author's newspaper *Notes to the People*, Jones references Byron in a concluding section that makes an argument for the public accessibility of art:

> As well might Byron's Harold,
> In one dark folio kept,
> In one man's sordid chamber
> Thro' endless years have slept. (ll. 689–93)[6]

The reference to *Childe Harold* is apt not just because of Byron's fame, but because of his method of addressing directly his readership, insisting on an interdependent relationship between art and the public. In the same poem, Jones's description of a character called 'Lady Devilson' echoes Byron's description of Don Juan's mother, Donna Inez, notoriously based on his ex-wife, Annabella Millbanke:

> But oh! beware how you approach her!
> No thorn so mangles an encroacher!
> She'll lure you on, with easy seeming,
> To drop some hint of doubtful meaning,
> Then turn, as hot as fire, to shew
> Her virtue's white and cold as snow;
> And, dragging you forth in a storm of laughter,
> Hurl the full weight of her chastity after.
> Such, no line is overdone,
> Is Lady Malice Devilson.
> ('The Painter of Florence', ll. 99–108)

> Morality's grim personification,
> In which not Envy's self a flaw discovers;
> To others' share let 'female errors fall,'
> For she had not even one — the worst of all.

> Oh! she was perfect past all parallel —
> Of any modern female saint's comparison:
> So far above the cunning powers of hell,
> Her guardian angel had given up his garrison.
> (*Don Juan*, I, 125–33)[7]

Although Lady Devilson's morality is a mechanism for hypocritical teasing, and Donna Inez (at least in this section) appears a paragon of virtue, both descriptions satirize the cultural pretensions of female chastity. Jones's rhyming of 'approach her' with 'encroacher' is eminently Byronic in its silliness, and the line 'Such, no line is overdone', with its air of a theatrical aside, is an example of the influence of the self-reflexive nature of Byron's later poetry. Given the detailed description of her personality, it is possible that Lady Devilson, like Donna Inez, was based on a real person.

There are also thematic examples of the influence of Byron in long Jones poems including 'The Painter of Florence' and 'The New World'. The former begins and ends in a contemporary setting but uses the speaker's after-dinner reverie to introduce a long, imaginary middle section that speculates on the origins of a Florentine painting hung in an English mansion. This section's narrative of a Renaissance Italian artist and his lover, and its depiction of the aftermath of a great battle on European soil, reflects the themes and images of Byron's poetry in its historical and geographical breadth. Although its title refers to America, 'The New World' consists partly of an account of an imagined revolution in British-held India, reflecting the orientalism of Byron's 'Turkish Tales' such as *The Giaour* (1813) and *The Bride of Abydos* (1813), or even Robert Southey's *The Curse of Kehama* (1810).[8] Like Byron's 'Turkish Tales', 'The New World' is composed in rhyming couplets, although Jones's lines are decasyllabic, while Byron's are octosyllabic. The poem's American sections, which envisage a future world dominated by the maturing republic, follow a tradition in British poetry including Southey's *Madoc* (1805) in which America represents a place of escape from the tradition-bound strictures of a crumbling Europe. *Madoc* explores this theme allegorically through its tale of twelfth-century warring Welsh royals (Madoc was a prince who, in Welsh folklore, discovered America in 1170); 'The New World' is a fantasy narrative whose purpose is both to celebrate American democracy and to warn the country about the dangers of European-style imperialism.

Southey's fellow Lake Poet, William Wordsworth, was Poet Laureate from 1843 until 1850, when he died at the age of eighty. Shortly after hearing of the latter's death Jones, while incarcerated in Westminster Prison, composed a short poem describing Wordsworth as a 'patriarch of modern song'.[9] Although the rest of the poem consists of rather mediocre elegiac material, Jones's description of Wordsworth was appropriate for a figure whose poetic influence reached back almost to the French Revolution. But Wordsworth's greatest influence on Jones came in the depiction of rural scenes and lifestyles. Jones's rustic poems, including 'The Cornfield and the Factory' and 'The Farmer' (later republished as 'The Peasant'), owed much to Wordsworth's elevation of the rural poor to an almost mythical nobility in works including 'Michael: A Pastoral Poem' (1800) or 'The Leech-Gatherer, or Resolution and Independence' (1807). Jones's elegy to Wordsworth may have shared its title with Shelley's mock-elegy, 'To Wordsworth' (1816), but it steered clear of the latter's accusations of religious and political conservatism. In this case Jones avoided Shelleyan iconoclasm, preferring to enlist the spirit of the young Wordsworth in the poetic battle for the enfranchisement of the rural and urban working class.

In spite of Shelley's atheism and stated pacifism, his writings proved a profound influence on the poetry of Ernest Jones. Shelley was eulogized in the pages of the

Chartist press for his support of democratic principles in his essays and poetry, and for his relinquishment of the privileges of his birth right in order to assume the role of a radical poet. In many ways, Shelley was perceived by Chartists as the archetypal 'gentleman radical', and it is not inconceivable that Jones identified himself with his poetic predecessor. At the end of his three-page introduction to 'The New World' (whose later title, *The Revolt of Hindostan*, deliberately alludes to Shelley's *The Revolt of Islam*, 1818), Jones addresses the American people:

> Free citizens of the republic! My country has been called the 'Ark of Freedom' — but in yours I see its Ararat, and to you, at whose hands Shelley looked for vindication and immortality, a humbler bard now dedicates his work.[10]

For Jones, and many other Chartist poets, Shelley was the radical poetic yardstick against which to be measured. The series of works that Shelley produced in response to the Peterloo Massacre of 1819 were particularly influential, partly because of their song-like nature. These demotic, or as Shelley termed them, 'exoteric', poems included 'The Mask of Anarchy', 'England in 1819', and 'Men of England: A Song'. Jones used the latter poem as the basis for his most anthologized work, 'The Song of the Low'.[11] The fifth stanza of Shelley's work emphasizes capitalism's exploitation of various trades:

> The seed ye sow, another reaps:
> The wealth ye find another keeps:
> The robes ye weave, another wears:
> The arms ye forge, another bears. (ll. 17–20)[12]

After an opening chorus which acts as a refrain, Jones takes each of these trades (agriculture, mining, textile, and arms) and creates a stanza from each of them, retaining the same order, but he inserts the building trade as the subject of the fourth stanza, reflecting the urban construction boom of the mid-nineteenth century. 'The Song of the Low' continues Shelley's theme of exploitation but adds a tone of ironic humour:

> We're low — we're low — we're very very low,
>   As low as low can be;
> The rich are high — for we make them so —
>   And a miserable lot are we!
>   And a miserable lot are we! are we!
>   A miserable lot are we!
>
> We plough and sow — we're so very very low,
>   That we delve in the dirty clay,
> Till we bless the plain with the golden grain,
>   And the vale with the fragrant hay.
> Our place we know — we're so very low,
>   'Tis down at the landlords' feet:
> We're not too low — the bread to grow,
>   But too low the bread to eat.
>   *We're low, we're low, etc.*
>
> ('The Song of the Low', ll. 1–15)

16   INFLUENCES AND EARLY POETRY (1840–45)

'The Song of the Low' diverges from the philosophies that underpin Shelley's poetry in the fifth stanza (or verse, when sung). Jones does not miss the opportunity to highlight the irony of a social class making the weapons that are used by another class to oppress it. In Shelley's 'The Mask of Anarchy' (1819) an imaginary Peterloo crowd is urged to use passive resistance when confronted with violence:

> With folded arms and steady eyes,
> And little fear, and less surprise,
> Look upon them as they slay
> Till their rage has died away.
>
> Then they will return with shame
> To the place from which they came,
> And the blood thus shed will speak
> In hot blushes on their cheek. (ll. 343–50)[13]

Jones is altogether less forgiving, but chooses his words carefully:

> We're low, we're low — we're very, very low,
>   And yet when the trumpets ring,
> The thrust of a poor man's arm will go
>   Through the heart of the proudest king!
> We're low, we're low — our place we know,
>   We're only the rank and file,
> We're not too low — to kill the foe,
>   But too low to touch the spoil.
>   ('The Song of the Low', ll. 61–69)

Jones's legal training probably made him aware that the wording of lines appearing to advocate regicide in his poem was ambiguous enough to be construed as referring to a foreign king being overthrown by a British army. Jones had not long since emerged from a prison sentence for seditious speech-making when he composed 'The Song of the Low'.

That Jones was capable of such skilful adaptation from Shelley makes his subsequent writing and publication of 'The Poet's Prayer to the Evening Wind' (1855) in the *Battle-Day: And Other Poems* collection all the more puzzling.[14] The poem reads almost like a foreign translation of Shelley's 'Ode to the West Wind' (1819) translated (albeit skilfully) back into English. As a tribute it is more than competent, there is real talent employed in the versification, but there is no acknowledgement of what is clearly its source, and no progression of the ideas from Shelley's original:

> Wild rider of grey clouds, beneath whose breath
>   The stars dissolve in mist, or rain, or sleet:
>   Who chariotest the scudding, years to death,
>   Beneath thy driven tempests' clanging feet!
>   ('The Poet's Prayer to the Evening Wind', ll.1–4)
>
> O, wild West Wind, thou breath of Autumn's being,
>   Thou, from whose unseen presence the leaves dead
> Are driven, like ghosts from an enchanter fleeing,
>
> Yellow, black, and pale, and hectic red,

Pestilence-stricken multitudes: O thou,
Who chariotest to their dark wintry bed.
('Ode to the West Wind', ll. 1–6)[15]

If 'The Poet's Prayer to the Evening Wind' is intended as an affectionate parody or homage to 'Ode to the West Wind' then it fails not just in its lack of acknowledgement, but in its lack of wit or invention. Shelley's succession of images is reproduced wholesale in much the same order but with, inevitably, less effect. If Jones wished to introduce Shelley's concepts of historical progression, revolutionary change, and personal poetic responsibility to a working-class audience he would have been better advised to direct them to the original. As Friedrich Engels noted in *The Condition of the Working Class in England*, Shelley and his fellow Romantic writers were hardly a closed book to the radical working-class population in mid-nineteenth-century England:

> It is the workers who are most familiar with the poetry of Shelley and Byron. Shelley's prophetic genius has caught their imagination, while Byron attracts their sympathy by his sensuous fire and by the virulence of his satire against the existing social order.[16]

It is possible that Jones's judgement in this matter was influenced by the preponderance of explicit imitations of Shelley which had appeared in the pages of the *Northern Star* during its run from 1838 to 1852. William S. Villiers Sankey, an influential leader of Scottish Chartism, produced a poem which he called 'Ode', which effectively consisted of extra verses for Shelley's 'Song to the Men of England':

> Men of England, wherefore plough
> For the lords who lay you low
> Wherefore weave with toil and care
> The rich robes your tyrants wear?
> ('Song to the Men England', ll. 1–4)[17]

> Men of England, ye are slaves,
> Though ye quell the roaring waves-
> Though ye boast, by land and sea,
> Britons everywhere are free.
> ('Ode', ll. 1–4)[18]

In a letter to James Leigh Hunt (1784–1859), the influential editor of the *Examiner*, Shelley wrote that he intended the short poems he composed in the aftermath of the Peterloo Massacre to be published 'in a little volume of *popular songs* wholly political, & destined to awaken & direct the imagination of the reformers'.[19] The volume never appeared during Shelley's lifetime, but a generation later these works became structural templates for part of the radical aesthetic of the poetry of Chartism. Beyond poetic form, what Shelley bequeathed to Chartist poets including Jones was the promise of deliverance that emerged from his essential idealism. Where Byron's cynicism and occasional misanthropy may have presented the status quo as an inevitable consequence of human nature, Shelley's faith in a Godwinian 'perfectibility' led him to produce a body of work that consistently raised the possibility of an escape from present political evils.[20]

18   INFLUENCES AND EARLY POETRY (1840–45)

What Engels describes as Shelley's 'prophetic genius' lies at the heart of Chartist perceptions of the Romantic poet. The figure of Shelley was surrounded with a form of secular mysticism which Shelley's own poetry, consciously or unconsciously, propagated. The concept of prophecy, in a non-religious sense that nevertheless utilized biblical forms and myth patterns, was never far from Shelley's poetry — from 'Ode to the West Wind''s 'trumpet of a prophecy' (l. 70), to 'The Mask of Anarchy''s dream-like re-imagining of a Peterloo scenario. Jones appropriated this concept of prophecy and applied it to his own radical poetry, presenting victory in the fight for the Charter as a political fait accompli, bolstered by Shelley's identification of the numerical advantage of the working class in 'The Mask of Anarchy': 'Ye are many — they are few' (ll. 155 & 372), and a mythic/historical idyll of rural self-determination. In 'Onward' (1846), eventual victory for the Chartist struggle is presented as an ineluctable historical outcome, and is compared to natural cycles of movement, growth, and decay.[21] The speaker ironically bids the forces of oppression to:

> Go stay the earthquake in the rock,
> Go quench the hot volcano's shock,
> And fast the foaming cataract lock.
> ('Onward', ll. 15–17)

Shelley's association of historical progression with a cyclical natural event in 'Ode to the West Wind', and his image of the inevitable decay of tyrannical ideology in 'Ozymandias' (1817) are brought together in Jones's poem to signal the end of industrial capitalism's social hegemony:

> Forbid the flowery mould to bloom,
> Where years have scathed a tyrant's tomb,
> And tell us slavery is our doom:
> E'en as the peaceful march of time
> Moulders the rampart's stony prime,
> So calm Progression's steady sway
> Shall sap and sweep your power away. (ll. 21–27)

In contrast to some of Jones's poems' use of more threatening language, the 'calm' of inevitable 'Progression' recalls Shelley's 'folded arms and steady eyes' in 'The Mask of Anarchy'. Addressing an audience split between arguments of physical and moral force, Jones's poetry occasionally alternated between advocacies of the two positions, suggesting that the failure of one approach might lead to the adoption of the other. Shelleyan pacifism and his identification of political cycles were useful concepts, but they relied on a patience many in the Chartist movement did not possess, and Shelley could not have taken into account the economic and social effects of the growth of industrial capitalism in the Victorian age. The quasi-militaristic tone of some of Jones's Chartist poetry was derived not from British Romanticism, but from fiercely patriotic elements in its German equivalent. The extent of Jones's immersion in this European literary tradition made him unique amongst British radical poets of the mid-nineteenth century.

German Romantic Influences

Aside from Ernest Jones's middle-class background with its aristocratic connections, a factor that set him apart from other politically active Chartists, and other Chartist poets, was his upbringing in the Duchy of Holstein, which at the time was a member of the German Confederation. Schooled at home between 1833 and 1835 by Friedrich Binge and Johann Schwarke, both of whom were theology graduates who went on to become Lutheran pastors, Jones's only exposure to institutional academia was at the exclusive St Michael's College in the Lower Saxony town of Luneburg. As a young man, Jones composed some of his own, unpublished, poetry in German. Once in Great Britain, his continued engagement with German poetry was demonstrated by the fact that between 1840 and 1842, more than three years before his involvement with radical politics, Jones translated the poetry of the German writers Ernst Moritz Arndt (1769–1860), Friedrich Leopold von Stolberg (1750–1819), Friedrich Rückert (1788–1866), Ludwig Ühland (1787–1862), and Friedrich Schiller (1755–1805) for publication in the *Court Journal* magazine. During this period the magazine also published twelve of Jones's own compositions. These submissions carried the Germanicized soubriquet, 'Karl'.

To a greater extent than other nineteenth-century figures including Samuel Taylor Coleridge, Thomas Carlyle, or George Eliot, who have been credited with the introduction of German tropes and thought into British literary theory and production, Jones viewed German literary traditions from the inside. Being an Englishman who did not live in England until he was nineteen years old, Jones was well-positioned to carry continental influences instilled from childhood into a British literary sphere which, although by no means alien to him, had previously been viewed from afar. This aspect of his poetic development is especially resonant given the relatively short space of time between the Jones family's eventual return to their home country in 1838 and his rapid rise as a celebrated Chartist political and poetic figure in the mid-1840s. Jones was just twenty-seven when he was first published in the *Northern Star*, and only twenty-nine when he was imprisoned for sedition after giving a speech to a Chartist crowd who subsequently rioted at Bishop Bonner's Fields in June 1848. The period between Jones's move to London and his involvement with Chartism saw the development of his early poetic voice, which carried distinct influences from the German literary tradition.

By the time of Jones's exposure to German Romantic literature it had largely worked through its troubled dialogue with the classicism of writers including Goethe and Schiller, and its younger generation of proponents were exploring themes of the self with relation to patriotism and nationhood. British Romanticism, as exemplified by Wordsworth's early radicalism and interest in the events of the French Revolution, Shelley's consistent calls for political reform, and Byron's qualified admiration for Napoleon, often formed its political stances in perceived opposition to British governmental interests, and was therefore labelled unpatriotic by the conservative British press. But British Romanticism's German equivalent expressed a longing for the ideal of a unification of German-speaking peoples, and nationalism therefore represented a radical position. Reflecting the German states' less industrialized landscape in the early years of the nineteenth century, idealized rural imagery dominated German Romantic poetry, and the construction of a re-imagined mythical Germanic past — which reached its creative apotheosis in Wagner's elaborate late nineteenth-century mythologies — began to emerge. According to George S. Williamson, 'this idea of a "new mythology" would exercise a powerful influence on German Romantic culture', and while Jones was familiar with the tropes and themes of British Romanticism, the effects of an engagement with the myths and motifs of German Romanticism can be clearly identified in his early poetry.[22] What is perhaps surprising is that these influences continued to operate and were brought to bear on his later Chartist poetry as a yet unexplored element of a European aesthetic incorporated into a British artistic response to a peculiarly British situation of political class.

A poem which emerges from the transitional phase between Jones's pre-Chartist and Chartist poetic careers is 'The Poet's Mission', which also provides evidence of its author's German literary inheritance. The piece was first published in the *Northern Star* on 17 October 1846, and this version of the poem assesses the poet's role in reflecting and guiding moral and intellectual thought in a cultural and historical context:

> Who is it rivets broken bands
> And stranger-hearts together,
> And builds with fast-decaying hands
> A home to last for ever?
>
> From thunder-clouds compels the light,
> And casts the bolt away,
> Upluring from the soulless night
> The soul's returning day?
>
> Who is it calls up glories past
> From tombs of churches old?
> And proudly bids the hero last,
> Tho' fades his grassy mould?
>
> Who is it, with age-vanquished form,
> Treads death's ascending path;
> Yet stronger than the fiery storm
> Of tyrants in their wrath?
>
> Whose voice, so low to human ears,
> Has still the strength sublime
> To ring thro' the advancing years —
> And history — and time?
>
> Who is it, in love's servitude,
> Devotes his generous life,
> And measures by his own heart's good
> A world with evil rife?
>
> The Bard — who walks earth's lonely length
> Till all his gifts are given;
> Makes others strong with his own strength,
> And then fleets back to Heaven.[23]

'The Poet's Mission' elevates the poet-figure to a position of historical and cultural importance. The first stanza's riveting together of 'broken bands' and 'stranger-hearts' appears to emphasize Chartist literature's socially cohesive function, its role in the formation of a common culture. Similarly, the contrast between the phrases 'fast-decaying hands' and 'a home to last for ever' highlight poetry's canonical potentiality, the possibility that it will outlast its creator and contribute to a state of cultural permanence. In the second stanza, the poet's ability to 'compel the light' of thunder, while at the same time casting 'the bolt away' would seem to symbolize literature's ability to utilize dangerous elements of societal friction in a non-violent, constructive manner by means of its interpretive, intellectual power. The poem is structured in such a way that its subject is only revealed in the last stanza, after a number of questions which detail the subject's attributes. This form of address encourages the reader to read over the poem again in light of the information presented at the conclusion. The poem as a whole contrasts the mortality of the poet with the potential immortality of the message he conveys; the 'strength' referred to in the last lines resonates with Shelley's ideas of poetic transmission expressed in 'Ode to the West Wind' and *A Defence of Poetry* (1819).

The draft manuscript of the work which became 'The Poet's Mission', however, reveals that it began its existence as a tribute to Louis Philippe (1773–1850), the 'King of the French' who abdicated during the 1848 Revolution. From the undated manuscript, it is clear that the transition from a poem supporting a perceived benevolent monarchy to a work which would have relevance to British working-class radicals necessitated only a few minor changes to five of the stanzas, and the replacement of two stanzas which identified its original subject. Because of this subject, it is almost certain that the draft manuscript dates from Jones's pre-Chartist career, especially given the fact that 'The Poet's Mission' was an early example of his Chartist output. This provides evidence that even before his Chartist period Jones was engaged with an aesthetics of message in his poetry, that he saw poetry not just as a purely artistic exercise, but as a means of conveying information about the external world within a particular frame. Jones, encouraged by the energetic and charismatic leader of the Chartists, Feargus O'Connor, presented a political persona that had undergone a Pauline conversion to the cause, having had no interest in politics before, to his first Chartist audiences. This narrative has been accepted by some Jones biographers: despite noting that Jones had written an anti-French Revolution poem as an adolescent just two pages beforehand, John Saville, in his introduction to *Ernest Jones: Chartist* confidently stated that, 'down to 1844, there is no evidence that Jones was in any way interested in politics'.[24] Jones's poetic persona, however, — as revealed by the progression of the ideological frames of his poetry before and during his Chartist period — proves to be nowhere near as naive as painted. It suited the Chartist movement to exhibit a refined, sensitive man with aristocratic connections who had been 'organically' drawn to the cause, but the truth was rather more complex. It will be shown that Jones's poetry engaged with politics and political figures before his Chartist involvement, and that whatever their political colour, these interests informed the development of his Chartist poetry.

The excised stanzas from 'To Louis Philippe' reveal a political worldview wholly different from Jones's Chartist persona. The original fifth stanza reads:

22 INFLUENCES AND EARLY POETRY (1840–45)

> Whose foot was on the earthquake's throes
> Whose seat the whirlpool's foam?
> Actions still could curb, 'mid foreign foes,
> The fiercer foe at home?[25]

The excised seventh stanza, the conclusion of the original work, could not be in greater contrast to much that democratic Chartism stood for:

> A monarch greater, than a throne
> Where earth's old glories dwell,
> Who reigns not over France alone
> But Frenchmen's souls as well.

The two added stanzas are in a different ink to the rest of the poem, indicating that they were inserted on a subsequent re-visiting of the poem, and the rejected stanzas are carefully deleted. The original title reads clearly as 'To Louis Philippe', but the monarch's name is crossed out in the same ink as the added sections and replaced with the name 'Byron', which is also crossed out, leaving this draft of the work untitled. Whether Jones's dedication of this poem to Lord Byron was a Chartist or pre-Chartist occurrence is not known, but it obviously represents a transitional stage between the poem's subject being a specific French monarch and an idealized poet-figure.

Jones's adaptation of a pro-monarchist poem for a Chartist publication meant that structural influences on the work remained as part of his newly-found radical voice. Where fellow Chartist poets including Thomas Cooper or William James Linton revealed the formal and tonal influences of British Romantic poets such as Shelley, Scott, or Byron, or the ballad traditions of eighteenth-century radical poetry, the structure of 'The Poet's Mission' resembles Ernst Moritz Arndt's patriotic 1813 poem, 'Was ist des Deutschen Vaterland?' (often translated as 'The German Fatherland'). Both poems employ an anaphoric series of rhetorical questions which are resolved in answers given after a volta towards the end of the poem. Arndt's work concerns the spiritual location of the German 'fatherland', and begins by listing historical areas of Germany and the natural scenery traditionally associated with them:

> Where is the German's fatherland?
> The Prussian land? The Swabian land?
> Where Rhine the vine-clad mountain laves?
> Where skims the gull the Baltic waves?
> Ah, no, no, no!
> His fatherland's not bounded so! (ll. 1–6)[26]

Jones's volta occurs at the beginning of the seventh and final stanza, when the question 'Who...?' is answered by revealing the 'Bard' as the poem's subject. Arndt, however, places his turn at the third line of the seventh of nine stanzas, allowing a triumphal crescendo to finish the poem; fitting for a work designed to arouse patriotic fervour in its readers:

> Where is the German's fatherland?
> Then name, oh, name the mighty land!
> Wherever is heard the German tongue,
> And German hymns to God are sung!

Influences and Early Poetry (1840–45) 23

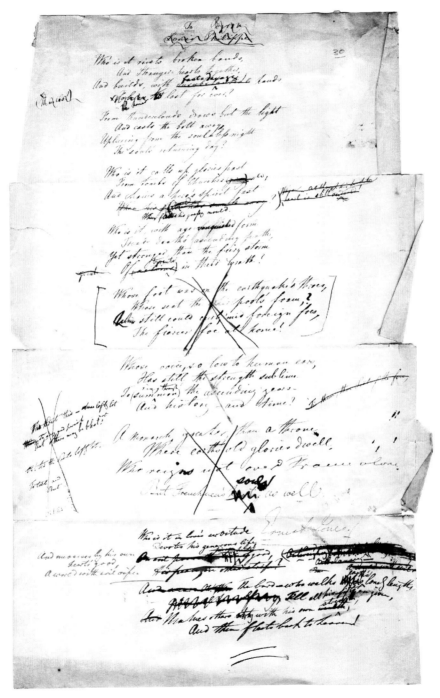

Fig. 1.1 Original manuscript of 'To Louis Philippe / To Byron / The Poet's Mission'. (Reproduced by kind permission of Archives and Local History, Manchester Central Library.)

24 INFLUENCES AND EARLY POETRY (1840–45)

This is the land, thy Hermann's land;
This, German, is thy fatherland.

This is the German's fatherland,
Where faith is in the plighted hand,
Where truth lives in each eye of blue,
And every heart is staunch and true.
This is the land, the honest land,
The honest German's fatherland.

This is the land, the one true land,
O God, to aid be thou at hand!
And fire each heart, and nerve each arm,
To shield our German homes from harm,
To shield the land, the one true land,
One Deutschland and one fatherland!

('The German Fatherland', ll. 37–54)

Arndt's anthem-like work answers its question, 'Where is the German fatherland?' with a declaration of linguistic, religious, and racial unity, aggressively reinforced by a declaration of militaristic national defence in the last stanza. As can be observed, there is little thematic, rhythmic, or formal similarity between Arndt's piece and that of Jones. But the connection lies in the particular mode of address, which establishes the works' thought structures. There is a level of control inherent in the use of the rhetorical question in poetry that increases the emphasis of the work's message. The poet formulates the question in a manner that increases the effectiveness of the resolving answer; the implied breadth of discourse holding more power than any simple declarative statement. While poems with individual rhetorical questions were not uncommon in Chartist poetry, the use of a series of questions to build up tension within the poem was rare. In Kovalev's anthology of Chartist literature, of the 116 poems not written by Jones, only the 1843 work 'Oppression' by 'D. C.' employs this method of creating poetic tension and release.[27] However, setting Jones's known familiarity with Arndt's output against 'D. C.s' relatively obscure work being printed in a periodical two years before Jones became interested in Chartism, and bearing in mind that 'The German Fatherland' was arguably Arndt's most famous work, it seems likely that the latter is where the inspiration for the structure of 'The Poet's Mission' arose. It is equally conceivable that Jones's legal training would have reinforced his penchant for this poetic method; he certainly used series of rhetorical questions to great effect in his Chartist oratory.

A further possible link between Jones's 'The Poet's Mission' and German Romantic poetry lies in the work's title. The title of Friedrich Hölderlin's 1800 poem 'Dichterberuf' is usually translated as 'The Poet's Vocation', or more uncommonly, 'The Poet's Calling'. While Hölderlin's intense, difficult poetry was not widely known until the middle of the nineteenth century, a collection of his work was put together and distributed by Schwab and Ühland in Germany in 1826. The latter poet was one of the writers whose work Jones translated for the *Court Journal*. While the similarity between the two poem's titles could be dismissed as coincidental, additional evidence for Jones's familiarity with the work is provided by the imagery of thunderstorms used to symbolize times of political disturbance initiated by a great spiritual force which galvanizes the poet into action. For Gunter Klabes, Hölderlin's use of thunder imagery in 'Dichterberuf' is analogous to Shelley's use of wind in 'Ode to the West Wind':

> The correlated phenomena of wind and thunderstorm, in which the divine manifests itself, are not conceptually limited to the physical world, but suggest images of the political turbulence of the era, of the cataclysmic events of the French Revolution and its aftermath.[28]

Where Hölderlin castigates some poets' dangerous or inappropriate use of the divine power of political upheaval symbolized by thunder: 'lately | Heard divine thunder ring out — to make a | Vile trade of it, exploiting the spirit',[29] Jones's poet-figure has righteous mastery over the elements, taming the natural force with his ability to 'compel the light' but 'cast the bolt away'; in the fourth stanza the poet is 'stronger than the fiery storm'. Jones's more positive utilization of the relationship between the poet and the storm's power also places more emphasis on the light created by the thunderstorm, suggesting metaphors of enlightenment, Promethean creativity, and inspiration. The fact that this image appears in one of the original stanzas of the poem, and remains essentially unchanged throughout the poem's transitional stages, suggests that Jones saw it as consecutively appropriate to Louis Philippe's attempts at political stabilization, Byron's satirical commentary on the events of the early nineteenth century, and the political agency of mid-nineteenth-century Chartist literature. Indeed, Jones used thunder as an image of revolutionary change again in 'Our Destiny': 'No! shouts the dreadful thunder, that teaches us to strike | The proud, for *one* usurping, what the Godhead meant for *all*' (ll. 19–20).[30] This invocation of natural forces as representative of an interventionist God is an example of natural theology expanded to encompass a political as well as moral authority. Jones's presumption to know the mind of God is thoroughly entangled with his characteristic equation of democracy with a Christian philosophy. Over and again Jones's poetry conflates political purpose with divine intent, elevating the Chartist cause by an implied endorsement from the highest possible authority.

The poetry of Ludwig Ühland, portions of which were translated into English during his lifetime by Thackeray and Longfellow, is characterized by song-like lyrics and balladic tales of courtly drama, often loaded with allegorical significance relating to issues of freedom, patriotism, or nationhood. Jones translated three of Ühland's poems for the *Court Journal* in the early 1840s — 'The Minstrel's Curse' ('Des Sängers Fluch'), 'The Monarch's Death-Prayer' ('Der Konig auf dem Thurme'), and 'The Boy's Mountain Song' ('Der Knabern Berglied') — although 'The Monarch's Death-Prayer' is a loose interpretation described as 'imitated', rather than 'translated', in Jones's introduction.

'The Minstrel's Curse' is a ballad relating the tale of two bards, an old man and a handsome youth, who travel to a great castle to entertain a tyrannical king at his court. The song they sing entrances the queen and the courtiers with its beauty, and the king, in a fit of jealous pique, runs the young bard through with his sword. As the grieving old bard leaves the castle he utters a curse on the tyrant and his kingdom:

26   INFLUENCES AND EARLY POETRY (1840–45)

> Woe! woe! ye mighty towers! no more your halls along
> Swell the sounds of melody, of minstrelsy or song!
> But timid steps of trembling slaves, and sigh, and shriek, and moan,
> Till vengeance' spirit tread to dust your battlements of stone! (ll. 45–48)[31]

Like Jones's own work, 'The Poet's Mission', this piece is intended to emphasize the importance of literature as a means of defining and memorializing a particular culture. An additional theme in 'The Minstrel's Curse', however, is that of freedom of speech and censorship. The king's murderous action simultaneously displays jealousy of the bard's popularity and failure to recognize the true significance of this popularity as a potential source of societal control. In this scenario governmental censorship becomes self-defeating in that it antagonizes a putative Fourth Estate, whose power as the dominant means of communication within society controls not just present perceptions, but those of the future. The absence of 'the sounds of melody, of minstrelsy or song' results in a 'desert silence' (l. 52), in which the king's legacy and legend are entirely lost to posterity, condemned to be 'buried and forgotten' (l. 65) forever.

It is not clear why Jones chose to adapt, rather than simply translate, another of Ühland's romantically medieval pieces, 'Der Konig auf dem Thurme' (1805). Jones calls his piece 'The Monarch's Death-Prayer', although the literal translation (and the one used by William Collett Landar in 1869) is 'The King on the Tower'. In both versions, this short lyric is a sympathetic portrayal of an aged king looking back over his reign and forward to his impending death, but Jones's poem is much more fatalistic and mournful in tone, and, in keeping with his change of title, more explicit regarding the king's fate. Jones also splits the voice of the poem so that the king's voice forming the third and fourth stanzas is within speech-marks, enclosed by the commentary of an omniscient narrator. Both the original and Landar's more faithful translation are spoken exclusively in the voice of the monarch. While Landar's king declares 'I have cared and striven for every one's sake, | I have drunk with sorrow the sparkling wine' (ll. 5–6),[32] Jones's speaker is more emphatic, and indeed, dramatic: 'My reign is o'er lengthened, my years are rife, | and in canker and care they were past' (ll. 11–12).[33] These differences represent an early example of Jones's tendency towards physically explicit imagery which sometimes verges on the visceral.

Some of Jones's cuttings from the *Court Journal* display handwritten revisions, as though the writer intended to edit them for future republication. The cutting of 'The Minstrel's Curse' is heavily annotated in Jones's own hand, and, tellingly, the word 'monarch', in the penultimate line, is crossed through and replaced with 'tyrant'. In an echo of his adaptation of the poem that became 'The Poet's Mission', Jones's revisions were intended to invest Ühland's poem with greater relevance for a Chartist audience, and the piece was re-published in his own periodical, *Notes to the People*, in 1851. The word 'monarch' then becomes, in the re-published version, 'tyrant-monarch'; a compound that keeps faith with Ühland's work while utilizing a familiar Chartist trope, broadening the poem's perceived message. *Notes to the People* also saw the republication of Jones's translation of E. M. Arndt's 'The Stars' ('Die Sterne'), with the archived cutting revision revealing only one excision of the adverb, 'fairly', which tightens up the metre.[34] This short, rather simplistic astronomical allegory exhibited enough ideological ambiguity to not require extensive revision.

Jones's *Court Journal* translation of 'The Boy's Mountain Song' retains the musicality of the original without straying too far from a literal interpretation, an achievement not replicated in William Collett Sandars's version of the poem in his 1869 collection of translated Ühland ballads and lyrics, 'The Herd Boy's Song'. The refrain which closes each stanza of the poem, 'Ich bin der Knab' vom berg', is distorted both rhythmically and semantically in Sandars's translation:

> Ich bin vom Berg der Hirtenknab',
> Seh' auf die Schlosser all herab;
> Die Sonne strahit am ersten hier'
> Am langsten weilet fie bei mir;
>> Ich bin der Knab' vom berg.
>> ('Der Knabern Berglied', ll. 1–5)[35]

> A mountain shepherd-boy am I,
> The castles far below I spy;
> The glorious sun I'm first to see,
> He lingers longest here with me,
> I am the mountain herd-boy.
>> ('The Herd Boy's Song', ll. 1–5)[36]

> The mountain shepherd boy am I,
> I look down on the castles high,
> The morning ray the first I see,
> The evening longest shines on me —
> I am the mountain boy.
>> ('The Boy's Mountain Song', ll.1–5)[37]

The German term *Knab'* equates most closely to the English 'lad', but Sandars insists on 'herd-boy', which is not only literally inaccurate but, by inserting an extra syllable, loses the original's distinctive rhythm of four lines of iambic tetrameter followed by an iambic trimetric refrain. Jones's lyrical instinct, when coupled with his familiarity with German as a second language, gives him a distinct advantage in the interpretation of German poetry.

The first four stanzas of 'The Boy's Mountain Song' stress its subject's unity with his natural surroundings and confer on him a noble individuality. In Jones's translation the boy drinks the stream's water 'fresh from the mother stone' (l. 7), signifying his closeness to nature's origins, 'aloft in the cloudless blue' (l. 17). The boy's power over nature is employed in the fourth stanza when he calls on passing storms 'spare ye my father's home' (l. 19), and this power becomes directed towards his kinsmen's (and, by extension, his nation's) enemies in the suddenly militaristic fifth and final stanza:

> And haply when alarm bells call,
> And beacons burn on the mountains all;
> Then I descend and join the file,
> And swing my sword and sing the while —
>> 'I am the mountain boy'. (ll. 21–25)

28   Influences and Early Poetry (1840–45)

The apparently seamless transition from shepherd to warrior is skilfully conveyed by the continuing refrain. This desire to utilize the 'natural' strengths of a nation's lower classes for righteous combat foreshadows Jones's later poetry when he calls on British working-class followers of Chartism to unite against the government. Parallels with the Irish patriotic ballad tradition can also be detected in Ühland's poem, and these persist in Jones's later work. The works of the poet and songwriter Thomas Moore (1779–1852), are recalled when reading 'The Boy's Mountain Song'. Many of his lyrics, including 'The Minstrel-Boy' (1798), elevate the status of Ireland's youth through a portrayal of a Romantic intimacy with nature, or the inheritance of a nation-specific bardic tradition. 'The Minstrel-Boy' concerns the transition between youth and soldiery, and celebrates the tradition of the 'warrior-bard', a theme that was to become central to much of Jones's work. Both in his oratory and in his poetry, Jones frequently romanticized and ennobled the peasantry and the working class, inverting aspects of his former monarchist politics while retaining much of the chivalric poetic imagery he inherited from German influences including Ühland. In the 1846 poem that celebrated his first open-air speech to a Chartist crowd, 'The Blackstone-Edge Gathering', Jones refers to 'the might of labour's chivalry', investing the workers with qualities traditionally associated with a medieval ruling class.[38]

An even more militaristic paean to German youth than Ühland's 'The Boy's Mountain Song' is Count Friedrich Leopold von Stolberg's 'The German Boy's Song'. Jones's choice of these overtly nationalistic works for translation suggests not just an interest in the transition from boyhood to manhood, but a correlated interest in the transition from a Romantic frame to military or political action. Stolberg's work begins and ends with the same stanza in which the eponymous youth declares his readiness for battle:

> My arm grows strong, my spirits soar!
>> Give me a sword to wield!
> Father! Despise my youth no more;
>> I'm worthy of the field. (ll. 1–4)[39]

At the side of his cutting of 'The German Boy's Song', Jones has written a note next to the third line of this stanza: 'Bold thoughts. My father! Scorn my youth no more'. This strongly indicates that the young Jones identified with the voice of the poem: the insertion of the term 'my' before 'father' into the note is especially interesting. The poem itself presents its speaker's childhood as merely a rehearsal for the role of warrior; maturity is simplistically equated with physical strength, patriotism is an instinctive, ever-present drive:

> Early in my childhood bright,
>> War was my sport by day, —
> Of perils I would dream by night,
>> Of wounds and wild affray! (ll. 9–12)

Describing a more complicated process, Jones returned to the theme of a youth readying himself for battle in the wider world in his 1846 work, 'The Better Hope.' In this poem the youth is quite explicitly Jones himself and the battle is the Chartist cause. 'The Better Hope' begins with a stanza that introduces its speaker as born into a social class characterized by its unfeeling separation from the masses:

> A child of the hard-hearted world was I,
>   And a worldling callous of heart,
> And eager to play with the thoughtless and gay,
>   As the lightest and gayest, a part. (ll. 1–4)[40]

The poem then continues with a romanticized, and it has to be said, largely inaccurate, description of Jones's childhood home, presented as a country seat with a 'lordly square' (l. 9), and 'sculptures rare'. In fact, Jones grew up on his father's relatively modest estate in Holstein before his family lived in a townhouse in London. It may be that Jones's failed attempt to buy a country house in his early twenties inspired this example of self-mythologizing; such a domicile certainly fitted the narrative of a child of the upper classes drawn to give up his privileges for the sake of righteous radicalism.

The speaker of the poem seeks to escape the emotionally constricted world of his peers to where 'beyond, in the broad, laughing world, | Men are happy in life's holiday!' (ll. 25–26). This characterization of the cheery lower classes at first seems to represent a reductive social determinism, but the speaker soon realizes that the effects of industrial capitalism are in the process of destroying the poor whom he had once romanticized. Jones's choice of words to describe the speaker's initial perception of the working population echoes the phrase 'man's holiday', which Feargus O'Connor repeatedly predicted as the state his Land Plan would achieve.[41] After describing the effects of a mechanized industrialism on the poor the poem closes with the speaker hesitating before deciding to join the fight for the oppressed:

> Oh! then I looked back for my cold, quiet home,
>   As the hell-bound looks back for the grave:
> But I heard my soul cry, Who but cowards can fly,
>   While a tyrant yet tramples a slave?
>
> Then I bound on my armour to face the rough world,
>   And I'm going to march with the rest,
> Against tyrants to fight — for the sake of the right,
>   And, if baffled, to fall with the best. (ll. 49–56)

That moment of hesitation, and its image of the 'hell-bound' looking 'back for the grave', is Jones's most explicit emotional expression of the dilemma he faced once he became radicalized in late 1845. His view of the class he was born into (though it was more 'middle' than 'upper') had been altered irrevocably, to such an extent that his involvement with Chartism became a morally driven fait accompli. In Jones's choice of poems to translate, and in his own work, we see an engagement with issues of self-development and the transition from youth to adulthood. These explorations of maturation can be related to the concept of *Bildungsroman* which saw its first example in Goethe's *Wilhelm Meister's Lehrjahre* (*The Apprenticeship of Wilhelm Meister*) in 1796; Thomas Carlyle's English translation of this novel in 1824 precipitated a Victorian pre-occupation with the concept.

INFLUENCES AND EARLY POETRY (1840–45)

Significantly, some of the last work that Jones published before his involvement with Chartism was composed in the German language. The *Deutsche Londoner Zeitung*, a German-language newspaper aimed at London's German diaspora, printed three of Jones's pieces in its 25 April 1845 issue. 'Licht und Sprache' ('Light and Speech') describes itself as 'Nach [After] Thomas Powell', and is a fairly standard Romantic celebration of the power of language, in particular its potential for poetry and the description of the sublime. 'Der Deutsche Sprachschatz' ('The German Vocabulary') appears by its title to pertain only to German and it identifies one compound term ('Auerpflanzstockbaumgedeihn' — a gardening term referring to dibbling for tree-planting) as a quintessentially German word, but its conclusion that language contains the whole world in its past, present, and future forms could equally apply to any language, and the poem is similarly standard Romantic fare.[42] 'Politisches' ('On Politics') is a highly metaphorical work that sees conflict as essentially instigated by a kind of autonomous mob mentality. In fairly close translation it reads thus:

> Two friends stood side by side,
> As brother would to brother;
> Until the mob surrounded them,
> And urged them 'gainst each other.
>
> It said, as it has always said,
> In its slick and foreign way:
> 'Just watch! You battling brothers!
> As we make your battles pay!'
>
> 'Let them beat themselves to pulp,
> These now so fresh and brave:
> It suits us fine to stand aside
> Before we rob the grave!'
>
> The fighters heard as though from far
> The scheming of the mass,
> And at the final moment stayed
> The deadly coup de grace.
>
> They offered hands of friendship,
> And pledged again as brothers,
> And ceased to fight, but stood to hear
> The fury of the others...
>
> ...the others who had lost the prize,
> But grudgingly declared:
> 'It's clear to see these friends are wise!'
> What lesson here is shared? (ll. 1–24)[43]

Given Jones's subsequent reputation as a political firebrand, the conciliatory manner of this work is worth noting. The poem is framed as though referring to politics in general, but its narrative can be read as symbolizing the effect of disruptive foreign involvement on German attempts at re-unification. This interpretation of the work is corroborated by the poem's publication in a German newspaper and, given the dearth of opportunities for German-language publishing in London (and the existence of fair copy manuscripts at the Manchester County Record Office dated just three days before publication), these works presumably were written specifically for the *Deutsche Londoner Zeitung*. Further corroboration is provided by the use of ambivalent language within the piece. The German term in the sixth line translated here as 'foreign' ('welschen') also has derogatory connotations relating to the French, Italians, or Romance-speaking nations in general. The poem can be read on two levels — as an allegory referring to the general nature of political confrontation and its possible resolution, or as an implicitly nationalist text blaming the lack of progress regarding aspirations for German re-unification on external European interference.

In some ways, Jones's decision to devote his political and poetic energies to the cause of Chartism was an embrace of the moral simplicity of poems such as 'The German Boy's Song' and 'The Boy's Mountain Song'. After the complexities of the myriad social stratifications of the British middle and upper classes, radicalism directed against the demonstrable injustices of the capitalist industrial system offered what appeared to be beguilingly simple truths. And to become a Chartist was to join a social class that was potentially universal. Poetically, Jones found in Chartism a unifying force analogous to the German patriotic drive of the poetry he had grown up reading. Jones's perorations in his Chartist speeches to 'Organise! Organise! Organise!' echoed the German desire for national unification;[44] the mythologization of a Romantic German past became the pre-capitalist rural ideals of Feargus O'Connor's Land Plan. Jones found various ways to use his early engagement with German poetry to form a radical English poetical aesthetic.

Original Poetry in the Pre-Chartist Period

Taken as a whole, what is remarkable about Jones's original *Court Journal* poems is their apolitical nature when compared with the nationalistic tone of many of the German poems that Jones translated and chose to publish concomitantly. Jones was clearly invigorated by the political fervour of the works of Arndt, Ühland, and von Stolberg, but his own work of this period remains strictly within the bounds of a post-Romantic aestheticism. Of the twelve original Jones poems published in the *Court Journal* between 1840 and 1842, only the love lyric 'To Her' was subsequently republished (ten years later in *Notes to the People*). This competent but unimaginative poem, with its Keatsian imagery, and somewhat self-defeating inclusion of the phrase 'sickly sentiment' (l. 9),[45] was footnoted in the *Court Journal* by a curious editorial statement that may have been intended as an encouragement to the young poet, but has almost the effect of a disclaimer:

> If these lines be not evidence of the advent of a true Poet, we are much mistaken. At all events, whatever may be the result, we shall have intimated our conviction on this subject.[46]

Though these early works by Jones exhibit a poetic confidence and grasp of form, their subject matter constrains the author, leading him towards deference, sentimentality, or the kind of derivative imitation common in young poets. 'Lines on Miss Adelaide Kemble' and 'Lines on Lady Stepney's New Work' are courtly

32   INFLUENCES AND EARLY POETRY (1840–45)

exercises in flattery, the latter an acrostic (LADY STEPNEY) spelling out the subject of its title, Catherine Stepney, who was Jones's artistic patroness at the time. 'The Sun' and 'The Rainbow of Hope' are evocations of natural splendour in the German Romantic tradition (Arndt's 'The Stars' is clearly the inspiration for the former), but their attempts to use imagery to signify aspects of the human condition, whether general or personal, are too obvious in the latter (clumsy colour metaphors are used), or too vague in the former.

'Lines on the Brocken' is a sonnet in rhyming couplets describing the highest peak in the Harz mountain range, in the North German state of Saxony-Anhalt, which provides the natural phenomenon known as the 'Brocken Spectre', a distortion and amplification of shadows on the mountain which features in many German legends. Perhaps the most famous nineteenth-century description of the Brocken was contained in the prose travel work, *Die Harzreise* (*The Harz Journey*) of 1824, by Heinrich Heine, with whom Jones would later share a mutual acquaintance, Karl Marx. The language of Jones's poem is ponderously Romantic, recalling the wealth of mountain imagery in German romanticism, or Alpine-related British works including Shelley's 'Mont Blanc' (1817). But where Shelley uses his depiction of the sublime in nature to question the existence of a caring deity, Jones employs a metaphor that is so vague it is difficult to determine whether it intends psychological, social, or political resonance. As the 'last rays' of a personified sun 'dissolve themselves in night' (l. 2), the great mountain causes them to cast a shadow 'eastward far' (l. 9), 'veiling the minor heights from mortal view' (l. 10).[47] The last four lines of the poem attempt to liken this phenomenon to aspects of human interaction, but the unspecified context renders the metaphor ineffectual:

> 'Tis thus the *earthly* great o'erwhelm the sight,
> By casting others in a nameless night:-
> They intercept rays the rest should share,
> And give, for light, but darkness and despair! (ll. 11–14)

'Lines on the Brocken' typifies the poorly thought-out resolutions of immature poetry but its final image was adapted and re-used by Jones three years later in the political poem 'The Cornfield and the Factory'.[48] This comparison between an idealized rural existence and the evils of industrial urbanization — a common theme in Jones's Chartist poetry — ends with a couplet describing the factory's effect on the rural landscape: ''*Tis this*, that wards the sunshine from the sod, | And intercepts the very smile of God!' (ll. 84–85).

'The Goodwin Sands' recalls in its subject matter Daniel Defoe's 1703 poem, 'The Storm', depicting the dangers to shipping, especially in wartime, of the nine-mile long sandbank off the coast of Kent. Jones's poem is the most promising of his *Court Journal* submissions in that it foreshadows his later use of song-like repetition to enhance the musical effect of his poetry:

> As sweeps that bark o'er the far off waves,
>   Yonder their buried dead
> Rise from their tempest-hollowed graves
>   With wet shrouds round them spread:
> And they point to the spot where their bark was lost

With their white, thin, spectral hands;
And the sailors deem it the breaker's foam
That warns off the Goodwin sands;
Nor know that the dead,
Arise from their bed,
To warn off the Goodwin sands! (ll. 19–27)[49]

Subtler evocations of the region are exampled by Matthew Arnold's 'Dover Beach' (1867), or Charlotte Smith's 'Beachy Head' (1807), but Jones's poem, published when he was twenty-two, displays the distinctive rhythms of his Chartist work. The quickening metrical effect of the shorter, pentasyllabic couplet lines twenty-five and twenty-six became a familiar feature of Jones's style, but whether he inherited this from German Romantics such as Ühland, or from English forms including the limerick, is not clear.

Three of Jones's *Court Journal* compositions have German titles, although the poems themselves are in English: 'Geister-Ahnung' ('Ghost-idea'), 'Der Glocken-ruf' ('The Bell-cry'), and 'Das Lebens-Ziel' ('Lifelong Goal'). 'Das Lebens-Ziel' is an aphoristic twelve-line lyric with a fatalistic tone and a slightly adolescent sense of impotent despair. Life is seen as 'but a Thought between | The Future and the Past', with 'Hopes ne'er to be fulfill'd'. In this moribund vision even the surety of a Christian afterlife holds little more than respite from life's disappointments:

We struggle through life's dreamy years,
With few glad visions blest;
And when our last *best* home appears,
We enter it, — to rest! (ll. 9–12)[50]

Although 'Das Lebens-Ziel' displays the familiar cantering rhythms and occasional exclamatory tone of Jones's later poetry, it typifies the work of his *Court Journal* period in the weakness of its subject matter. With hindsight it is possible to see in these works a good poet in search of a worthy subject, but the lack of distinctive quality could just as easily be attributed to simple poetic immaturity.

Of the German-titled *Court Journal* poems, the piece that most obviously foreshadows Jones's later work is 'Geister-Ahnung'. The speaker in this work passes a 'ruined mansion hall' (l. 2) which natural phenomena seem to re-animate:

The boughs at the casements whisper,
Like lovers at the dance;
And flitting shadows, one by one,
O'er the marble pavement glance.

From vault and arch and column,
Deep echoes come like laughter;
And fitfully a deadened sound,
Like sighs, glides stealing after. (ll. 5–12)[51]

Although there is little in itself that is remarkable in this poem's Gothic imagery, its relationship to 'The Better Hope', a poem written some years after, raises interesting thematic issues. The later poem's image of 'my father's hall' (l. 13), a 'cold, quiet home' (l. 49) where 'a laugh cannot pass through a marbly mass' (l. 23), is an inversion of the picture presented in 'Geister-Ahnung'. The earlier poem's

34 INFLUENCES AND EARLY POETRY (1840–45)

mansion is uninhabited but imbued with a ghostly life; the house in the later piece is inhabited but strangely empty of human emotion. A sense of dislocation pervades both works, and the presence of 'a dark old wood' (l. 14) in 'The Better Hope' is paralleled by the speaker's situation travelling through a 'forest hoar and thin' (l. 14) in 'Geister-Ahnung'. The latter image betrays a sense of vulnerability in the speaker which is confirmed by his closing declaration: 'I ne'er again at midnight hour, | Trod o'er that mansion grey!' (ll. 19–20); a rejection, though presumably born of fear, that pre-figures the fully conscious rejection of an upper-class environment by the speaker of 'The Better Hope'. Even in the early 1840s, the Jones family's relationship with the aristocracy was a troubled one, due to Charles Jones's long-running dispute with his former employer, King Ernst of Hanover (the erstwhile Duke of Cumberland).

The 13 December 1843 issue of the *Morning Post* sees the first publication of an original English-language poem by Jones that explicitly concerns a political subject. 'To Chateaubriand: A Voice from England to the Stranger Bard' is a eulogy to the aging father-figure of French Romanticism that conflates its subject's literary and political endeavours, characterizing his increasingly isolated existence in France as a form of imprisonment: 'still through the prison bars the angel sings' (l. 7).[52] In fact, François-René de Chateaubriand (1768–1848), though exiled several times during his eventful life, was never imprisoned. A complex character, Chateaubriand found himself in and out of favour with various powerful figures in French politics through the early nineteenth century, from Napoleon to Louis XVIII, and ended his days in opposition to Louis Philippe, the subject of praise in Jones's original version of 'The Poet's Mission'. Perhaps what drew Jones to Chateaubriand as a political figure was his residual, instinctive monarchism combined with a strong sense of Christian justification for increased democracy. While the former reflected Jones's own political stance at the time, the latter increasingly became a feature of both his poetry and his later Chartist oratory. Using the familiar Shelleyan mechanism of volcanic imagery Jones's poem asserts the moral agency of its subject's literary work:

> Forth, o'er the coldness of the outer world,
> Burst, from his deep heart feelings' fiery flow;
> Thus, from the volcano's rim, unfurled
> The lava banner's waves o'er ice and snow.
>
> Hail to the bard, who ever sung the right;
> Hail to the river on a desert roll'd;
> Hail to the veteran from the Titan fight
> Hail to the heart that dies but grows not old!
>
> ('To Chateaubriand', ll. 9–16)

Twelve years after it appeared in the *Morning Post*, 'To Chateaubriand', under the new title of 'The Poet's Death', became part of the 'Poet' section of *The Battle-Day: And Other Poems* (1855). In this guise it differed very little from the original, excepting minor changes to grammar and punctuation, and to the second line, 'grown white-haired in the service of his lyre' being changed to 'grown *grey*-haired in the service of his lyre' (my emphasis).[53] What is implicit in this change is that

Jones himself potentially becomes the subject of the work. Jones was only thirty-six when this poem was re-published (Chateaubriand died in 1848, aged seventy-nine), but it was commonly thought that his imprisonment from 1848 to 1850 had had a deleterious effect on his health. Indeed, many claimed that the experience led to his relatively early death in 1869: the grey hair referred to in the poem could easily be imagined as his own. With the adaptation of this poem from a work dedicated to a real historical figure to one relating to a general poet-figure (a process familiar from 'To Louis Philippe'/'To Byron'/'The Poet's Mission'), it seems clear that Jones intended his audience to identify himself in this poet-figure. Beyond mere egotism, and a tendency toward self-mythologization, this tacit utilization of personal experience reaches back to Romantic explorations of the self as employed by Wordsworth, Coleridge, Keats, Byron, and Shelley. The latter two in particular recorded their own experiences, both actual and psychological, in a consciously mythopoeic manner. Forty years before 'The Poet's Death', no attentive reader was in any doubt as to the implicit identity of Childe Harold or Don Juan, and alter-egos of Shelley appear in works including 'Julian and Maddalo: A Conversation' (1818) and *Adonais* (1821). Jones inherited this method of treating himself as representative of a universal poet-figure from illustrious predecessors.

Given that the *Morning Post* was hardly an obscure publication, and that *The Battle-Day* sold well as a collection just twelve years later, it seems remarkable that no-one appears to have noticed or commented on the fact that 'To Chateaubriand' and 'The Poet's Death' are essentially the same poem. It is also remarkable that four poems Jones had published in the *Morning Post* shortly before his Chartist period have been omitted from all previous bibliographies. The *Morning Post* published 'Echoes No. I — The Golden Harp', 'Echoes No. II — The Cornfield and the Factory', 'Echoes No. III — The Farmer', and 'Peace to Earth'.[54] All these works provide evidence of an increasing engagement with politics which runs counter to contemporary accounts of Jones's previous ideological naivety before his involvement with radical politics, and subsequent biographical acceptance of these accounts.

'Peace to Earth' describes, in elevated poetic language, the international mood during and following the Bombardment of Mogador, part of the first Franco-Moroccan War, which had taken place the previous month. Mogador, the Portuguese name for the modern Moroccan city of Essaouira, was an important trading port attacked by the French fleet in retaliation for Morocco's support of Algeria in resistance against the French. What heightened international interest in this incident was both the presence of several European elements in the port at the time and Mogador's important trade relations with Europe. Tensions between Britain and France were exacerbated by the conflict, and many observers feared the two nations were on the brink of war. The poem begins by portraying war as a constant presence in international relations, and identifies the conflict as a brief but dangerous unleashing of a monstrous personification:

> The baying of the wolf of war
> > Was heard across the startled world —
> > His wild defiance hurled
> > At England's cliffs from Afric far;

36 INFLUENCES AND EARLY POETRY (1840–45)

> And fierce the restless monster shook his chain,
> When, beaten by the hand of peace,
> Murmuring he sought his sullen lair again,
> And the vexed world breathed in its short release.
> ('Peace to Earth', ll. 1–8)

Despite the heavy metaphors employed, this is a long way from the abstractions, word-plays, and interiorities of Jones's original *Court Journal* poems. Although 'Peace to Earth' may have been written partly to reflect the more politically engaged editorial profile of the *Morning Post*, it is possible to see over the period 1840–44 Jones's transition from poetic debutant to a writer of serious ambition, creating work which engaged with external realities. In contrast to Jones's later, fiercely internationalist and anti-imperialist politics, England is sympathetically portrayed, in this first stanza at least, as an unwilling participant in a possible global conflict: the 'wild defiance' of 'the wolf of war' is 'hurled | At England's cliffs'. Jones's sense of twin nationhood emerges in his evocations of England's and Germany's potential influence in the conflict:

> Then had fiery-eyed impatience urged
> The *Lion* o'er the precipice he verged,
> Or bade the *Eagle* wave his restless wing:
> Discord had sate on ruin as its king.
> [...]
> The German Alps from every towering branch
> Had shaken down their living avalanche,
> And England sent, with doom-denouncing breath,
> Her floating archipelagos of death! (ll. 9–12, 19–22)

As the poem progresses the mood of the two nations becomes more aggressive: England's '*Lion*' has a 'fiery-eyed impatience', while the German '*Eagle*' has a 'restless wing'. What is interesting about this poem is that France, the aggressor in the conflict which had awakened these sleeping giants, is not referred to at all, either directly or emblematically. It is as though Jones takes it for granted that *Morning Post* readers would subscribe to a general English antipathy towards its European neighbour. But it is also possible that Jones wished to avoid any jingoistic reaction to his work by keeping the focus away from a potential enemy. Ultimately, the tone of Jones's poem is not militaristic in that it reflects the prevailing mood of international observers in wishing to avoid an escalation of conflict.

The metaphor of 'floating archipelagos of death' to represent the British naval fleet that was sent to the Mediterranean during the escalating crisis is, poetically speaking, the highpoint in terms of imagery in the work. It works not just as a visual image but as an effective representation of battleships as sovereign extensions of the islands of Britain, physical symbols of the nation. England's 'doom-denouncing breath' implies that English involvement in the conflict, though limited to implicit threat, was both justified and diplomatically effective; but this patriotic representation is undermined by ambiguity in the poem's conclusion. After a description of the brief ferocity of the Bombardment of Mogador this essentially anti-war poem concludes with an uneasy celebration of an avoidance of international conflict: 'And God's own peace, unfathomed and unbought, | Broods dovelike o'er the wondering earth again' (ll. 45–46). The slightly menacing tone of these final lines is formed by the sense that the mechanisms for peace in this instance are not understood, and can therefore not necessarily be repeated in the future. The double connotation of nurture and resentment inherent in the use of the verb 'brood' serves to enhance the conclusion's sense of unease.

The three poems that make up the 'Echoes' series are significant in that they show Jones poetically engaged with domestic political subjects for the first time, and the subsequent re-publishing of the last two raises interesting issues concerning Jones's conception of the mobility of poetic subjects. 'The Golden Harp', as its title suggests, deals with the question of Ireland; 'The Cornfield and the Factory' contrasts perceptions of a healthy rural lifestyle with that of industry-blighted urban environments; and 'The Farmer' tackles the issue of political agitation in rural Britain. 'The Golden Harp' is Jones's interpretation of the events of 1843, 'the Repeal Year', when some observers feared that increased political activity and agitation in Ireland had brought Britain close to civil war. Daniel O'Connell (1775–1847), the leader of the Repeal Association, had enjoined calls for simple repeal of the Union with the proposal of agrarian reforms which would end the landlord-tenant system which over much of Ireland consisted of Irish Catholic peasants working only to pay rents to absentee Protestant landlords. O'Connell, the respected politician who had successfully campaigned for Catholic emancipation in the preceding decades, was fiercely opposed to violent agitation of any form, but the radicals of the Young Ireland movement were more ambiguous and varied in their approaches, and their newspaper, the *Nation*, was an influential voice in the debates over Irish issues. The year 1843 ended with the setting up by Parliament of the Devon Commission to look into the issues surrounding Irish land leases. O'Connell was doubtful about the commission's ability to deal with the problem but the government's action was partially successful in dampening the revolutionary flavour of some pockets of agitation.[55]

'The Golden Harp', like 'Peace to Earth', celebrates the withdrawal of the threat of violence. But in terms of the contemporary issues affecting Ireland it is difficult to tell where the writer's political sympathies lie. This ambiguity is less a deliberate obfuscation than a result of the confusing use of multiple metaphors and imagery which Jones uses to approach his difficult subject. 'A beautiful Spirit' (l. 2) plays a 'golden harp' (l. 14) in response to a thunderous storm in which are heard the shouts of millions, 'like the cry of a nation's despair' (l. 13). This music has the effect of waking the people 'from their sleep of long years' (l. 20), but there is no echo, a lack of response occasioned apparently by a lack of leadership: 'That *coward heart* shrunk at the storm it had called, | And the legions they *doubt*, for the leader's appalled!' (ll. 28–29). The tempest passes and the beautiful Spirit is left to quench the flames caused by the lightning's blasts with her tears. She then gazes on a dull flower, which turns out to be no less than a shamrock, who then declares that after the defeat of treachery 'the spirit of ERIN shall summon again | From her golden lyre a golden strain' (ll. 55–56). The shamrock then closes the poem with a pair of aphoristic couplets of a distinctly anti-revolutionary bent:

38 INFLUENCES AND EARLY POETRY (1840–45)

> The sun shines but when tempests cease,
> *Freedom* only lives in *Peace*.
> It is not discord, fear, and ire
> Can raise the *flower* or wake the *lyre*.
> ('Peace to Earth', ll. 57–60)

The problem with this poem, apart from its use of national and poetic clichés, is that the reader barely has time to establish the symbolic nature of one metaphor before another comes along to confuse the picture. The tempest is clearly emblematic of revolutionary fervour, but it is difficult to pin down with any degree of certainty what the other images denote. If the 'coward heart' is meant to represent O'Connell, or perhaps the leaders of the Young Ireland movement, it is still difficult to determine whether the voice of the poet is speaking on behalf of the oppressed of Ireland in condemnatory sympathy with their cause, or crowing over the failure of nerve of an attempted insurrection.

'The Golden Harp' is important, however, in that it establishes Jones's early engagement with domestic political issues almost two years before his involvement with Chartism, and highlights Ireland as an important context with regards to wider political agitation throughout Britain. In the post-Chartist period, Jones wrote an article entitled 'To the Men of Ireland', published in the *People's Paper* on 8 March 1856, equating the plight of the Irish people with that of the English working class:

> Grievously, indeed, has Ireland suffered at the hands of England, but who inflicted that suffering? Was it the English people? Never! Those who slew you at Rathcormac, slew us at Peterloo; those who imprisoned you in the DUBLIN Newgate, imprisoned us in the London one. Those who passed the curfew laws for you, passed the six-acts for us. Those who robbed you of your lands robbed us as well. Those who ejected the cottar in Ireland, created the pauper in Great Britain.[56]

This reference to the cottars, or cottiers, whose systematic eviction in Ireland throughout the first half of the nineteenth century subsequently exacerbated the effects of famine, was an attempt to draw an analogy between the Irish peasant class and the English rural populations whose lives had been disrupted by repeated Inclosure Acts and the rapid urbanization caused by industrialization.

'The Cornfield and the Factory' and 'The Farmer' both contain images of rural life and were both subsequently republished in the 1855 *Battle-Day* collection (the former was also published in the *Northern Star* edition of 27 June 1846) as part of a four–poem section titled 'Plough and Loom', although 'The Farmer' is truncated and re-titled 'The Peasant'.[57] 'The Cornfield and the Factory' is reproduced in its entirety in the collection and appears, as a poem contrasting the healthy bucolic lifestyle with the urban hell created by rapid industrialization, in perfect keeping with Chartist and post-Chartist radicalism, condemning the excesses of capitalism and harking back to the agrarian aspirations of Feargus O'Connor's Land Plan. In the *Morning Post* in 1844, before Jones had any contact with radical politics, the same work appears to mourn the loss of an ideal vision of England that is quintessentially Tory in its mythology:

> Oh! what is so blithe as through cornfields to roam,
>> When the lark is in heaven and laughter on earth?
> Oh! what is so blithe as the glad harvest-home,
>> When the lads are all frolic — the lasses all mirth? (ll. 1–4)[58]

This mobility of subject is an especially strong aspect of Jones's poetic career because of the ideological volte-face represented by his defection to the ranks of Chartism in late 1845. Although Jones's poetry was well-received by the mainstream literary press throughout his career, after 1845 most of his readership would have been radical. And due to Jones's involvement with various newspapers, the pressures of creative production led him to re-use poetry written before his Chartist 'conversion'. These examples can illuminate areas where 'Olde England' Toryism and radical politics partially shared an agenda in opposition to the laissez-faire economic capitalism represented by the Whigs. When 'The Cornfield and the Factory' abandons the song-like structure of its pastoral section and uses dense heroic couplets to describe the ravages on landscape and people of the industrial revolution, the agendas of elements of both right-wing and left-wing politics are served:

> Care-stricken forms the street's long darkness fill,
> Embodied dreams of misery and ill!
> A more than Cain-like mark their foreheads bear,
> For sin's their only respite from despair!
> And in each sunken eye's unhallowed cell
> The fever flashes, not of life, but hell.
> Oaths upon infant lips, and, loathsome sight!
> The eyes of childhood without childhood's light. (ll. 58–65)

The moral outrage inherent in this depiction of the human degradation caused by the urban factory system is part of a 'state of the nation' address that transfers easily across a broadly anti-industrial political spectrum.

In the form it appears in the *Morning Post* in 1844, 'The Farmer' is ideologically by far the most reactionary of Jones's pre-Chartist productions. It begins in much the same vein as 'The Cornfield and the Factory', contrasting the nobility and purity of rural labour with the plight of the industrial labourer:

> For *him* the orchards bloom, the cornfields nod,
> And these are the altars where he worships God.
> Not thus the pale mechanic, hapless slave,
> Digs for a master's wealth his own dark grave.
> ('The Farmer', ll. 12–15)

But a note of unease begins to enter the rural idyll when Jones describes the farmer's cottage and the economic plight of its tenants. The farmer's wife has 'a dying heart beside a darkening hearth' (l. 26), and the farmer himself is described as 'now careworn and thin' (l. 41). The causes of this financial misery are not specified but 'The Peasant', which is the *Battle-Day* version of the poem, ends with the following pair of couplets:

> His heart a prison, with a chaos fraught,
> His hearth neglected, and his brain untaught,
> Half-stifled curses smouldering in his breast,

40   INFLUENCES AND EARLY POETRY (1840–45)

> 'Tis thus the British peasant seeks his rest.
> ('The Peasant', ll. 49–52)

At this point the sympathy of the reader lies squarely with the poem's protagonist, and the only difference between this version and the original is the replacement of the terms 'yeoman' and 'farmer' with 'peasant'. The latter term becomes the title of the 1855 work, presumably in an attempt to lower the social status of the subject to attract sympathy from a radical or working-class audience. But the subsequently excised twenty-six-line denouement of the original *Morning Post* poem begins by raising the image of the 'stormy spirit' (l. 53) familiar from 'The Golden Harp'. This time the spirit is positively identified as 'AGITATION' (l. 58), which calls the farmer from his work, leaving his fields untilled; he:

> *Neglects* the soil, and *wonders that he wants*,
> Blames *others* for the wreck *himself* has made,
> And clasps the *knife*, when he should grasp the *spade!*'
> ('The Farmer', ll. 60–62)

The poem ends by describing yet another withdrawal from violence, where 'the voice of honest worth again is heard' (l. 69), and significantly, a variation on Shelley's revolutionary formula from 'The Mask of Anarchy' of 'ye are many — they are few' is invoked to bolster the wisdom of conforming to the status quo: 'Numbers are safety — unity is force!' (l. 73).

With its outright condemnation of political agitation, despite the apparent cause of financial hardship, it is not difficult to see why Jones did not re-publish 'The Farmer' in its original form; a work more antithetical to the Chartist ethos could hardly be imagined. But what made him decide to re-work the poem in its truncated form in 1855? Was he simply running out of material? Certainly to modern eyes, reversing a poem's ideological position by omitting its original final section (without at least acknowledging the fact) might seem aesthetically, or even politically, dishonest, the literary equivalent of a Stalinist re-writing of history. But there is a counter argument: if Jones had wished to suppress the earlier poem, he could easily just have left it alone. It is possible to detect bravery and even a distorted integrity in his revisionist actions. His re-working of the piece was perhaps an exorcism of the ghosts of his former political self, and an implicit recognition that the seeds of his future radicalism were present in his pre-Chartist poetry, disguised though they may have been by a generally conservative outlook.

By analyzing the development of Ernest Jones's poetic voice from the early 1840s it becomes clear how his celebrated Chartist works emerged not from a spontaneous poetic 'reinvention', but from a progression of tropes and themes that already existed in his work. It is possible to detect a narrowing of political focus in his work from his translations of German patriotic poetry, through the literary/political subject of 'To Chateaubriand' to the domestic political concerns of 'The Golden Harp' and 'The Farmer'. Re-worked poems including 'The Poet's Mission' prove how effectively, and with relatively little revision, early pieces could be adopted for use within radical contexts of publication. The rural idealism of 'The Cornfield and the Factory' goes further by indicating that Jones's Chartist 'conversion' was not quite

INFLUENCES AND EARLY POETRY (1840–45)   41

the complete ideological reversal it first appears. Jones's demonstrable inheritance of a wider European Romantic influence than his contemporaries perhaps provides some explanation of the essential 'difference' of Jones's voice within Chartist poetry; 'difference' surely being one of the factors that increases a poet's standing amongst his peers. By the time Jones's poetry began to appear in the *Northern Star* in the mid-1840s, he was already a widely-published minor poet, with some good reviews endorsing his work. The purpose and focus of the cause of Chartism raised his literary profile still further, and enabled him to utilize his poetic talents to create a body of work that inspired a generation of working-class radicals.

Notes to Chapter 1

1. Leon Gottfried, *Matthew Arnold and the Romantics* (London: Routledge & Keegan Paul, 1963), p. 3.
2. Andrew Radford and Mark Sandy (eds.), 'Introduction', in *Romantic Echoes in the Victorian Era* (Aldershot: Ashgate, 2008), p. 3.
3. Sanders, p. 78.
4. Thomas Frost, 'Scott, Byron, and Shelley', *Northern Star*, 2 January 1847. Hereafter, quotations from the *Northern Star* will be indicated by the initials *NS* followed by the date of publication.
5. For a variety of interpretations of the complex cultural relationship between Victorian Britain and the previous century, see Francis O'Gorman and Katherine Turner (eds.), *The Victorians and the Eighteenth Century: Reassessing the Tradition* (Aldershot: Ashgate, 2004).
6. Ernest Jones, 'The Painter of Florence: A Domestic Poem', in *NP* (1851), I, 41–47.
7. George Gordon Byron (Baron), *Don Juan*, ed. by Truman Guy Steffan and Willis W. Pratt, 4 vols (Austin: University of Texas Press, 1957), II, 29–30.
8. After the real Indian Uprising of 1857, 'The New World' was re-published separately under the title *The Revolt of Hindostan*.
9. Ernest Jones, 'To Wordsworth', in *NP* (1851), I, 69.
10. Ernest Jones, 'Introduction', in 'The New World', in *NP* (1851), I, 4.
11. Ernest Jones, 'The Song of the Low', in *NP* (1852), II, 953 (in Kovalev, pp. 174–76).
12. Percy Bysshe Shelley, 'Men of England: A Song', in *Shelley: Poetical Works*, ed. by Thomas Hutchinson (London: Oxford University Press, 1967), p. 572.
13. Percy Bysshe Shelley, 'The Mask of Anarchy', in *Shelley: Poetical Works*, pp. 340–44.
14. Ernest Jones, 'The Poet's Prayer to the Evening Wind', in *The Battle-Day: And Other Poems* (London: Routledge, 1855), p. 61–62. Hereafter *The Battle-Day* is referred to as *BD*.
15. Percy Bysshe Shelley, 'Ode to the West Wind', in *Shelley: Poetical Works*, pp. 577–79.
16. Friedrich Engels, *The Condition of the Working Class in England*, eds. and trans. by W. O. Henderson and W. H. Chaloner (Oxford: Blackwell, 1958), p. 273.
17. Percy Bysshe Shelley, 'Song to the Men of England', in *Shelley: Poetical Works*, pp. 572–73.
18. William S. Villiers Sankey, 'Ode', in Kovalev, p. 76.
19. Shelley, *The Letters of Percy Bysshe Shelley*, ed. Frederick L. Jones, 2 vols (Oxford: Clarendon, 1964), II, 141.
20. For a poetic account of the difference between Shelley's and Byron's social and political philosophies, see Shelley's 'Julian and Maddalo: A Conversation' (1818–19).
21. Ernest Jones, 'Onward', *Labourer*, I (1847), 234 (in Kovalev, p. 150).
22. George S. Williamson, *The Longing for Myth in Germany: Religion and Aesthetic Culture from Romanticism to Nietzsche* (Chicago: University of Chicago Press, 2004), p. 23.
23. Ernest Jones, 'The Poet's Mission', *NS* 17/10/1846 (in Kovalev, p. 179).
24. Saville, p. 15.
25. Ernest Jones, 'To [Names of Byron and Louis-Philippe crossed out]', Ernest Jones Manuscript Poems, Manchester County Record Office, MS. f281.89 J5/30 (hereafter referred to as EJMP MCRO).

42   INFLUENCES AND EARLY POETRY (1840–45)

26. Ernst Moritz Arndt, 'The German Fatherland', in *The World's Story: A History of the World in Story, Song and Art*, ed. by Eva March Tappan, 14 vols (Boston: Houghton Mifflin, 1914), VII, 276–78.

27. Kovalev, p. 58.

28. Gunter Klabes, 'Political Reality and Poetic Mission: Hölderlin's and Shelley's Heterocosm', in *English and German Romanticism: Cross-Currents and Controversies*, ed. by James Pipkin (Heidelberg: Winter, 1985), pp. 301–21 (p. 310).

29. Friedrich Hölderlin, 'The Poet's Vocation', in *Friedrich Hölderlin: Poems and Fragments*, trans. by Michael Hamburger (London: Routledge, 1966,) p. 175.

30. Ernest Jones, 'Our Destiny', NS 11/7/1846 (in Kovalev, p. 137).

31. Ernest Jones (trans. from Ludwig Ühland), 'The Minstrel's Curse', *Court Journal*, 4 December 1841, cutting in EJMP MCRO, MS. f281.89 J5/95. Hereafter quotations from the *Court Journal* will be indicated by the initials *CJ* followed by the date of publication.

32. Ludwig Ühland, 'The King on the Tower', in *The Poems of Ludwig Ühland*, trans. by William Collett Sandars (London: Ridgway, 1869), p. 29.

33. Ernest Jones (trans. from Ludwig Ühland), 'The Monarch's Death-Prayer', *CJ* 25/12/1841, cutting in EJMP MCRO, MS. f281.89 J5/95.

34. Ernest Jones (trans. from Ernst Moritz Arndt), 'The Stars', *CJ* 9/10/1841, cutting in EJMP MCRO, MS. f281.89 J5/95.

35. Ludwig Ühland, 'Der Knabern Berglied', in *Poems of Ühland*, ed. by Waterman T. Hewett (London: Macmillan, 1904), pp. 18–19.

36. Ludwig Ühland, 'The Herd Boy's Song', in *The Poems of Ühland*, trans. by William Collett Sandars, pp. 38–39.

37. Ernest Jones (trans. from Ludwig Ühland), 'The Boy's Mountain Song', *CJ* 18/10/1841, cutting in EJMP MCRO, MS. f281.89 J5/95.

38. Ernest Jones, 'The Blackstone Edge Gathering', NS 22/8/1846 (in Kovalev, pp. 140–41).

39. Ernest Jones (trans. from Count Friedrich Leopold von Stolberg), 'The German Boy's Song', *CJ*, undated cutting in EJMP MCRO, MS. f281.89 J5/95.

40. Ernest Jones, 'The Better Hope', NS 5/9/1846.

41. Donald Read and Eric Glasgow, *Feargus O'Connor: Irishman and Chartist* (London: Edward Arnold Ltd. 1961), p. 109. See Chapter 3 for further discussion of the Land Plan.

42. Ernest Jones, 'Der Deutsche Sprachschatz', *Deutsche Londoner Zeitung*, 25 April 1845

43. Ernest Jones, 'Politisches', *Deutsche Londoner Zeitung*, 25 April 1845. Translated from the original German by Simon Rennie and Adrian Knapp (University of Leeds).

44. Ernest Jones, Speech at Manchester, 20 October 1850, cited in Saville, p. 113.

45. Ernest Jones, 'To Her', *CJ* 8/11/1842, cutting in EJMP MCRO, MS. f281.89 J5/95.

46. Ibid., editorial statement.

47. Ernest Jones, 'Lines on the Brocken', *CJ* 22/5/1841, cutting in EJMP MCRO, MS. f281.89 J5/95.

48. Ernest Jones, 'The Cornfield and the Factory', *Morning Post*, 20 January 1844. Hereafter quotations from the *Morning Post* will be indicated by the initials *MP* followed by the date of publication.

49. Ernest Jones, 'The Goodwin Sands', *CJ* 2/10/1841, cutting in EJMP MCRO, MS. f281.89 J5/95.

50. Ernest Jones, 'Das Lebens-Ziel', *CJ* 2/7/1842, cutting in EJMP MCRO, MS. f281.89 J5/95.

51. Ernest Jones, 'Geister-Ahnung', *CJ* 5/3/1842, cutting in EJMP MRCO, MS. f281.89 J5/95.

52. Ernest Jones, 'To Chateaubriand: A Voice from England to the Stranger Bard', *MP* 13/12/1843.

53. Ernest Jones, 'The Poet's Death', BD, p. 66 (in Kovalev, pp. 178–79).

54. Ernest Jones, 'Echoes No. I — The Golden Harp', *MP* 19/1/1844; 'Echoes No. II — The Cornfield and the Factory, *MP* 20/1/1844; 'Echoes No. III — The Farmer', *MP* 6/2/1844; 'Peace to Earth', *MP* 26/9/1844.

55. For a summary of the events leading up to the years of the Irish Famine, see Peter Gray, *Famine, Land and Politics: British Government and Irish Society* (Dublin: Irish Academic Press, 1999), pp. 41–78.

56. Ernest Jones, 'To the Men of Ireland', in Saville, pp. 216–18 (p. 216).

57. Ernest Jones, 'The Peasant', in *BD*, pp. 47–48. In Miles Taylor's bibliography at the end of *Ernest Jones, Chartism, and the Romance of Politics 1819–1869* (Oxford: Oxford University Press, 2003), p. 264, 'The Cornfield and the Factory' is listed as 'The Cottage and the Factory'.
58. Ernest Jones, 'Echoes No. 11: The Cornfield and the Factory', *MP* 20/1/1844.

CHAPTER 2

Jones and Myth
1846–48

From the mid-1840s it becomes increasingly difficult to separate Ernest Jones's literary life from his political activity. When Jones first approached Christopher Shackleton, who ran the Chartist Hall in Holborn, on 28 January 1846, he did so 'clutching a sheaf of poetry'.[1] His introduction to the *Northern Star* a few months later was by means of a long poem in the form of a dramatic monologue, *My Life*, which had been published by T. C. Newby the previous year. While his introductory letter to his 'Brother Chartists', declaring his political credentials and offering himself as a delegate to the National Convention, was printed on the front page of the newspaper on 9 May 1846, the same issue carried within a longer introduction written by the editors of the poetry page. The piece made much of a review of *My Life* in the *New Quarterly Review* of the previous January. These words in a radical newspaper lifted from the pages of a well-regarded conservative literary journal leave the reader in no doubt that Chartism has acquired a rising literary star:

> The first part of this pleasing work lies before us. It contains more pregnant thoughts, more bursts of lyric power, more, in fine, of the purely grand and beautiful, than any poetical work which has made its appearance for years, if we except the magnificent productions of Browning, and perhaps the lays of Tennyson.[2]

The use of Tennyson as a poetic benchmark in the mid-1840s is understandable, but Robert Browning was not yet a widely-admired literary figure by January 1846. His inclusion in this comparative context can probably be attributed to early recognition by the *New Quarterly Review* of his mastery of the dramatic monologue — the poetic form of *My Life*.

Less than two months after his introduction to the readers of the newspaper, the poetry page of the *Northern Star* preceded the publication of 'The Cornfield and the Factory' (a pre-Chartist poem which had already appeared in the *Morning Post*) with the following paragraph:

> From a considerable number of original pieces with which our political friends have favoured us, we have selected the best. We commence our selection with the following poem which too truly pictures the withering influence of the accursed factory system; the author is already a favourite with our readers, his name is sufficient introduction.[3]

Jones's swift popularity with the Chartist readership may seem strange given that he had no previous experience of radical politics or radical literature, but he instinctively understood what his readers wanted to hear, and gradually formed a bond with them that reached across class boundaries. That 'The Cornfield and the Factory' (discussed in the previous chapter), a poem written before his Chartist involvement, could appeal to a radical working-class audience suggests that Jones's earlier imaginative development had begun to converge independently with radical poetics. This can be attributed to the nature of Tory opposition to the increasing industrialization and urbanization of England, and Jones's absorption prior to 1846 of this opposition's imaginative expression in terms of 'Golden Age' myths. Jones adapted these and other myths to synthesize a specifically Chartist mythic vision which formed the basis of his poetry for the rest of his career.

During the early part of Jones's Chartist career, before his imprisonment in 1848, his poetry reflected that period's Chartist pre-occupation with Feargus O'Connor's ambitious Land Plan, which was intended to provide viable agricultural plots and residences for urban workers through a subscription scheme. O'Connor, Chartism's charismatic Irish leader, saw a potentially powerful ally in the young and talented Ernest Jones, and Jones repaid the compliment with praise of O'Connor in speech, prose, and verse, and vociferous support of the Land Plan. The agrarian ambition of O'Connor's scheme drew on nostalgia for pre-industrial, non-urban landscapes and lifestyles whose evocations of simplicity, natural bounty, and wholesomeness proved a rich source of poetic material for Jones and other Chartist poets including Allen Davenport (1775–1846), William James Linton (1812–97), and Ebenezer Jones (1820–60). This nostalgia was not confined to the radical working class but found its expression in all areas of society where scepticism of the capitalist mantras of economic advancement and technological progress existed. The recovery of past values became a recurrent theme as the transformation of the industrial landscape became linked with anxieties regarding social and moral degeneration. The year before Victoria's accession to the throne a sense of contemporary devaluation pervades the preface of the self-published first edition of Augustus W. N. Pugin's *Contrasts* (1836), which compares modern and medieval architecture:

> I hope this Work will prove how little title this Age has to be one of improvement on the score of architectural excellence, when, in truth, that science is at a very low ebb; in which state, I fear, it will remain, unless the same feelings which influenced the old designers in the composition of their Works, can be restored: — a result which, though I most fervently wish, I dare not at present hope for. But I feel thoroughly convinced, that it is only by similar glorious feelings that similar glorious results can be obtained.[4]

Although this work's concern is the state of modern architecture, its emphasis on the recovery of the past's 'glorious feelings' is representative of wider Victorian anxieties that their society was culturally inferior, and that the basis of a remedy lay in a form of active retrospection. For Pugin, simply emulating medieval methods of construction is not enough; in order to create a modern architecture of similar aesthetic standard to that of the past, modern designers must recover an ancestral ethos and rework it through modern sensibilities. This process inevitably involves deconstruction, and for radical Chartists seeking a similar return to past values the edifice to be deconstructed was society itself. For Chartist poets the expression of the means of this deconstruction, and subsequent re-building, began with the creation of a mythic narrative that explained the present and predicted the future through reference to the past. Ernest Jones, to a greater degree than other Chartist poets, made use of language associated with an indeterminately–situated medieval past to encourage a return to its perceived values. Examination of Jones's poetry of this period reveals the role of poetry in Chartist political discourse and the formation of Chartist culture, but also illuminates its mythic consistency and ambition.

'The Two Races', History, and Myths of Deliverance

'The Two Races' is a poem that explores a contemporary social duality.[5] Its title may be a reference to Benjamin Disraeli's novel *Sybil, or The Two Nations* (1845). Indeed, it is worth speculating that Jones's poem might be an ironic elaboration of the ideas in Disraeli's novel, given that there is evidence that these two literary–political figures of the period not only knew each other, but were to become unlikely, if only occasional, allies. According to G. J. Holyoake, certainly by the 1850s, Jones's debt to his politically complex Tory contemporary went beyond the latter's support for voting reform in Parliament:

> On one occasion when I printed for him [Jones], and he was considerably in arrears, he said, 'I must go to my friend Disraeli.' An hour later he returned, and handed my brother Austin three of several £5 notes. He had others in his hand. That politic Minister inspired many Chartists with hatred of the Whigs, whom he himself disliked, because they did not favour his circuitous pretensions; and when he found Chartists of genius having the same hatred, he would supply them with money, the better to give effect to it.[6]

The accuracy of this account of clandestine collusion between Tory and Chartist might be called into question given Holyoake's eventual Whig sympathies and the general clamour of conflicting histories and memoirs in the post-Chartist period. But Holyoake was by no means as hostile towards Jones as R. G. Gammage (*History of the Chartist Movement 1837–1854*), and is usually regarded as one of the least partial Chartist memoirists.

Jones's initial method of examining the 'Condition of England' is to focus on the shift of power between the old aristocratic class and the relatively new merchant/industrial class, and it is these social groups that comprise 'The Two Races'. Within the poem Jones evokes a Golden Age by comparing the present with a mythical past, a partially imaginary composite that represents a political ideal. The binary structure of the poem is similar to that of 'The Cornfield and the Factory' (which contrasts the rural lifestyle with urban industrial squalor) in that both comprise two distinct parts; but both works yearn for a return to past values, idealizing the past in comparison to an unjust and socially destructive present. 'The Two Races' seeks an alliance between the aristocracy and the workers to defeat the usurping 'lords of trade' (l. 29). To this end, Part I is addressed to the 'Gentlemen of England', while Part II lists the moral deficiencies of the new industrialist class and predicts the emerging ascendancy of a third class of workers. In an adaptation of the concept of benevolent monarchy that features in some early Jones poetry the historical proto-democratic credentials of the aristocracy are highlighted in Part I. This is achieved by reference to the political checking of the excessive powers of the Church and the monarchy, and the perceived social balance effected by acts of benevolence in the tradition of *noblesse oblige*:

> Ye sons of Saxon chivalry,
> And hospitable state;
> Those champions of old liberty,
> When kings had grown too great.
>
> Who boarded bluff King Harry,
> And John on Runnymede;
> Who tamed the tyrant's tyranny,
> And soothed the people's need.
>
> Who welcomed honest poverty
> To shelter and to feast,
> And broke on his own infamy,
> The crozier of the priest.
>
> ('The Two Races', ll. 9–20)

Allusions to specific historical figures and events including Henry VIII and the probable locality of the signing by King John of the Magna Carta in 1215 make this poem slightly atypical of Jones's poetic Chartist output. However, the function of these references within the context of the work is in keeping with Jones's habitually mythic treatment of history as a justification for political radicalism. The fact that Jones lists specific historical figures and events alongside generalized references to the alleged benevolence of the former ruling class suggests a strategy of conflation of the historic and the apocryphal. For Jones, the past is an imaginative construct: it is sequential, in the sense that it is part of a seemingly inevitable progression, but it is also material that is malleable within the context of the creative imagination. The myth of a 'Saxon Constitution', a pre-1066 essentially English version of natural law, is opposed to the myth of the 'Norman Yoke' imposed by foreign invaders.

The appeal to the aristocracy to assist in the struggle for the Charter in 'The Two Races' is framed as a natural continuation of noble deeds carried out in the past. Unrestrained capitalism is characterized as undermining English society from its central position in the social spectrum:

> Arise! If ye are nobles
> In nature as in name:
> There's misery to banish!
> There's tyranny to tame!
>
> For the lords of trade are stirring
> With their treasures, far and nigh;
> They are trampling on the lowly,
> They are spurning at the high. (ll. 21–28)

Although there is a hint of mockery in Jones's use of the word traditionally associated with the ceremonial act of knighthood, 'Arise!', the request for assistance in opposition to the upstart class of industrialists seems genuine. In an example of adaptive mythopoeia that transfers the perceived sins of the old class onto the new, Part II of the poem sees Jones take the traditional image of the morally corrupt, effete aristocrat from popular fable and literature and transpose it onto the new industrialist class. It is now they who are 'lurers of the village maid' (l. 67) and have 'buried all their manhood | In silk, and plume, and gem' (ll. 81–82). The word 'silk' has a particular symbolic resonance for Jones; it appears in eight of his Chartist poems, almost always in association with effeminacy or decadence.[7]

Brian Maidment asserts in *The Poorhouse Fugitives* that threat is an important function of many Chartist lyrics beyond an attempt to 'create and extend group identity and political solidarity'.[8] In Jones's work this threat is almost always directed towards the capitalist class or its perceived enablers in the established Church or the government, but in the final stanzas of 'The Two Races' it becomes apparent that Jones's appeal to the old aristocracy in Part I masks an implicit threat to them as well; the imminent triumph of the working class will demand submission or allegiance from all:

> But another strain is sounding,
>   In music fresh and clear;
> And the nation's hearts are bounding,
>   That glorious psalm to hear.
>
> It tells, a race has risen,
>   Of more than knightly worth;
> Forth-breaking from its prison,
>   In the dungeons of the earth.
>
> And not by lance or sabre,
>   *These* nobles hold their lands, —
> But by the right of labour,
>   And the work of honest hands.
>
> And not for crown and crozier,
>   They till the sacred sod;
> But the liege-lord of their holding,
>   Is the lord of nature: — God. (ll. 89–104)

In an open letter to the *Northern Star* published on 1 April 1848 Jones suggests that Chartists must 'show to all sections of the community, how their just interests are identical with those of the working classes, and how the people are in truth prepared to act up their expressions of fraternity'.[9] Elements of this inclusivity are reflected in the first part of 'The Two Races', but the last stanzas take language traditionally associated with the aristocracy ('knightly', 'nobles', 'liege-lord') and apply it to the working class; a linguistic appropriation that both inverts traditional associative values ascribed to different classes, and pre-figures real social, and presumably economic, appropriation through political action. The usurpation of the dominant social position of the aristocrat by the industrialist class which is detailed by much of the poem is now to be superseded by the rise of the working class — the work does not concern two 'races' but three. The poem begins to work on levels of multiple address: as an appeal to the aristocracy; as a threat to both the aristocracy and the industrialist class; and as an encouragement of the revolutionary or reformist ideals of the radical working class. In common with 'Our Cheer' the work ends with a divine justification for radical political action and an invocation of natural justice: God is 'the lord of nature', the earth that is farmed by the workers is 'sacred', and the rise of the working class is accompanied by a 'glorious psalm'. Indeed, the implication of the final lines is that the divine right of kings has been transmuted into the divine right of the working man. The divine approval of this predicted historical phase suggests that not only is it a return to the natural state of things, but that it is to be a state of permanence. By ending the poem with the emphatic monosyllable, 'God', preceded by a heavily indicated pause, Jones suggests an unarguable finality.[10]

Jones's characterization of social classes as 'races' indicates, in the context of Victorian taboos regarding miscegenation, not only a lack of mobility between the classes, but the lack of a desire for such mobility. Beyond this, the use of racial terminology imposed on social groups implies their separate origins; it is a historical description which says as much about the past as about the present. But it is a past that is obstinately indeterminate. In 'The Two Races' Jones manipulates a narrative that exists partly in the collective imagination of his readership, and partly in his own conception of the progression of British history. The poem operates in the space between these two ideas, drawing on mythical constructs validated by real historical events or figures and by their apocryphal equivalents gleaned from popular culture. This shifting between fictional and non-fictional contextual loci ensures that the poem's imaginative focus remains at the liminal level in the reader's experience. The nature of poetry is such that it can encompass quasi-historical narratives by mere allusion, blending them at will to form myths that, even if they only have integrity within the space of the poem, nevertheless are capable of emotionally engaging an audience. Jones's apparently blithe bringing together of Henry VIII, King John, and the benevolence of an unspecified Saxon aristocracy evokes a mythic nationalist narrative whose plastic nature allows it to interpret traditionally conservative subjects as inspirations for a radical ideology. Jones draws on the wider narrative implied by the poem; a narrative whose insistence that it is unfinished locates the present, and by extension its readership, within its confines.

The Land Plan, Ireland, and Myths of Fertility

'The Factory Town', a relatively long poem consisting of thirty-six song-like quatrains, retains the use of mythic narrative patterns and imagery, but focuses more exclusively on contemporary concerns.[11] The work reinterprets the conventional Victorian myth of technological and economic progress as part of an immoral system that enslaves and de-humanizes vast swathes of the population. Shelley's re-imagining of the Peterloo Massacre, *The Mask of Anarchy* (1819), is not only a formal model for the poem — both are based on a four-beat quatrain structure — but inspires some of the work's highly imaginative metaphors, diabolical imagery, and, perhaps more tellingly, its initial dream-like quality:

> The night had sunk along the city,
>   It was a bleak and cheerless hour;
> The wild-winds sung their solemn ditty
>   To cold, grey wall and blackened tower.
>
> The factories gave forth lurid fires
>   From pent-up hells within their breast;
> E'en Ætna's burning wrath expires,
>   But man's volcanoes never rest.
>
> Women, children, men were toiling,
>   Locked in dungeons close and black,
> Life's fast-failing thread uncoiling
>   Round the wheel, the modern rack!
>
> E'en the very stars seemed troubled
>   With the mingled fume and roar;
> The city like a cauldron bubbled,
>   With its poison boiling o'er.
>
> For the reeking walls environ
>   Mingled groups of death and life
> Fellow-workmen, flesh and iron,
>   Side by side in deadly strife.
>
> ('The Factory Town', ll. 1–20)

Although he is clearly referring to contemporary urban industrial conditions Jones uses a past tense that de-familiarizes his subject, creating a temporal distance that gives the reader the impression of a more detached standpoint. There are fairy-tale connotations to the line, 'It was a bleak and cheerless hour', and these associations are strengthened by the use of terms including 'dungeon', 'poison', and 'cauldron'. There is a mordant pun through reference to the textile industry in the line 'life's fast-failing thread uncoiling', and the machinery in the factory is compared to the rack — the most metaphorically evoked instrument of medieval torture. The dehumanizing effects of this industrial system are such that humans and machines ('flesh and iron') have become indistinguishable, they are 'fellow-workmen'. This vision of workers as automata enhances the horrific tone of these opening stanzas, and is even more explicitly stated in the tenth stanza:

> Yet the master proudly shows
>   To foreign strangers factory scenes:
> 'These are men — and engines those'
>   'I see nothing but — machines!' (ll. 41–44)

The introduction into the poem of 'foreign strangers' serves to further de-familiarize, encouraging the reader to witness the scene of industrial squalor from an external perspective. Beyond its inherent horror, this representation of the mechanization of humanity through the industrial process relates to the issue of agency. Jones's claim that 'red Mammon's hand was robbing | God's thought-treasure from their brain' (ll. 35–36) is an observation that has political as well as existential implications. Indeed, when, later in the poem, it is suggested to the workers that 'The strongest chains by which you're bound, | Are but the chains of your own fear' (ll. 91–92), freedom is associated with an altered consciousness which is a return to essential humanity.[12] In an echo of the accusatory language of 'Our Cheer' ('the living — our disgrace!'), 'The Factory Town' implies that escape from the present economic system is more than simply a political goal, it is a moral imperative. Failure to act constitutes a fatal transgression:

> Still, the reign of guilt to further,
>   Lord and slave the crime divide:
> For the master's sin is murder,
>   And the workman's — suicide! (ll. 97–100)

In reference to this stanza Anne Janowitz has suggested that 'in the false morality of the economy of boss and labour, the despair that leads the factory workers to suicide is reckoned to be a sin'.[13] However, the preceding stanza highlights the deadly effects of the factory system: 'weavers! 'tis your shrouds you're weaving, | labourers! 'tis your graves you ope' (ll. 93–94). It is more likely that rather than a literal act of suicide Jones is referring to the effective suicide of the factory workers' passive acceptance of their lot: the sin lies in the workers' political apathy, their tacit collusion with their bosses' exploitation of them. In this instance the responsibility for political action is placed squarely on the shoulders of the working class; its members are the agents of potential change and change begins with their consciousness of this fact.

The ultimate result of subjective realization of the true nature of the capitalist economic system is collective action in the form of a workers' revolt. In an echo of the passive resistance advocated by Shelley in *The Mask of Anarchy*, this revolt need not be violent, and its eventual outcome will be a return to a bucolic idyll of the type promised by Feargus O'Connor's Chartist Land Plan:

> Up in factory! Up in mill!
>   Freedom's mighty phalanx swell!
> You have God and Nature still.
>   What have they, but Gold and Hell.
>
> Fear ye not your masters' power;
>   Men are strong when men unite;
> Fear ye not one stormy hour:
>   Banded millions need not fight.
>
> Then, how many a happy village
>   Shall be smiling o'er the plain,
> Amid the corn-field's pleasant tillage,
>   And the orchard's rich domain!
>
> While, with rotting roof and rafter,
>   Drops the factory, stone by stone,
> Echoing loud with childhood's laughter,
>   Where it rung with manhood's groan! (ll. 101–16)

Janowitz has observed that 'while the central sections of "The Factory Town" probe at the meaning of consciousness on the shop floor, the conclusion of the poem winds round to the communitarian rhetoric of the commoner's fantasy'.[14]

The poem begins with the nightmarish imagery that describes conditions on the factory floor and the polluting effects on the city before a perspectival narrowing leads to an examination of the thought-processes of the workers. The perspective of the poem then opens out again when the attainment of true consciousness in the individual is translated into collective action and in turn transforms the political, and actual, landscape. The poem travels from a negative mythic scenario to a positive mythic scenario by means of a transformation in subjective human consciousness for which the poem itself is, in part, intended to be an agent of change.

While the pre-Chartist poem 'The Cornfield and the Factory' similarly contrasted a hellish urban industrial landscape with that of an idyllic countryside, its function was observational, it offered no political solution. 'The Factory Town' suggests that the transformation of one way of life into the other can be initiated by a simple act of will. The eventual rewards of collective political action are associated with a state of natural growth and fertility. The working class is told that, while the factory owners have 'but Gold and Hell', they 'have God and Nature still'. The more sophisticated conclusion of this poem, however, is that the return to a more natural way of life will dissolve many of the social problems associated with the industrial economic system:

> And flowers will grow in blooming-time,
>> Where prison-doors their jarring cease:
> For liberty will banish crime —
>> *Contentment* is the best *Police*. (ll. 117–20)

The pun on the word 'jarring' is intended to suggest that most crime originates from unnatural sources — that political and economic injustice are at the root of most criminal behaviour. In what could be seen as an appeal to perennial middle-class Victorian anxieties regarding law and order it is predicted that greater political representation for the working class will reduce criminal behaviour to the extent that society will be able to regulate itself. The prophetic tone is sustained to the end of the work as the implications of the poem's political message reveal its relevance to further areas of society:

> While art may still its votaries call;
>> Commerce claim and give its due;
> Supplying still the wants of all,
>> But not the wastings of the few.
>
> Gathering fleets may still resort,
>> With snowy canvass proudly bent,
> For bearing wealth from port to port
>> But not for war or banishment!
>
> Then up, in one united band,
>> Both farming slave and factory-martyr!
> Remember, that, *to keep the* LAND,
>> The best way is — *to gain the* CHARTER!   (ll. 133–44)

Art, commerce, and foreign trade are variously assured that a society controlled by, or at least more representative of, the workers need not descend into chaos.

The British way of life need not be totally transformed if there is a substantial redistribution of wealth, or if British ships are used only for trade rather than the enhancement of imperial ambition or the transportation of political undesirables. It appears that, aware of the power of his potentially revolutionary earlier stanzas, Jones felt the need to emphasize the political pragmatism and cultural continuity offered by the Chartist vision. The last stanza re-emphasizes Jones's habitual call for unity between rural and urban workers, and strongly associates the 'CHARTER' with the 'LAND' by the full capitalization of both words. In this sense the term 'land' is intended to evoke the Land Plan, as well as its more general agricultural and nationalist associations.

It is worth contrasting Jones's mythic representation of the 'land' with that of James Clarence Mangan (1803–49), and by extension, English representations of this period with those of the Irish. For Mangan, whose poetic career was contemporaneous with Jones's, and was similarly affected by his eventual involvement with radical politics (in Mangan's case, Irish nationalism), the land is more a spiritual entity than the subject of agrarian fantasy. The emphasis is less on the land's inherent usefulness than on the poetic speaker's relationship with it. Nowhere is this more apparent than in Mangan's most anthologized translation from a traditional Gaelic lyric, 'Dark Rosaleen' (Roisin Dubh), to the extent that the land is mystically personified as a beautiful female:

> O! the Erne shall run red
> With redundance of blood
> The earth shall rock beneath our tread
> And flames wrap hill and wood
>
> And gun-peal, and slogan-cry,
> Wake many a glen serene,
> Ere you shall fade, ere you shall die,
> My Dark Rosaleen! (ll. 72–79)[15]

While much of the poem utilizes the sense of dislocation and yearning that traditional unrequited love lyrics express to represent the longing for a free Ireland, this stanza more overtly associates the figure of the woman with topographical land imagery. The physicality of the imagery in the poem leaves one in no doubt that the work refers to the land, rather than merely the concept of nationhood — in a later stanza the speaker refers to 'your emerald bowers'.

Jones's Chartist poetry was written chiefly for an urban working-class readership whose cultural and ancestral roots were often obscured by the lack of credible genealogy or written history, and the dislocating process of the shift from a largely agricultural to a largely industrial economy. For this reason, Jones's use of the term 'land' is connotative of a peculiarly English view of the countryside, in explicit contrast to urban landscapes. It is also the case that, although estrangement from rural lifestyles is regularly pointed to in his poetry, this estrangement is almost always presented as a temporary, even artificial, state. The attainment of control of the land in Jones's work is always within grasp, if only the readership would realize it. There is none of the air of fatalism that tinges the hope for a free Ireland expressed in the work of Mangan. It may well be that these differing emotional registers can be attributed to the darkening shadow of the Irish Famine, or differences between contemporaneous perceptions of the probabilities of achievement of a free Ireland or a People's Charter.

In 'The Lovely Land', which appeared in the Irish nationalist publication the *Nation* on 18 July 1846, Mangan describes viewing a painting of an Irish landscape by Daniel Maclise (1806–70), but thinking at first that the landscape must be Italian or French. His shame on realizing he is looking at a pictorial representation of his homeland is more personal and subjective than the feelings of shame Jones hoped to induce in his English working-class readership for their relinquishment of a natural lifestyle, or their unwillingness to overthrow their oppressors:

> Shame on me, my own, my sire-land,
> Not to know thy soil and skies!
> Shame that through Maclise's eyes
> I first see thee, Ireland!
> ('The Lovely Land', ll. 33–36)

In terms of voice, the great difference between this approach to political poetry and that of Jones or most other Chartist writers is the intensely individual nature of Mangan's subjectivity. In this poem the speaker's relationship with the land is one of personal estrangement redoubled by the revelation that the land is 'first see[n]' in pictorial form. There is almost the sense that the land of Ireland cannot be viewed directly, that its perception must be mediated through cultural filters including paintings, or, in the case of 'Dark Rosaleen', love songs. Given the emotional register of these works it is possible to assume that the purpose of these mediations is at least in part analgesic.

This indirect viewing of Ireland is taken a step further by Mangan in poems that he claimed were translated from languages such as Turkish ('The Karamanian Exile' — *Dublin University Magazine*, 1844) and Arabic ('The Time of the Barmecides' — *Dublin University Magazine*, 1839, 1840). In fact, although he knew German, Mangan did not speak either of these languages, and the 'translations' were poetic hoaxes which, according to Henry J. Donaghy, used 'a mythic golden past to visualize a supposedly similar golden past of Ireland's'.[16] Mangan and Jones both use their mythic visions of the past to defamiliarize the present, but Mangan adds an exoticism with his strategy of geographical, as well as temporal, dislocation:[17]

> Then youth was mine, and a fierce wild will,
> And an iron arm in war,
> And a fleet foot high upon ISHKAR's hill,
> When the watch-lights glimmered afar,
> And a barb as fiery as any I know
> That Khoord or Beddaween rides,
> Ere my friends lay low, — long, long ago,
> In the time of the Barmecides,
> Ere my friends lay low, — long, long ago,
> In the time of the Barmecides. (ll. 11–20)[18]

The references to exotic people and places may bring to mind the Romantic fashion of Orientalism exploited in the Eastern-themed poetry of Byron and Southey in particular, but the anapaestic rhythms in this work are typically anglophone, while the repetition and subject matter recall the tropes of German Romantic poetry. The analogous association of youth and nationalism in German and Irish verse has been noted in the previous chapter (in this context, the associative implications of the growth of the *Young* Ireland Movement from the Repeal Association should be noted), and indeed, the first two lines of the above stanza bear a striking resemblance to the first stanza of 'The German Boy's Song' by von Stolberg discussed previously. This may not be a coincidence; Mangan was an avid translator of German literature. David Lloyd has noted that:

> Mangan's translations from and articles on German literature of the late eighteenth and early nineteenth centuries constitute the greater part of his literary output. [...] The material he translated is remarkably various, ranging from the work of familiar figures such as Goethe, Schiller, Jean Paul, Novalis, and Heine to lesser known writers including Justinus Kerner, Cristoph Tiedge, and Friedrich De La Motte Fouqué.[19]

Mangan also translated poems by Friedrich Rückert and Ernst Moritz Arndt, whose work Jones also translated for the *Morning Post*. Indeed, in 1844, Mangan published a loose translation of Arndt's 'Was ist des Deutschen Vaterland' (which he stripped of German references and re-named 'Our Fatherland'), a work discussed in the previous chapter.

It is tempting to see in this convergence of poetic interest between Jones and Mangan a triangulation of influence and inspiration, and indeed an interchange of mythic figures and narratives, between German romanticism, British Chartism, and Irish nationalism in the mid-nineteenth century. But while the literary traffic between the German states and the British Isles might be imagined to have been largely one way (westwards, of course), there is evidence to support the contention that the interplay between the radical poetics of Britain and Ireland echoed the well-documented political discourse between Chartism and Irish nationalism at the time. Dorothy Thompson notes that:

> In British radical politics, Ireland stood for several things. On the grounds of natural justice and human rights, Ireland had the right to her own government. Most radicals believed that universal suffrage would produce a repeal of the Act of Union.[20]

It is significant with regard to Jones's engagement with Irish issues that his rise to prominence within Chartism, politically and poetically, coincided with the occurrence of the Irish Famine and the death of Daniel O'Connell, the leader of the Repeal Association. According to Malcolm Chase, O'Connell's death '[brought] to a close one of the most significant and turbulent careers in Irish politics but also open[ed] up a real possibility of co-operation between Irish nationalists and British Chartists.'[21] In a broader sense, this co-operation would have been a continuation of a previous trend. Paul A. Pickering has noted that 'the 1842 National Petition, which had been signed by millions of working people in England, called for the repeal of the Union as well as the implementation of the Charter', and Chartist recognition of the plight of Ireland was reflected in poems throughout the Chartist period that depicted the Irish people as subjects of the same oppressing forces under whom the English working class suffered.[22] William James Linton, though an English (and eventually American) Chartist poet, spoke as an Irishman for his 'Irish Harvest Song', which was first published in the *English Republic* magazine in 1851. The poem blends the familiar tropes of Chartist land poetry with an appeal for an Irish national identity and recognition of the English financial mismanagement that exacerbated the effects of the Irish Famine:

> This land is ours, — God gave it us;
>   We will maintain our own;
> This land is ours, — we will not starve
>   Where corn is grown;
> We will not starve in harvest-time
>   Because some alien-born
>   Would speculate in corn. (ll. 1–7)[23]

Long after the demise of Chartism, and probably to capitalize on the growing East Coast Irish diaspora of the time, this poem was republished in 1867 in New York after Linton emigrated to America. It appeared in a brochure entitled *Ireland for the Irish, Rhymes and Reasons against Landlordism, with a Preface on Fenianism and Republicanism.*

An even more direct association between Irish and English political concerns is evidenced by Allen Davenport's 'Ireland in Chains'.[24] The poem is framed as an appeal to 'Britons' to intervene in the ongoing oppression of Ireland, the implication being that Ireland's suffering is a distorted mirror of Britain's own:

> Rise, Britons, rise! with indignation, —
> Hark! hark!! I hear the clanking chains,
> That bind a brave and generous nation,
> Where martial law and terror reign;
> Her gallant sons demand assistance,
> Can British hearts refuse the call?
> Behold them struggling for existence,
> Shall Ireland, or her tyrants fall?
>   See! see! the fiends of war
>   Have seized on Liberty;
>   Then rise, and as one man declare,
>   That Ireland shall be free! (ll. 1–12)[25]

Written and published at the height of the famine, this poem sees the Irish situation as a possible trigger for revolt in Britain, presenting a stark choice between the demise of Ireland or of 'her tyrants'. Jones himself saw a similar link between the Irish and British political situations, and sought to forge an alliance between the working classes of both nations. 'The March of Freedom', celebrates the momentum of democratic revolt through many European countries in its fifty-two quatrain stanzas, but its final stanzas are reserved for Ireland.[26] After a refrain of 'Cry: "Liberty to Erin!"', the physical barrier of the Irish Sea is symbolically bridged by the intertwining political ambitions of Chartism and Irish nationalism:

Athwart that famous 'gulf,'
　　Though swift its current hies,
We soon can build a bridge
　　With dead monopolies.

For hark! to Freedom's call
　　The fatal spell is broke;
Repeal means — *Union* of the slaves,
　　And *reverence* of the *yoke*.

Then, Hurrah for the Charter,
　　On Shannon, Thames, and Tweed;
Now, scythemen! to the harvest!
　　Reap! you who sowed the seed.

　　　　　　　('The March of Freedom', ll. 197–208)

Similarly, 'A Song for the People' ends a general call for freedom and democracy by highlighting the situation in Ireland.[27] Throughout the work, the refrain 'For the world shall see — that we will be free, | And free be the sister-isle' is incorporated, indicating an apparently symbiotic relationship between the political goals of the radical elements of both nations.

At the time that Chartist poets were incorporating Ireland into their work, Irish nationalist poets were writing radical pieces advocating the overthrow of tyranny in general terms which would have relevance across the British Isles. John de Jean Frazer (?1804–52), an Irish nationalist poet known pseudonymously as 'Jean de Jean', published a collection called *Poems for the People* (published in Dublin in 1845) which included the poem, 'A Word to the People'.[28] This poem, with its plea for solidarity amongst the oppressed, speculation of a future of liberty, and connotations of divine approval of radicalism in the term 'anointed', could read as a Chartist text:

Oh! could we thus in concord live,
　　As brother should with brother;
And, with no sordid feelings, give
　　Our efforts to each other:
With hands so strong, and hearts so firm,
　　By freedom's cause anointed,
How soon would be a stinted term
　　To tyranny appointed! (ll. 9–16)[29]

In the throes of the horrific aftermath of the Irish Famine, as ruling classes across Europe fell to popular revolt, the same poet published a work called 'Harvest Pledge' in the *Nation* of 8 July 1848 — three weeks before the paper was seized and suppressed by the authorities for over a year. The manner of this work was distinctly more threatening than that of 'A Word to the People', reflecting what Mike Sanders identifies as 'a much less inhibited attitude towards violence within Irish nationalism',[30] but its language also provides the perfect Irish analogue to Ernest Jones's brand of radical poetic medievalism:

So the serfs, in the face of the Lord of the Manor
Set a spear for a shaft and a sheaf for a banner;
And said, 'If we choose, from the sward to the sky,
From centre to shore, thou shouldst yield — or die!' (ll. 21–24)[31]

There are clearly many points of contact, both poetic and mythopoeic, between Jones and the Irish poets Mangan and Frazer. The starkest difference, however, is biographical, and illustrates the reason why events in Ireland were considered by Chartists to be indicative of the contempt the ruling classes held for all the working people of the British Isles. Melissa Fegan writes:

> Many Famine poets were certainly not middle-class professionals: James Clarence Mangan worked only periodically as a clerk and transcriber, John Keegan was a hedge-school teacher, John de Jean Frazer was a carpenter. All three died in penury — Mangan and Keegan in 1849, Frazer in 1852. All three deaths could be related to the Famine they chronicled. There was not always a disparity between the poet and his subject.[32]

Radical Medievalism and Chartist Mythopoeia

The selection of Ernest Jones poems analyzed in the preceding pages is fairly representative of his early Chartist poetry. The works articulate varying approaches to the subject of the struggle for the People's Charter, but where their images and narratives intersect, distinct patterns begin to emerge. Themes of divine approval and purpose, historical progression, the awakening of political consciousness, and the link between idyllic pasts and futures are prevalent. In essence, Chartist poetry, by definition, concerns the attainment of political representation for the working class. But the nature of Jones's Chartist poetry is such that even its inconsistencies (which include fluctuations between the positions of the 'moral force' and 'physical force' arguments, or the lack of identification of the precise level of political agency attributed to the working-class population) fit within a wider narrative pattern — a meta-narrative. In mythic terms this narrative, quite naturally, overwhelmingly represents a deliverance paradigm, but in relation to political regeneration and agency, elements of fertility and hero myths are also identifiable within the works. By dedicating his work to a specific political movement which, despite links with earlier radical movements, was a relatively recent phenomenon, Jones was forced to be both adaptive and creative in his use of myth.[33] Indeed, adapted narratives and images from scriptural, historical, literary, and popular sources were synthesized to create a specifically Chartist myth which explained present circumstances in relation to the past, and predicted the future. Jones instinctively understood that myth is a powerful form of cultural narrative that operates on a largely emotional level, and that poetry is the perfect method of delivery for myth in a new age of mass communication that gave the working class access to relatively cheap and instantaneous news and literature.

By the time of Jones's involvement with Chartism, its establishment of working-class cultural forms was well-advanced. The pioneering labour historian Dorothy Thompson writes:

> Working people in all parts of the island — in Scotland and Wales as well as in England — demonstrated in favour of a political programme, formed organisations to promote it and in many ways set up a whole alternative culture in the process. A mass of published material was produced, newspapers, pamphlets, broadsides, placards and books were circulated, sermons were preached, plays

and pageants performed, hymns and songs were written and performed. Traditional forms were adopted alongside new forms of organisation and demonstration.[34]

As Chartism began to create a culture with its own literature and historical perspective, it began to form mythic narratives to explain its origins and destiny; and in common with many other cultures, poetry played a large part in this process. Industrial areas in particular were fertile grounds for the formation of Chartist culture due to the economic and geographic displacements that occurred in their populations. The establishment of the *Northern Star* weekly newspaper by Feargus O'Connor in 1838 was explicitly intended to give the working class its own politically conscious voice. In 1847, within a year of joining the Chartist movement, Ernest Jones worked with O'Connor to produce the *Labourer*, a monthly companion magazine to the *Northern Star* which intended to place 'poetry and romance side by side with politics and history'.[35] The association of poetry with politics seems natural enough within a movement that had long recognized the social function of verse, but the suggested correlation between 'romance' and history is especially interesting, implying a narrative approach to historical understanding. Within the pages of the *Labourer* Jones published his own historical morality tales including 'The Confessions of a King' and 'The Romance of a People', which, though they were set in an indeterminate past, seemed to attempt the same function as Harriet Martineau's *Illustrations of Political Economy* (1832) in the sense that they were narratives addressing the complexities of current economic and social problems. In a series in the *Labourer* entitled 'The Insurrections of the Working Classes' Jones effectively attempted a rewriting of European history from a radical perspective which was intended 'to distinguish the delicate whisper of truth amid the din of conflicting testimony'.[36] The implied historical narrative presented to the reader through the body of Jones's Chartist poetry is an extension of this alternative view of history which attempts to create a new myth relevant to the historical experience of a social stratum that had been under-represented by the cultural hegemonies of successive ruling classes.

Jones's much-vaunted previous connections with the aristocracy not only helped inspire but gave associative credence to frequent references in his poetry to a noble, chivalric, English past. Although such romantic references were not unknown in the works of other Chartist poets (C. Westray addressed the 'Sons of Albion'; Charles Cole suggested that a 'swain is higher than a king'), it was Jones who persistently harked back to an indeterminate historical period when relations between England's classes were apparently on a more equal, or at least fairer, footing.[37] For Miles Taylor, Jones's '"olden time" sense of history' is indicative of political naivety:

> Jones's vision of modern industry, as far as he had a coherent view of it, was derived not from an understanding of the class struggles of the 1830s and 1840s, nor even from a radical agrarian tradition embodied in the idea of the people's farm. Rather, depiction of class relations in the hungry 'forties rested on a quaint but idealized view of the collapse of the medieval social order, whereby the labouring poor had been deserted by the nobility and the church.[38]

60 JONES AND MYTH (1846–48)

This extrapolation of a comment on the level of Jones's political sophistication from his poetic imagery fails to take into account the mythopoeic aspects and functions of Jones's Chartist poetry, or that of political poetry in general. While there may have been a correlation between the real political goals of the Chartist Land Plan and the rural imagery associated with Jones's poetic medievalism, the relation between the two is rarely more than symbolic. The pastoral vision in Jones's poetry acts less as an explicit commentary on contemporary political themes than as a symbolic indicator of a possible future through mythopoeic reference. Yet even in this, Jones's use of medieval tropes in his poetry might partially trace its radical roots in works of revisionist history including William Cobbett's *History of the Protestant Reformation* (1824–26), whose anterior function was to address perceived contemporary injustice (in this case Catholic Emancipation) through the prism of historical narrative.

The roots of the wider literary fashion of Victorian medievalism are sometimes identified in the influence of Sir Walter Scott's *Ivanhoe* (1820), but it is likely that Jones's German upbringing and education familiarized him with an earlier example of literary medievalism in Goethe's dramatic work *Goetz von Berlichingen* (1773), which made a considerable cultural impact in the German-speaking world. The character of Goetz, certainly as presented in the first scenes of the play, is a rebellious free-spirit and there is evidence to suggest that Jones's conception of England's mythical past contains an implicit commentary on the conservatism inherent in mainstream Victorian medievalism. Within the pages of the *Labourer* Jones questions the worth of nostalgic literary fashion when it is divorced from contemporary political realities:

> What is Robert Browning doing? He, who could fire the soul of a Luria, and develop the characters of a Victor and a Charles, — he, who could depict nature's nobility in a Colombe, — has he nothing to say for popular rights? Let him eschew his kings, and queens, — let him quit the pageantry of the courts — and *ascend* into the cottage of the poor. [...] Can Tennyson do no more than troll a courtly lay? His oak could tell other tales beside a love story. [...] Can Knowles but stalk upon his stilts of Arragon, go hunting with his feudal falconers, or make a princess condescend to love a serf?[39]

This analysis of contemporary literary medievalism, written near the beginning of his Chartist poetic career, suggests that Jones was well aware of the ideological pitfalls of an unfocused historical nostalgia. Indeed, the same year saw Tennyson attempt to answer similar accusations that his poetry did not deal with more weighty issues with the publication of *The Princess* (1847), a blank verse narrative addressing the problems of female education and advancement. In a later issue of the *Labourer* Jones did give credit to mainstream contemporary writers' expressions of democratic ideals, even if he argued with the form of these expressions. Taylor writes:

> In his first major literary survey Jones noted that a 'democratic tendency' had begun to pervade English literature, commencing with Byron and Shelley, and now to be found in Elizabeth Barrett Browning, Tennyson, and even Bulwer-Lytton. Jones singled out for praise Barrett Browning's 'Lady Geraldine', as well as Tennyson's 'Lady Vere de Vere'. At the same time he lamented the simplistic and unrealistic treatment of ordinary people which often lay at the heart of these works.[40]

Jones's evocations of a mythical English past are filtered through a radical politicization that critiques, rather than subscribes to, mainstream Victorian exercises in sentiment and nostalgia. Terms such as 'manhood' refer less to an old-fashioned sense of chivalry and masculinity than to the development of political consciousness and the willingness to see this through to its active conclusion:

> Working men, working men — stand by your Charter,
> *Themselves* say — without you their efforts are nought.
> Freedom and Right are not things you can barter;
> Then rally the phalanx of *manhood* and *thought*!
> ('Our Trust', ll. 33–36)[41]

When it came to terms which were even more richly connotative of medieval values Jones's usage is remarkable not only for its frequency but for its context. 'Gallant' as a term appears fifteen times across ten of the thirty-seven poems that Jones published in the *Northern Star* between 1846 and 1848. The word becomes part of phrases including 'gallant band', 'gallant hosts', and 'gallant hearts' which emphasize gallantry as a collective quality rather than the expression of a traditionally individual attitude.[42]

Throughout Jones's early Chartist poetic career, his use of medieval imagery and vocabulary, along with their nationalist and mythic associations, becomes part of a strategy to create a poetic voice that melds a Romantic individualism with the radical communitarian tradition represented by older Chartist poets such as Allen Davenport. As Janowitz observes, the search for an effective poetic voice is crucial for Jones due to his unusual social background amongst Chartist activists:

> Jones poetically carves out a place for his lyrical singularity to become part of a larger collective subjectivity, as he reaches across from his élite educated background to the political movement in front of him. Through his attempt to forge his own links with a movement to which he has become affiliated rather than into which he was born, Jones brings the resistant edge of individualism to bear on the residual voice of the tradition of song and oral lyrics.[43]

Jones's German upbringing and social origins in the minor gentry and military classes not only help to inform his particular medievalist vision, but are instrumental in broadening the Chartist poetic to enhance what Janowitz appositely terms a 'collective subjectivity'. Mythic medievalism forms the quasi-historical basis for Jones's conception of the Chartist 'we'.

The paradox at the heart of radical medievalism is that it is steeped in nostalgia, which is an essentially conservative impulse in that it expresses a desire for the recovery of a former state. But for Jones, the symbols and mythologies already embedded in British culture were sometimes capable of forming part of a radical narrative, whether or not they originally emerged from conservative ideologies. If, as Maidment has suggested, one of the primary functions of Chartist poetry was to encourage political solidarity, then it is worth considering Mircea Eliade's assertion that 'myth assures man that what he is about to do *has already been done*, in other words, it helps him to overcome doubts as to the results of his undertaking'.[44] In this sense the actions that the readers are being encouraged to perform in mythopoeic political poetry are presented as the equivalent of the repetition of experiments that have already been proven successful. Jones's poetry of this period not only promises his readers a 'brave new world', but, in the tradition of deliverance narratives stretching back to Exodus, offers a return to the values of an old world with which his readers should be instinctively familiar. The cyclical nature of the mythic narratives Jones employed in his poetry meant that however far the personal ideological leap might have been from conservative monarchist to active radical, the corresponding poetic journey was never as long. Janus-like, Jones's poetry looked simultaneously into the past and the future, with radical eyes emboldened by the tacit support of conservative traditions.

Nicholas Dames writes of the cultural predilections of the Victorian period as being 'toward a nostalgic *evasion* of both what came before it and what, as yet unforeseen, was to come after it'.[45] Although the Chartist vision, even in its most nostalgic forms, can appear less blinkered than mainstream Victorian culture in that its defining characteristic is forward-looking, it remains the case that myth, the filter through which to a large degree that vision was perceived, defines itself by its unstable relationship with veracity. The distorted emphases that myth places on the past and the future necessarily involve the diminution of certain elements, and the complete evasion of others. Jones's mythical conception of Britain's political landscape, like corresponding conservative mythical conceptions, is just as much about forgetting as about remembering. In 'England', the emphasis is on the present's dislocation from both the past and a potentially liberated future;[46] amnesia is a temporally reversible affliction in the slave-like existence of the working population:

> Oh! England, my country, I see thee with sorrow,
> Still toiling and moiling 'mid sadness and pain;
> In fears of *to-day* still forgetting *tomorrow*,
> Though freedom's young lion is clanking thy chain.
> ('England', ll. 1–4)

Freedom is endowed with leonine power (the image containing an implicitly nationalist reference to the figure of Britannia) and yet its youth suggests not only vitality but a lack of memory that may be a pre-requisite for radical action. Jones's poetry of this period is torn between providing the mythopoeic memory of an idyllic former state and encouraging the forgetting of generations of culturally dominant, conservative ideologies that might suppress the impulse for political change. It is in the nature of mythopoeia, whether that means the making or the adaptation of myth, that its productions should appear unauthored, that they are presented as pre-existent narratives, only ever *referred to* by the writer. This strategy relieves the myth-maker of responsibility for the distortions inherent in a form that exists in the space between truth dressed as fiction, and fiction dressed as truth.

Chartist poetry is an emotional trigger, one of whose intended functions is to instigate political action. This action may be to consolidate an existing structure, or may be more explicitly transformative, but the purpose of poetry in this context is, through imaginative expression, to provide the emotional basis for future achievement. For Sanders, Chartist poet Gerald Massey (1828–1907) confronted similar issues with regard to the nature of the relationship between the past and the present, but the treatment of the former is as much a process of 're-incarnation' than mere evocation:

> The political challenge for Massey is to find a means of making the current generation a conductor of the past's messianic power, and it is memory [...] which he considers capable of fulfilling this task. For Massey, memory is not simply a matter of recalling a past event or hero. Rather, it is to re-incarnate the political energies stored in the past.[47]

In keeping with this idea of a radical utilization of historic agency, the third stanza of 'England' provides perhaps Jones's most explicit contrast between the present and an exemplary yet indeterminate past, and expresses an assertive impatience with the complications that lead to political indecision:

> What say those whitefaces so dim and downcast?
> > What mouth ye, what mean ye, with 'buts' and, with 'ifs?'
> Give me ten thousand bold hearts from the Past,
> > And I'd chase the oppressor right over the cliffs. (ll. 9–12)

Only poetry could compress this level of emotional manipulation and mythical reference into such a short space. Indeed, it is in the elements of compression and the manipulation of emotion that poetry and myth are to some degree intertwined. While myth involves the compression of narrative through the relationship of symbolic figures, poetry is the compression of language itself. In poetry, just as in myth, such compression places increased emphasis on its figures and images, suggesting the paradigmatic or the universal. And myth, in dealing with ideals, paradigms, and journeys toward perfection, is, like poetry, an important expression of emotion in the form of imaginative desire. In political poetry we see an increased emphasis on the concept of human perfectibility, and a corresponding increase in the use of mythic patterns, reference, and language.

Throughout the twentieth century observers including Kenneth Burke, Northrop Frye, Mircea Eliade, and Frederick Clarke Prescott argued, in their different ways, for recognition of the close relationship between myth and poetry; but none of these writers examined the use of myth in political poetry.[48] It almost goes without saying that, given its more general critical neglect, mythopoeia in Chartist poetry has not been studied. In Ernest Jones's Chartist work we see a particular concentration of the use of mythopoeia due to the combination of several factors. Beyond political poetry's characteristic use of mythic deliverance narratives, Chartist poetry had a more specific use for myth in its role as part of wider Chartist attempts to create an alternative working-class culture. Into this existing poetic tradition Jones brought a poetic voice already steeped in the patriotic myths of Romantic German poetry. This inheritance was filtered through, and reinforced by, the concurrent vogue in Victorian poetry for medievalism (itself a form of mythopoeia), which Jones found a way to critique and adapt into a complex, radical re-reading of history. The effects of radicalization on Jones's poetry were transformative in terms of the re-orientation of its ideological perspective, but many of its themes and imagery were carried over from his early influences.

64   JONES AND MYTH (1846–48)

Finally, Jones's separation in terms of social status from the class for whom he was writing gave him a uniquely discrete perspective that enabled the construction of a mythic narrative based on what he saw. This separation meant that, for very obvious reasons, he could not write about the plight of the working class from experience, and so was forced to compose poetry drawing on the symbols, abstractions, and figures characteristic of mythic writing. As much as the contemporary political situation demanded it, the mythopoeic aspects of the Chartist poetry Ernest Jones wrote between 1846 and 1848 emerged from who he was, and where he had been. Bearing in mind Jones's essential difference from his readership, the following chapter examines the role of his poetry in negotiating his relationship with the Chartist body.

Notes to Chapter 2

1. Taylor, p. 77.
2. *New Quarterly Review* quoted in *NS* 9/5/1846.
3. *NS* 27/6/1846.
4. A. W. N. Pugin, 'Preface', in *Contrasts: Or, a Parallel Between the Noble Edifices of the Middle Ages, and Similar Buildings of the Present Day* (London: [self-published], 1836), p. iii.
5. Ernest Jones, 'The Two Races', *NS* 12/9/1846.
6. G. J. Holyoake, *Sixty Years of an Agitator's Life*, 2 vols (London: Fisher Unwin, 1892), II, 250.
7. For example: 'Onward', *NS* 10/7/1847, 'Think not your paltry silken bands | Can bind Progression's giant hands' (l. 16); and 'Our Trust', *NS* 27/5/1848, 'The soft silken hand of the vile profit-monger' (l. 21).
8. Maidment, p. 37.
9. Ernest Jones, 'Soldier and Citizen: to the Oppressed of Either Class', *NS* 1/4/1848.
10. Across the thirty-seven poems by Jones published in the *Northern Star* between 1846 and 1848, the term 'god' appears thirty-four times.
11. Ernest Jones, 'The Factory Town', *NS* 13/2/1847 (in Kovalev, pp. 141–45).
12. The similarity, particularly in an industrial context, between these lines and Blake's 'mind-forged manacles' (in his poem 'London') may be an example of convergent literary evolution. Blake's work was not well known at this point and his critical re-discovery was only established in the 1860s.
13. Janowitz, *Lyric and Labour in the Romantic Tradition*, p. 182.
14. Ibid., p. 183.
15. James Clarence Mangan, 'Dark Rosaleen', in *The Collected Works of James Clarence Mangan*, ed. by Jacques Chuto and others, 4 vols (Dublin: Irish Academic Press, 1996–99), III, 169–70.
16. Henry J. Donaghy, *James Clarence Mangan* (New York: Twayne, 1974), p. 35.
17. It is also worth noting at this point the similarity between Mangan and Jones in their occasionally cavalier attitude to poetic production. Both were capable of misrepresenting the origins of their poetry, whether overtly or implicitly.
18. James Clarence Mangan, 'The Time of the Barmecides', in *The Collected Works of James Clarence Mangan*, ed. by Jacques Chuto and others, II, 169.
19. David Lloyd, *Nationalism and Minor Literature: James Clarence Mangan and the Emergence of Irish Cultural Nationalism* (Berkeley: University of California Press, 1987), p. 129.
20. Thompson, p. 16.
21. Chase, p. 271.
22. Paul A. Pickering '"Repeal and the Suffrage": Feargus O'Connor's Irish "Mission", 1849–50', in *The Chartist Legacy*, ed. by Ashton, Fryson & Roberts, pp. 119–46 (p. 119).
23. William James Linton, 'Irish Harvest Song', in Kovalev, p. 201.
24. Allen Davenport, 'Ireland in Chains', *NS* 25/4/1846.
25. Allen Davenport, 'Ireland in Chains', in Kovalev, p. 123.

26. Ernest Jones, 'The March of Freedom', *NS* 18/3/1848 (in Kovalev, pp. 152–57).

27. Ernest Jones, 'A Song for the People', *NS* 4/3/1848 (in Kovalev, pp. 151–52).

28. It is worth speculating that Jones's 1851 *Notes to the People* journal took its name in part from Frazer's collection. Jones's interest in Irish nationalist literature pre-dated his involvement with Chartism (see Taylor, pp. 75–76), and he is likely to have been familiar with Frazer's work.

29. John de Jean Frazer, 'A Word to the People', in *Political Verse and Song from Britain and Ireland*, ed. by Ashraf, p. 190.

30. Sanders, p. 172.

31. John de Jean Frazer, 'Harvest Pledge', *Nation* 8/7/1848.

32. Melissa Fegan, *Literature and the Irish Famine 1845–1919* (Oxford: Clarendon Press, 2002) p. 167.

33. The distinctions between the 'adaptive' and 'creative' employment of mythopoeia in poetry have been recognized since at least the first century BC. In his masterly critical poem 'Ars Poetica', Horace (65–8 BC) is dismissive of the former when he instructs potential poets to 'either follow tradition or invent a consistent story'.

34. Thompson, p. [ix].

35. 'Preface', *The Labourer: A Monthly Magazine of Politics, Literature, Poetry*, January 1847, i-vi.

36. Ernest Jones, 'The Insurrections of the Working Classes', *Labourer*, January 1847, 11.

37. Charles Cole, 'The Strength of Tyranny', *NS* 9/5/1846; C. Westray, 'To the Chartists', *NS* 20/2/1841.

38. Taylor, p. 85.

39. Ernest Jones, 'Literary Review', *Labourer*, 1847, 94.

40. Taylor, p. 96.

41. Ernest Jones, 'Our Trust', *NS* 27/5/1848.

42. Ernest Jones, 'A Chartist Chorus', *NS* 6/6/1846, ll. 1 & 31 (in Kovalev, p. 136); 'England's Greatness', *NS* 4/7/1846, l. 2; 'The Factory Town', *NS* 13/2/1847, l. 90, respectively.

43. Janowitz, *Lyric and Labour in the Romantic Tradition*, p. 166.

44. Mircea Eliade, *Myth and Reality*, trans. by Willard R. Trask (New York: Harper & Row, 1968), p. 141.

45. Nicholas Dames, *Amnesiac Selves: Nostalgia, Forgetting, and British Fiction, 1810–1870* (Oxford: Oxford University Press, 2001) p. 11.

46. Ernest Jones, 'England', *NS* 23/1/1847.

47. Sanders, p. 217.

48. Kenneth Burke, *A Rhetoric of Motives* (New York: Prentice Hall, 1950); Northrop Frye, *Fables of Identity: Studies in Poetic Mythology* (New York: Harcourt Brace, 1991); Eliade, *Myth and Reality*; Frederick Clarke Prescott, *Poetry and Myth* (New York: Macmillan, 1927).

CHAPTER 3

The 'Mighty Mind'
1846–48

> I am pouring the tide of my songs over England, forming the tone of the mighty mind of the people.[1]

These words from Jones's diary entry of October 1846 were written in the midst of the first flush of his Chartist poetic success. Perhaps the first thing that strikes the modern reader is the apparent privilege, or even primacy, attributed to the position of the author. Indeed, the relative status of the author is only enhanced by the description of the imagined collective readership as 'the mighty mind'. Moreover, the statement suggests that, early in his Chartist career, Jones perceived the role of poetry as much more than simply a commentary on, or passive reflection of, contemporary events and issues, but as an active element of political discourse. Descriptions of actions of 'pouring ... over' and 'forming the tone' are unequivocal in their indication of influence and agency, reflecting the general Chartist perception of the active role of poetry within the movement which was formed prior to Jones's involvement around a favoured group of poets including Allen Davenport, Benjamin Stott, and Thomas Cooper.[2] This attitude in turn reflects the wider early Victorian awareness of the importance of the relationship between society and culture as explored by writers such as Thomas Carlyle (1795–1881) and the emergent John Ruskin (1819–1900).

The essentially Romantic view of art as a shaping influence on society was echoed by late twentieth-century critical shifts away from formalist reductions of poetry's extra-literary contexts. Anthony H. Harrison's *Victorian Poets and the Politics of Culture: Discourse and Ideology* (1998) is part of wider efforts by many modern critics to emphasize the social function of poetry:

> I consider poems as social and cultural artifacts of historical importance in part because they display subtle describable categories of cultural power by transmitting ideology. They do so under the guise of eliciting pleasure. 'A thing of Beauty' may be a 'joy forever,' but literary texts also act as material forces in the world and mold readers' values, expectations, and behaviour in reality; they thus advance not only the fame of their authors but also their power in society.[3]

The idea that literary texts might 'mold readers' values, expectations, and behaviour in reality' is easily equated with Jones's view that he was 'forming the tone' of his readership. However, it is symptomatic of the critical neglect of Chartist poetry in the late twentieth century that a work with a title such as Harrison's should briefly acknowledge Chartism as 'a highly controversial topic of political discourse in these years',[4] and yet fail to mention the phenomenon of Chartist poetry, even as context to the ideological implications of the work of canonical writers such as Alfred Lord Tennyson, Elizabeth Barrett Browning, Matthew Arnold, and Christina Rossetti who form the book's focus. The overtly political nature of the Chartist poem does not mean that the 'describable categories of cultural power' displayed are any less subtle, only that they are, in many cases, more readily identifiable. The ideological variations and tensions within the Chartist movement itself generate a complex nexus of 'interpretive communities'. Jones's position and status within this nexus in the period leading up to his imprisonment in 1848 will be the topic of this chapter.

The Chartist Response

Jones's apparent privileging of the author's status, even taking into account its appearance as an exuberant entry in the diary of a newly famous young man, brings into focus another twentieth-century reaction to formalism: that of reader-response theory. Whether the intended function of Chartist poetry is to encourage, condemn, or discuss, its success relies on the reader's response to its political meaning. While Jones may be correct in assuming that his Chartist poetry will have more demonstrable effect on the real world than his *Court Journal* publications, it is also true that the nature and magnitude of that influence is dependant wholly on his readers' interpretation of his works. The model of Georges Poulet's phenomenological approach to the reading process, whereby an almost mystical melding of consciousnesses occurs to produce a new pseudo-consciousness located in the text, is particularly appropriate to the Chartist reading experience for two reasons. Firstly, the more or less equal weight given to the input into the process by the author and the reader mirrors the fact that, unlike traditional poet-reader relationships, in this case the communication is first and foremost between fellow Chartists: equivalence between the producer and consumer is inherent in the nature of the process of transmission. The second reason relates to the apparent autonomy that Poulet's conception of the reading process bestows on the actual text, which 'becomes (at the expense of the reader whose own life it suspends) a sort of human being [...] a mind conscious of itself and constituting itself in me as the subject of its own objects'.[5] The polemical nature of Chartist poetry enhances the agency of the text: a poem that contributes to active political debate can truly be said to have *done* something; its *affect* produces a more demonstrable *effect* than that of less overtly functional poetry.

In his seminal collection of examples of 'self-taught' Victorian poetry, *The Poorhouse Fugitives*, Brian Maidment suggests that the recitation of Chartist poetry in social situations operated to suppress the drive for political action through its substitutive nature. This argument implies that language's symbolic form of action emotionally deflects the necessity for its actual equivalent:

In my view, this close connection between reading and doing was seldom properly established because the recitation of the poem often seems to have served a *cathartic* effect rather than a persuasive one, so that the social aggression in the poem was sublimated or acted out rather than developed into action beyond the poem. Reading became to some extent a substitute for action, a self-contained political act without further implications.[6]

The lack of historical evidence for a direct link between the recitation of Chartist poetry and Chartist political action is perhaps unsurprising given that it is difficult to imagine where the smoking gun would be located. The slippery and heterogeneous nature of any definition of 'political action' only complicates the search for a direct causal link. A political act might range from armed insurrection to the mere signing of a petition. The focus of Maidment's assertion is on the momentary effect of a reading or recitation, which excludes the possible effects of the re-reading of favoured Chartist poems which was common practice. In its review of Jones's first collection of Chartist poetry the *Northern Star* suggests that at least one poem had already entered the Chartist consciousness: 'these poems consist of, first, 'The Better Hope', the concluding verses of which have been so often repeated by Mr. O'Connor'.[7] The effects of poetry, political or otherwise, on the consciousness of the reader are often residual, or even atemporal. Francis O'Gorman's essay 'Matthew Arnold and Rereading' highlights a Victorian lack of critical recognition of the complexities of the effects of the re-reading process:

In the critical prose of the mid-nineteenth century, it is hard to find a sense of the mobility of reading; a recognition that a text may look different when it is read again; that one reading is not all a text can or even must accommodate; that texts develop implications in an extended way beyond a single acquaintance; that their significance can be drawn out over time that is drawn out; and that what and how they mean, and what and how they feel, is in a complicated and hard-to-analyse relationship with temporality.[8]

This multiplicity of effects of re-visited texts would suggest that the after-life of Jones's poetry was not characterized by a simple repetition of emotional experiences and political meanings, but rather a contributive relationship with the evolving consciousness of the individual and collective reader/ship. Maidment notes the variety of Chartist periodicals 'where the enormous number of these lyrics testifies to their importance in the wider development of Chartist modes of political consciousness'.[9] It is through the enhancement and alteration of the Chartist political consciousness that Chartist poetry had its 'further implications', but the employment of newly established means of mass communication accelerated this process.[10]

The poetry that Ernest Jones and his contemporaries published in the *Northern Star* in the 1840s has ready answers for the question posed by Andrew Franta with regard to the political nature of Shelley's poetry:

However critics frame the opposition between poetry and politics, they have continued to ask: why did a writer committed to many of the tenets of radical political reform choose poetry as his vehicle? In short, if your aim is to change the world, why choose a form of expression with a severely limited and, in many ways, radically inappropriate audience?[11]

THE 'MIGHTY MIND' (1846–48)   69

Franta's answer in the case of Shelley revolves around the longevity of poetry and the peculiarly intergenerational nature of much of its transmission: Shelley was, in effect, prepared to wait for the next generation of readers to interpret the political meaning of his works.[12] The political poets of the Chartist era could not afford to wait for their poetry to take its effect, nor did they need to. The readership of radical journals and newspapers in the 1840s was neither 'severely limited' nor 'radically inappropriate'; the rise of working-class literacy rates and means of mass communication created a relatively politically astute, ready-made audience for whom poetry was still an important method of discourse. In July 1840 the unstamped Glasgow-published weekly newspaper the *Chartist Circular* began a series entitled 'The Politics of Poets' with an insistent justification of poetic engagement with the business of society:

> The Gentleman critics complain that the union of poetry with politics is always hurtful to the politics, and fatal to the poetry. But these great connoisseurs must be wrong, if Homer, Dante, Shakespeare, Milton, Cowper, and Burns were poets. Why should the sensitive bard take less interest than other men in those things which most nearly concern mankind. The contrary ought to be, and is true. What is poetry but impassioned truth — philosophy in its essence — the spirit of that bright consummate flower that is in our bosoms?[13]

This suggests a division of attitudes towards the political relevance of poetry along class boundaries. The writer is derisive of attempts to isolate poetry from societal concerns; there is a denial of poetry's 'ivory tower' associations. The mocking use of the French loan word 'connoisseur' accentuates the isolationist refinement of those 'Gentlemen critics' (the capitalization is deliberately connotative of a cohesive group) who consider poetry to be a rarefied pursuit, essentially esoteric in nature. Through the recognition of the political relevance of great poets throughout history there is an implicit attempt to contemporize poetry's political effect; to update the Shelleyan ideas of poetic universality and posterity as put forward in *A Defence of Poetry* (1821). The acceptance of poetry as a prime ulterior intellectual force leads to a recognition of poetry's contemporary political agency. Beyond its relation to skill or virtuosity, the use of the word 'consummate' suggests that poetry somehow completes something within human souls and minds.

The two seemingly antithetical figures of the Poet who emerged as the mythic legacy of the Romantic period — the Poet as solitary, self-absorbed individual, and the Poet as worldly, politically-engaged champion of liberty — can, with significant degrees of cross-contamination, be seen to have had a part in dividing early Victorian poetics along class lines. Middle-class poets including Tennyson, Browning, Barrett Browning, and Clough all, in their own ways, dealt with matters of political significance, but the allegorical, and sometimes downright difficult, nature of their approaches could have the effect of obscuring or diluting the political meaning of their works in favour of a largely aesthetic, politically neutral, reading. The inheritors of the attempted social inclusivity of early Wordsworth and Coleridge, the acid directness of Byron, or the impassioned political engagement of Shelley were the poets of Victorian working-class protest, who enriched a tradition of broadside ballad, hymn, and folk verse with Romantic forms and tropes. They shared none of the reticence of 'Gentleman critics' with regard to the mixing of poetry and politics. Indeed, the political leaders of Chartism appeared to have little doubt regarding the political relevance and influence of poetry. In *The Poetry of Chartism*, Mike Sanders notes that, alongside Feargus O'Connor, George Julian Harney (1817–97), Peter Murray McDouall (1814–54), and Samuel Kydd (1815–92) all wrote poetry occasionally and published at least one poem in the *Northern Star*.[14] For Sanders, part of the function of Chartist poetry, through its role in shaping what he terms the 'Chartist imaginary', is to provide a vital forum of discourse between the various ideologically diverse sectors within the broad church of which the Chartist body is comprised:

> It does this partly by the 'simple' act of representing discrete fractions of the movement, thereby making them more intelligible to other parts. Moreover, precisely by representing these same fractions as fractions of the same movement, an underlying shared identity is adumbrated even whilst it remains undefined. The polysemic nature of poetry clearly assists in this; the creation of multiple points of identification, the ability of the word to carry shades of meaning, facilitates the process whereby group x comes to recognise aspects of group y as consonant with its own aspirations and values. Beyond this, poetry's affective capacity helps to generate the emotional bonds, the common feelings, which are as necessary a part of any movement's infrastructure as its organisational forms.[15]

Importantly, Sanders also foregrounds:

> [The] belief that there is a vital relation between the poetical and political condition of the Chartist movement. Put simply, Chartists argued that the capacity of the working classes both to recognize and produce good poetry demonstrated their fitness for the franchise.[16]

It was Chartist culture's instinct to generate radical equivalents of mainstream cultural forms, but beyond this Chartist poetry set free the political imagination to roam where it may. Poetry's inherently rhetorical nature, its infinite and subtly shifting masks of poetic voice, and its occasionally indeterminate use of language allowed statements to be made that might have been open to prosecution if made in more conventional forms. The freedoms intrinsic to poetic form were powerful analogues for the societal, political freedoms sought by the Chartist movement.

The problem for the twenty-first-century reader of Chartist poetry is in one sense common to all readers of historical texts: the awareness that the variations of the multiplicity of possible readings over the intervening period (complicated by the inevitable variety of possible critical perspectives) point to a creeping invalidity that always threatens the present interpretation. The occasional nature of Chartist poetry complicates the reading process still further for the modern reader. The central and defining function of Chartist poetry — the achievement of the adoption by Parliament of the six points of the Charter — has been irrelevant for a century and a half. The fact that its *raison d'être* is long gone diminishes its power as an artefact, leaving it to rely on aesthetic qualities that were never meant to stand alone. The only way for the modern reader to negotiate this obstacle is to admit an imagined Chartist reader as a fourth consciousness into Poulet's ghostly triumvirate of author-reader-text. The modern reader, in an attempt to render the text intelligible, assumes the identity of an imaginary contemporary reader, or at least uses that identity as a guide through the text. The obvious pitfall of this approach is the inauthentic nature of the twenty-first-century imagined Chartist reader, but the historical and political distance between the modern reader and the Chartist text is already inevitable. Without this attempt to engage with Chartist poetry from the inside it runs the risk of being viewed only from what Matthew Reynolds terms the 'poetry-as-journalism' approach, whose emphasis is on the interpretation of poetry with reference to detailed historical contextualization.[17] This approach may be appropriate for works of political prose, but would exclude pertinent interrogation of the emotional and occasionally indeterminate nature of works of political poetry. Reynolds rightly cites Tennyson's objection to overly empiricist critical approaches: 'I hate to be tied down to say, "*This* means *that*," because the thought within the image is much more than any one interpretation'.[18] This admittance of critical indeterminacy is just as relevant to the reading of Jones's poetry. Indeed, through a curious inversion, the method of reading through an imaginary Chartist reader perhaps provides a balance against the process by which Jones, at least initially, wrote for an imagined audience with whom he had virtually no prior social contact. It is certainly the case that the first qualification that Jones had to establish on his entry into the Chartist movement, both politically and poetically, was that of authenticity. A similar problem of authenticity dogs the modern reader who attempts to interpret poetry from a Chartist tradition that has had relatively little critical exposure throughout the twentieth century. Leaving aside the problematic question of perceived poetic quality or the obstacle of formal unfamiliarity, such troubled negotiations across historico-critical lacunae illuminate by way of contrast the way we are in some senses *taught* how to read Victorian poetry that has long been accepted into the canon.

Poetic Negotiations

From the beginning of his Chartist career Jones negotiated a relationship with his audience through his poetry (in conjunction with his skills as an orator and a journalist) that either emphasized or diminished his social difference in order to suit the particular issue being addressed. The quasi-fictitious nature of the poetic voice served as a filter through which Jones could communicate ideas to his audience from varying social standpoints. The speaker of 'The Two Races' uses the privilege of familiarity with the 'Gentlemen of England' (l. 1) to plead for their assistance in the battle against a growing industrialist hegemony; the relatively long poem 'England's Greatness' reflects its writer's level of education in its geographical expansiveness. But Jones's introductory poem, published in the *Northern Star* on 16 May 1846 was 'Our Summons', the first of four pieces that summer ('Our Summons', 'Our Destiny', 'Our Warning', and 'Our Cheer') whose titles begin with that defiantly self-conscious first person plural.[19] From the outset Jones begins to establish himself as part of the democratic *cognoscenti* as his first poems perform multiple functions as letters of introduction, curriculum vitae, and political rallying cries.

72   The 'Mighty Mind' (1846–48)

Taken as a group, the four 'Our...' poems document the subtly changing relation-ship between Jones and his largely working-class audience in the early months of his Chartist career. Given Jones's recent introduction to the Chartist movement it is reasonable to assume that these poems were composed in much the same order they first appeared in the *Northern Star*, although they appeared grouped but in a different order when published in the *Chartist Lyrics and Fugitive Pieces* pamphlet later in the year. Despite the inclusivity of its title, the mode of address in 'Our Summons' separates the speaker from the addressees: the 'men of honest heart' (l. 1). The poem is intensely class-conscious, relying on Jones's characteristic inversion of the relative nobility of the upper and lower strata of social class as the basis for its moral vision:

> 'Tis not to dig the grave,
>   Where the dying miner delves;
> 'Tis not to toil for others
>   But to labour for yourselves.
>
> And nobler coin will pay you,
>   Than Kings did e'er award
> To the men, they hired to murder,
>   The brothers they should guard.
>
> No glittering stars of knighthood,
>   Shall soil your simple vest —
> But the better star of honour
>   Brave heart in honest breast.
>
> No changing Norman titles,
>   To hide your English name —
> But the better one of freemen,
>   With its blazoning of fame.

('Our Summons', ll. 21–36)

Jones, the trained barrister, compares the imperative of Chartist political action to a 'summons'. Although the work's title declares it be part of a communitarian discourse, its speaker is not included in the political relationships detailed by the second person address but represents either an omniscient narrator or Jones himself, assuming a pose of disinterestedness. The tension between the modes of address of the title and the body of the poem suggests the tentative positioning that a young man in Jones's situation might have felt obliged to adopt, drawn to a struggle between two classes of which he had little experience, in a country with whose social traditions he was only lately familiar.

Something significant happens halfway through 'Our Destiny', the second poem of the group. An epiphanic volta switches the mode of address mid-poem from second person to first person, deftly inserting the speaker into the social sphere of the poem. Jones achieves this by masking his sleight-of-hand in the fervid register of religious revelation. Where the iambic 'Our Summons' has a bouncing, song-like rhythm, 'Our Destiny' begins with heavy trochees and drawn-out anapaests, and this, along with the liberal use of exclamation marks, gives the poem's opening an urgent, insistent feel. The mode of address in the first two stanzas is a continuation of the second person of 'Our Summons', with the addition of 'ye', the archaic second person plural, enhancing the millenarian register of the poem:

> Labour! labour! labour! toil! toil! toil!
>   With the wearing of the bone and the drowning of the mind;
> Sink like shrivelled parchment in the flesh-devouring soil;
>   And die, when ye have shouted it till centuries shall hear!
>   Pass away unheeded like the waving of the wind!
>
> Build the marble palace! sound the hollow fame!
>   Be the trodden pathway for a conqueror's career!
> Exhale your million breathings to elevate one name!
>   And die, when ye have shouted it till centuries shall hear!
>
>   ('Our Destiny', ll. 1–9)

The first line's hammer-like repetitions are abandoned for the ensuing stanzas, but it nevertheless begins an interlocking rhyme scheme that links the first and second stanzas. The flurry of exclamation marks lends a desperate mood to the ironic encouragement to continue working for the benefit of a privileged few. The volta falls between the two following stanzas which introduce a divine justification for political action; 'ye' is replaced by 'us' and the speaker becomes part of the second half of the poem's response to the first half:

> 'By right divine we rule ye. God made ye but for us!'
>   Thus cry the lords of nations to the slaves whom they subdue.
> Unclasp God's book of nature — its writings read not thus!
>   Hear! tramplers of the millions! — Hear! benders to the few!
>
> God gave us hearts of ardour — God gave us noble forms —
>   And God has poured around us his paradise of light!
> Has he bade us sow the sunshine, and only reap the storms?
>   Created us in glory, to pass away in night? (ll. 10–17)

The repetition of the term 'Hear!' in the thirteenth line echoes, perhaps, Shelley's similar use of the term as a refrain in the psalmic 'Ode to the West Wind': 'Destroyer and preserver; hear, O hear!' (l. 14).[20] Jones employs the evangelical power of the term to provide the need for a self-justifying response that includes the speaker in the number of the oppressed 'millions'. The speaker becomes part of the divinely elected band whose message of change is echoed by the elemental forces of the natural world, and accompanied by an implicit threat:

> No! say the sunny heavens, that smile on all alike;
>   The waves, that upbear navies, yet hold them in their thrall;
> No! shouts the dreadful thunder, that teaches us to strike
>   The proud, for one usurping, what the Godhead meant for all.
>
> No! no! we cry united by our suffering's mighty length:
>   Ye — ye have ruled for ages — now we will rule as well!
> No! no! we cry triumphant in our right's resistless strength;
>   We — we will share your heaven — or ye shall share our hell! (ll. 18–25)

The speaker's shift from observer to participant is disguised by the magnitude of the righteous indignation the poem expresses. The repeated, exclamatory anaphoric negatives that punctuate the final lines of the poem bring an even greater emphasis to an already emphatic piece. The repetition of the term 'we' in the final line, in oppositional relation to the repetition of 'ye' two lines earlier (which now denotes the oppressors rather than the oppressed), reinforces the speaker's association with the poem's protagonists.

The third of the *Northern Star* 'Our...' poems, 'Our Warning', is unequivocal in its mode of address. 'Ye' refers to the ruling class of the country, and 'we' to a potential working-class army, recruiting from every corner of the British Isles:

> Ye lords of golden argosies!
>   And Prelate, prince, and peer;
> And members all of Parliament,
>   In rich St. Stephens, hear!
>
> We are gathering up through England,
>   All the bravest and the best;
> From the heather-hills of Scotland,
>   To the green Isle of the West.
>
> From the corn field and the factory,
>   To the coal-belt's hollow zone;
> From the cellars of the city,
>   To the mountain's quarried stone.
>
> ('Our Warning', ll. 1–12)

There is little doubt that the call to the ruling class contained in the first stanza would have had more resonance for the readers of the *Northern Star* who knew that Jones had been associated with that social sphere. Jones's condemnation of the establishment was all the more effective for him formerly having been part of it. These poems were published during Jones's rapid rise through the political ranks of the Chartist movement and it was at this point that Jones's poetry began to enjoy a closer relationship with his political life. Jones's most recent biographer, Miles Taylor, has written that 'Jones's poetry [...] catapulted him from relative obscurity into the Chartist leadership'.[21] But throughout Jones's political career it must have been an advantage to be able to make political points through the medium of poetry, in the guise of various poetic voices. In 'Our Warning' the perennial Chartist issue of physical force versus moral force is addressed. John Saville contends that Jones 'always [...] refused to accept what he considered to be the false dilemma between moral and physical force, responsible for so much of the disunity of the movement since its early years'.[22] In his speeches and in his poetry violence was a threat of last resort, yet the threat was real and consistently forceful:

> We seek to injure no man;
>   We ask but for our right;
> We hold out to the foeman
>   The hand that he would smite!
>
> And, if ye mean it truly,
>   The storm may yet be laid,
> And we will aid you duly,
>   As brothers brothers aid; —

> But, *if ye falsely play us,*
>   And if ye but possess
> The poor daring to betray us,
>   Not the courage to redress;
>
> Then your armies shall be scattered, —
>   If at us their steel be thrust, —
> And your fortresses be battered,
>   Like atoms in the dust!
>
> And the anger of the nation
>   Across the land shall sweep,
> Like a mighty Devastation
>   Of the winds upon the deep! (ll. 21–40)

The message of peace in the sixth stanza ('we seek to injure no man') is conditional upon the behaviour of the opposition, but the proximity of violence is implied by the fact that 'the storm may *yet* be laid' (my emphasis). The numerical advantage of the working class is used in the last two stanzas as an opportunity to employ Old Testament language of battle and destruction; 'the anger of the nation' seemingly sufficient to produce an inevitable victory. The lack of an apparent material destructive agent or method recalls the collapse of the walls of Jericho in the penultimate stanza, while the imagery of the wind's effect on the ocean in the last stanza is almost certainly derived from the third canto of Shelley's 'Ode to the West Wind':

> The sea-blooms and the oozy woods which wear
>   The sapless foliage of the ocean, know
> Thy voice, and suddenly grow grey with fear,
>   And tremble and despoil themselves.
>   ('Ode to the West Wind', ll. 39–42)

Shelley's elemental representation of revolutionary historical cycles was prominent in the public consciousness of the time; although first published in *Prometheus Unbound* of 1820, 'Ode to the West Wind', along with most of Shelley's work, benefitted from Mary Shelley's championing and collecting of his *oeuvre* in the late 1830s and early 1840s. This association in poetic language between natural and political transformation was readily absorbed by Chartist writers. In *The Poetry of Chartism*, Sanders notes the tendency of poetry associated with the movement to 'use natural metaphors to encode political struggle'.[23] Similarly, Maidment observes, 'the symbols [in Chartist poetry] draw heavily on processes of change within nature — fire, floods, earthquakes, even glaciers — to stress the "naturalness of the revolutionary process"'.[24] In the Chartist Lyrics section of Maidment's *The Poorhouse Fugitives* anthology the first poem is Ebeneezer Jones's 'When the World is Burning' (1845), and the second is W. J. Linton's 'The Gathering of the People' (1851), which subtitles itself as 'A Storm-song'.[25] Although there is a clear philosophical discrepancy between Shelley's pacifism and Jones's more equivocal attitude to the use of violence for revolutionary or reformist ends, the depiction of the forces of change as natural phenomena served them both. For Jones, the Shelleyan tropes of naturalization of revolutionary action which were frequently used in his work not only assured his readers of probable success in their political pursuits, but absolved them of any moral censure by aligning their actions with an historical inevitability. Jones had certainly visited this area before in the natural theology contained in his translations of German Romantic poets including Ernst Moritz Arndt and Ludwig Ühland.

By the fourth poem in the 'Our...' series, 'Our Cheer', Jones has, by the accretion of poetic familiarity, built up the confidence to criticize his readership and consequently steps outside the action again. But this time the second person address is infused with a register of patriotic outrage:

> My countrymen! why languish
>   Like outcasts of the earth,
> And drown in tears of anguish
>   The glory of your birth?
>
> Ye were a free-born people
>   And heroes were your race:
> The dead, they are our freemen,
>   The living — our disgrace!

> ('Our Cheer', ll. 1–8)

It is extraordinary testament to the regard with which Jones was held by the *Northern Star* readership at this time, just a few months after his introduction to the Chartist movement, that he could berate his new audience in such vehement terms without damaging his political and poetic reputation. Despite the coalescent element of the Chartist political cause, the complex nature of this audience must still have been largely imagined by Jones, and its probable response would therefore have been unknown. It is possible that poems such as this operate by a diffusion of censure, whereby each individual reader considers the poem to be primarily addressed to others, but nevertheless is affected by the message it imparts. There is also an element of 'good cop/bad cop' in the focal shifts employed by the poem. The opening stanzas of 'Our Cheer' at once denigrate the slavish behaviour of the working class while elevating its status through the use of terms including 'glory', 'free-born', and 'heroes'. But as the poem continues, the aggressive element intensifies: the last five stanzas of the poem pile religious, social, patriotic, sexual, and historical pressure on the readership to encourage decisive political action:

> He shall not be a Briton
>   Who dares to be a slave!
> An alien to our country!
>   And a mockery to the brave!
>
> Down with the cup untasted!
>   Its draught is not for thee.
> Its generous strength were wasted
>   On all, but on the free!
>
> Turn from the altar, bondsman!
>   Nor touch a British bride!
> What? Wouldst thou bear her blushing
>   For thee at thine own side?

> Back from the church door, craven!
>   The great dead sleep beneath,
> And liberty is graven
>   On every sculptured wreath.
>
> For whom shall lips of beauty,
>   And history's glories be?
> For whom the pledge of friendship?
>   For the free! the free! the free! (ll. 21–40)

The inclusive and often celebratory nature of much Chartist poetry is revealed here to contain underlying elements of exclusion and threat. The individual reader is presented with a form of coercive interpellation: the poem details the social consequences of a lack of self-identity as a Chartist. Unusually, acceptance of the role of poetic addressee in this case leads to a loss of identity as defined by the community. The favoured position of the reader is beside the poem, castigating those who do not fully support the Chartist cause. Political exclusion is equated with sexual, religious, and social exclusion.

Within these poems' over-riding concerns with inclusion, their privileging of plural terms, and their gradual positioning of the author within the imagined readers' community, it is possible to read elements of the social anxiety that a man in Jones's situation might have felt. By disturbing the equilibrium of a highly stratified Victorian society, Jones's renegade behaviour had left him (and his family) vulnerable to similar levels of social exclusion that his poetry prescribes for those who do not support the Chartist cause. Viewed in this light, the aggression identified in some of these poems can be seen as part of a strategy of deflection, or even, in more explicitly psychoanalytic terms, a displacement of anxiety. Jones's poetry in this initial Chartist period appears an attempt, through language, to will into being a relationship with his audience. In a most concrete way, language becomes, in Kenneth Burke's phrase, 'symbolic action'.[26] The linguistic repetition of the author's inclusion in his readers' community through the terms 'we', 'us', and 'our' initiates and potentially consolidates a process of real social inclusion. The gradual nature of the poet-figure's absorption into the Chartist body in these early *Northern Star* pieces perhaps reflects Jones's anxiety that his entry into Chartism from a relatively 'superior' social position should not be seen as coercive.

With the possible exception of 'The Song of the Low' (1851), the most performed work by Jones in the twenty-first century is 'The Blackstone Edge Gathering', which commemorates its author's first outdoor address to a Chartist audience. The meeting of 2 August 1846 was attended by thirty thousand Chartist sympathizers and was such a success that it became known as 'the birthday of renewed Chartism'.[27] The event initiated a connection between Jones and the people of the north of England (in particular, the industrial towns of Halifax and Manchester) which lasted the rest of his life. Although in terms of its mode of address the voice of the poem maintains a distance from the events described, the aim of the work is to evoke the sense of community that such meetings involved. What the voice's narrative detachment cannot disguise is Jones's sense of excitement, power, and wonderment after the experience of addressing thousands of Chartists from the spectacular backdrop of Blackstone Edge's natural amphitheatre:

> O'er plains and cities far away,
> All lorn and lost the morning lay,
> When sunk the sun at break of day,
>   In smoke of mill and factory.
>
> But waved the wind on Blackstone height
> A standard of the broad sunlight,
> And sung, that morn, with trumpet might,
>   A sounding song of Liberty.
>
> And grew the glorious music higher,
> When pouring with his heart on fire,
> Old *Yorkshire* came, with *Lancashire*,
>   And all its noblest chivalry.
>
> ('The Blackstone Edge Gathering', ll. 1–12)

The topography of Blackstone Edge and the human event it hosts counter the alienating effects of industry, and this restorative quality is extended to diminish the historical rivalry between the two largest counties of northern England. Terms including 'music', 'song', and 'trumpet' imply a harmonic resonance that is both provided by and sustains the meeting. The knightly quality of 'chivalry' is appropriated to refer to working-class subjects, but it is the collective strength of these subjects that is celebrated by the poem, in contrast to the personal quality of chivalry indicated by traditional medieval narratives. Subsequent stanzas emphasize the peaceful but resolute nature of the gathering, in spite of the ruinous effects of industrial conditions and economic privation:

> So brave a host hath never met,
> For truth shall be their bayonet,
> Whose bloodless thrusts shall scatter yet
>   The force of false finality!
>
> Though hunger stamped each forehead spare,
> And eyes were dim with factory glare,
> Loud swelled the nation's battle prayer,
>   Of — death to class monopoly!   (ll. 17–24)

Jones's statement to his audience in this poem is at its broadest in terms of its emphasis on the numerical advantage of the disaffected working class but certain phrases make specific political and ideological points that are worthy of note. 'False finality' (l. 20) would appear to refer to the artificial naturalization of the present economic system, the ideological assertion that the present is a natural culmination of, and therefore an improvement on, the events of the past. This poem disputes the idea that this is 'the best of all possible worlds', the philosophy of Gottfried Leibniz (1646–1716) that Voltaire satirized in *Candide, ou l'Optimisme* (1759). The central theme of both *Candide* and 'The Blackstone Edge Gathering' is the largely unnecessary nature of human suffering and the demystification of the laissez faire attitudes that contribute to it. The force of the message is amplified by the poem's inflated identification of the Blackstone gathering as the 'nation', whose 'battle prayer' appropriates concepts of military might and religious justification for its cause. The phrase 'class monopoly', especially when considered alongside the

Fig 3.1. Blackstone Edge, near the traditional border between Lancashire and Yorkshire. (Photograph taken by Author.)

80   THE 'MIGHTY MIND' (1846–48)

similarity of the phrase 'false finality' to 'false consciousness', might indicate an individual anticipation of Marxian philosophy on Jones's part, but phrases of this type were in common usage amongst radicals of the 1840s. The eventual historical consequences of Marx and Engel's synthesis of these concepts into a more integrated philosophical system in the later part of the decade and beyond naturally affect a modern audience's reading of these phrases.

The final stanzas of 'The Blackstone Edge Gathering' consolidate the musical motifs of the earlier part of the work and make a bold attack on the established Church that provides evidence of the strength of the links between Chartism and Nonconformist Christianity:

> And up to Heaven the descant ran,
> With no cold roof 'twixt God and man,
> To dash back from its frowning span,
>   A church prayer's listless blasphemy.
>
> How distant cities quaked to hear,
> When rolled from that high hill the cheer,
> Of — Hope to slaves! to tyrants fear!
>   And God and man for liberty! (ll. 29–36)

Jones's identification of 'a church prayer's listless blasphemy' emerges from his Nonconformist opposition to Anglicanism, and it is likely that the confidence with which he attacks the established Church's perceived part in the exploitation of the working class relates to broader poetic expressions of Christian unease on these issues from outside the Chartist movement. One of the most articulate poetic voices expressing middle-class anxieties regarding the deleterious physical and spiritual effects of the factory system at the time belonged to Elizabeth Barrett Browning (1806–61), a poet whom Jones approvingly identified as displaying a 'democratic tendency'.[28] Her work 'The Cry of the Children' (1844) contains a critique of the Church of England's perceived abandonment of child labourers in industrial areas that similarly emerges from a Dissenting tradition. The eleventh stanza of the poem emphasizes, in terms analogous to Jones's 'cold roof 'twixt God and man', the spiritual distance between the human and the divine that attends the physical suffering caused by industrial conditions. The children working in factories no longer pray because their prayers are not answered:

> 'But no!' say the children, weeping faster,
>   'He is speechless as a stone:
> And they tell us, of His image is the master
>   Who commands us to work on.
> Go to!' say the children, — 'up in Heaven,
>   Dark, wheel-like, turning clouds are all we find.
> Do not mock us; grief has made us unbelieving:
>   We look up for God, but tears have made us blind.'
> Do you hear the children weeping and disproving,
>   O my brothers, what ye preach?
> For God's possible is taught by His world's loving,
>   And the children doubt of each. (ll. 125–36)[29]

These last lines' refusal to dissociate the spiritual and material is illustrated by the imagery of heavenly clouds transformed into 'dark, wheel-like' industrial shapes in the imaginations of the children. Significantly, the prayer to which God fails to respond is The Lord's Prayer, the invocation that is perhaps the most universally accepted across Christian denominations. While the sentiment, and the religious foundation of that sentiment, might be similar to that of Jones, Barrett Browning was writing for a primarily middle-class audience, and this poem's specific appeal was for reform of legislation with respect to child labour. 'The Blackstone Edge Gathering', while it may contain an element of multiple address to all layers of society, was composed for the largely working-class readership of the *Northern Star*, and explicitly calls for a root and branch reorganization of British society.

If 'The Better Hope', which was analyzed in Chapter 1, is a poem that details Jones's emotional journey towards radicalism in the fashionable *Bildungsroman* style of the day, then 'The Working-Man's Song' sees an apparent absorption, in terms of both identity and form, of its author into its subject.[30] Its title declares its intention to serve as an anthem, and could be read as the deliberate assumption of the artifice of a poetic voice, but its first lines reveal its possessive form to be part of an individualizing and interpellating process that includes its author. Its plurals, which move through class and nationhood to a radical internationalism that becomes an increasingly prominent feature of Jones's Chartist poetry, are significantly reached via a first person voice. Again, political action is sanctioned by divine justification:

> The Land is my birthright — the beautiful land!
> By the promise that God gave to man,
> When creation first came from the Lifegiver's hand,
> And the arc of the rainbow the waterwaste spanned,
> And the green earth to brighten began.
>
> They have torn me away from its mother-like breast,
> And forth on a wilderness cast;
> A slave, or a trampler of slaves, at the best,
> To conquer the earth at a master's behest,
> And die as a pauper at last.
>
> ('The Working-Man's Song', ll. 1–10)

The use of the land in this poem as the connective element between 'working-men' celebrates O'Connor's Land Plan, but also implicitly incorporates into its narrative anyone born in the land in question, including its author. The interruption of the maternal relationship referred to in the sixth line symbolizes the emergence of an unnatural state in which the ordained role of the individual is distorted by the economic system. 'Wilderness' serves as the antithesis of civilization and therefore order. A simple distinction between slaves and oppressors is rejected by the inclusion of 'trampler[s] of slaves' as part of the oppressed group, who in turn 'conquer the earth at a master's behest'. In its more sophisticated analysis of the socio-economic system than the simply oppositional relationships characterized in some of Jones's (and other Chartists') poetry, this could be interpreted by the Chartist reader as an encouragement to embrace as fellow sufferers those who serve as oppressors and then subsequently mend their ways. For all their occasionally aggressive revolutionary language, a feature of many of Jones's Chartist poems was the depiction of the permeability of class boundaries. The chairman of a Chartist memorial meeting at Rawtenstall, Lancashire, in 1877 recalled Jones as 'a man who sought to do away with any bickering between class and class — one who did more than any man he knew of to bridge the gulf between the middle and the working classes'.[31] This strategy of rapprochement served the wider Chartist purpose in that it encouraged middle-class support for the cause of working-class enfranchisement, but it also justified Jones's personal involvement with a political community with which his social links were originally non-existent.

The images of creation myth in the first stanza of 'The Working-Man's Song' introduce within the poem oppositional tensions between expansion and contraction, and between fertility and desolation. In the next stanzas the introduction of the first person plural accompanies an account of the contrast between what the working-man has achieved, and what he has received:

> The cities of England are grand to behold,
>   Her harvests their plenty reveal;
> On channels of iron roll treasures of gold,
> And argosies proudly their banners unfold:
>   We see them — from gaol and Bastile!
>
> When the foemen of England were thick on the sea,
>   And their legions were lining the shore,
> Who came to the rescue? — the conquerors are we!
> The tamers are tamed and the captives are free!
>   And we are but slaves as before!
>
> In the mart and the mill where the foreigner tried
>   To outvie us with glittering store,
> We poured in our labour — we humbled his pride,
> And where is a nation can march by our side?
>   Yet we are as poor as before! (ll. 9–25)

The achievements of English industry, agriculture, military and foreign trade detailed in each stanza are contrasted with the last lines' summary of the experience of the working class. The poem simultaneously opposes and employs the kind of Victorian propaganda that trumpets the imperial might of Britain by encouraging the Chartist reader paradoxically to separate his destiny from that of the nation while celebrating his part in that nation's achievement. This ironic treatment of the dominant ideology is analogous to Jones's appropriation and adaptation of conservative medieval nostalgias to create a Chartist-specific origin myth of an idyllic rural past. But in this case an inverse relationship between the expansion of empire and the contraction of working-class choice, freedom, and prosperity is identified that nevertheless utilizes patriotic rhetoric as its basis. However, by the end of the poem the distinctions created by national boundaries are proved to be false, and in an internationalism that is as much post-Shelleyan as it is pre-Marxian, the workers are encouraged to take control in Europe by the might of their labour rather than by more violent means:[32]

> The land is my birthright — then on — in a band,
>   Battalions of progress! advance,
> I take my invincible armour in hand,
> For the spade, after all, is the lord of the land,
>   And the sickle shall baffle the lance.
>
> For now we have learned the great lesson aright,
>   That Frank — Briton — Teuton, are one;
> That their interest is not to *compete* — but *unite*!
> Till nations combining leave tyrants to fight
>   By the light of young liberty's sun! (ll. 41–50)

The emphasis on internationalism contained in Jones's Chartist poetry reflects his European upbringing and is a continuation of the impulse that led him to write about the figure of Chateaubriand in 1843. The equation of the 'Frank', 'Briton', and 'Teuton', while retaining the nomenclature of standard nineteenth-century racial classifications, is an implicit rejection of the parochial view of national difference that patriotic narratives tend to promulgate. Within a year of publishing this poem Jones was in Paris meeting the German Karl Marx, whose *Communist Manifesto* saw its first periodical publication in 1848 in the *Deutsche Londoner Zeitung*, the British German-language newspaper that had published the last poetry of Jones's pre-Chartist period in 1845.

If Jones's early Chartist poetry represented in part an attempt to will into being a relationship between himself and his readership, it also attempted to provide that readership with an image of the model Chartist, or at least as Jones envisaged that figure. The necessity of this project, which was after all political rather than poetic in nature, precluded the kind of subtleties found in some contemporary poetic treatments of the political upheavals taking place across Europe at the time. Jones could not afford the layers of detachment displayed by Arthur Hugh Clough's epistolary novel in verse, *Amours de voyage* (1849), whose account of the Siege of the Rome (1849), despite its author's political interest, forms a backdrop to an ironic, hesitant love story. Jones's more direct poetic appraisals of contemporary geopolitics were founded in political expediency: the hope was that a pan-European revolutionary chain reaction would force democratic change onto the London government. Part of Jones's mission was to encourage his readership to identify themselves with, and therefore as, European revolutionaries. Long before the phrase was coined by Friedrich Engels, Jones was combating an insular 'false consciousness' that, in his view, used patriotic ideologies to inflate national difference in order to disguise the fact that democracy should be a wider European goal, and that if the workers of various nations might not '*compete* — but *unite*', then their goal would be all the more achievable. 'The Working-Man's Song' interpellates its readership as European, but balances this potentially dangerous strategy with a substitution of the term 'land' for 'nation', which allows for a patriotism accompanied by more vague (and hence more malleable) ideological baggage than conventional nationalist narratives. The conservative variant of this kind of 'internationalist patriotism' is illustrated by the fact that in Dorothea Felicia Hemans's much-parodied 1826 patriotic ballad 'Casabianca' ('The boy stood on the burning deck...') the boy in question is actually French.[33]

84   THE 'MIGHTY MIND' (1846–48)

The year 1847 saw Jones begin to publish poetry in the *Northern Star* that portrayed Chartism as part of a Europe-wide movement towards greater political representation for the people. Poems including 'The New Year's Song of Our Exile', which satirizes the British political situation from the perspective of a *faux naïf* expatriate, and 'England', which compares the revolutionary movements of the Continent with historical English political events including the Peasants' Revolt of 1381, start to set the Chartist struggle in the context of an international democratic trend.[34] The social flexibility of the poetic voice of Jones's first Chartist poems becomes a pan-national flexibility, and the poems begin to take on a somewhat didactic flavour. 'Poland's Hope', which was written between the Wielkopolska Uprising of 1846 and the Greater Poland Uprising of 1848, is as much an instructional text for a British working-class readership as any real attempt to encourage military resolve in Polish revolutionaries:[35]

> Poles! be free. The words are spoken;
> Battles lost and treaties broken,
>   Ratify the great decree;
> Not the warhorse madly prancing,
> Not the bayonet redly glancing,
> But the march of mind advancing,
>   Says: Be free! Poles, be free!
>
> Yet we say not: Peace! — to them!
> Peace? It is a costly gem,
> That a slave cannot afford;
>   While the Vistula's great waters
> Swell with tears of Poland's daughters,
> And with blood of Russian slaughters,
>   Never — never sheathe the sword.

('Poland's Hope', ll. 1–14)

The barely disguised subtext of this work is centred on the term 'slave', which Jones habitually uses to describe members of the British working class: the implication is that the situation in Poland, along with its concomitant violent imperatives, is interchangeable with that of Britain. As Jones's frustration with the intractability of the British government grew, and successive European administrations required more oppressive measures to counter radicals in their own countries, his poetry abandoned the 'men of peace' message that had characterized some of his early Chartist pieces, and began to make a case for the use of force that often walked a fine line between the pragmatism of a radical anticipation of *Realpolitik* and an impatient belligerence.[36]

The Domestication of Revolt

'The Age of Peace' appeals to its readers to interrogate the popular concept of *Pax Britannica*, which suggests that the British naval superiority evident throughout the world since the Battle of Waterloo in 1815 effectively secures and upholds a universal peace for global benefit.[37] The register of the poem is one of heavy irony as it lists the many regions in the world riven by conflict, and details the misery caused by an economy failing despite Britain's commercial monopolies. The first two stanzas act as a call and response, with the poem opening in a parodic approximation of the dominant ideology, and then quickly shifting to a revelatory critique of that ideology's myth of British peace and wealth:

> Men! exult with one another,
>   See how wrong and bloodshed cease!
> Man in man beholds a brother —
>   'Tis — oh! 'tis the age of peace!
>
> Peace! ha! ha! be wind and vapour,
>   Foolish thought of feeble soul,
> Keep alight thy twinkling taper,
>   While the whirlwind seeks its goal!
>
> ('The Age of Peace', ll. 1–8)

The idea of a cordial and prosperous British Empire presiding over a newly harmonious world is lambasted in a series of subsequent stanzas that cover an extraordinary geographical range as they depict a global picture of myriad regional and national disputes, wars, and annexations:

> Hark! from distant eastern waters,
>   To the farthest western wave,
> Comes the voice of many slaughters,
>   O'er the earth's unclosing grave.
>
> Hark! in seas of China booming,
>   How the loud artillery roars;
> And a thousand mast are looming
>   On La Plata's battered shores.
>
> Hark! the Caffir groans unheeded,
>   Scourged by strong invader's band;
> And the Indian lance is needed
>   To defend the Afghan's land.
>
> Hark! along the wide Zahara,
>   Rings the volley — flames the steel;
> From Morocco to Boccara,
>   Columns march and squadrons wheel.
>
> Hark! by Otaheite's garden,
>   Threats and flames the French corvette;
> And the blackened bodies harden,
>   Where the west its wigwam set. (ll. 11–28)

The work continues to list further sites of conflict in New Zealand, Madagascar, Greece, Albania, Circassia, Poland, Ferrara, Messina, Naples, Sicily, Spain, the Asturias, Oporto, Switzerland, Paris, Mexico, and Ireland. This apparently exhaustive tour of international misery expands the Chartist poetic imagination far beyond its domestic borders partly to encourage solidarity with direct or indirect foreign victims of the policies of the British ruling class, but also to contextualize the struggle for British suffrage. The Chartist reader is assured by what seems insurmountable evidence that if he is 'rocking the boat' then, in reality, the boat is close to sinking anyway:

> Hark to England's voice of wailing!
>   Not alone the people rue;
> Commerce tarries — banks are failing,
>   And the smiter's smitten too.
>
> Baffled League and palsied faction,
>   Lords of land and lords of trade,
> Stagger 'neath the vast reaction
>   Of the ruin they have made. (ll. 105–12)

This kind of justification was necessary to counter the conservative media's portrayal of Chartist agitation as destabilizing and therefore unpatriotic. Part of the function of Jones's poetry of this period was to help to realign his readership's notion of patriotism so that it encompassed a radical vision. This was achieved through a sometimes unsteady balance of pre-Marxian demystification of economic realities and the celebration of a vigorously imagined working-class origin myth. The 'nation' becomes 'the land' or 'the people', and the term 'England' shifts its meaning according to poetic context in order to denote either the people who comprise it (the vast majority of whom, of course, are working-class), or the seat of military and commercial force whose policies heap misery on its own people and across the world. The indeterminacy, and therefore the flexibility, of poetic language becomes an important tool for the subtle adjustment of political perceptions, including what Anne Janowitz sees as a reclamation of the landscape (and, by extension, popular sovereignty) by Chartist poets from Romantic tropes: 'a tradition which had been virtually overgrown by the detemporalizing and individualizing picturesque sensibility of meditative poetry'.[38] In opposition to parliamentary use of the term 'people' as a pejorative, Chartism, whilst re-aligning the concept of sovereignty, sometimes deliberately conflates it with 'land' and 'nation'.[39]

'The Age of Peace' could almost be read as a millenarian text, predicting a transformative global event by its foregrounding of military instability and economic downturn. This interpretation is not discouraged by its typically rousing finale that ends the poem with a circular re-reading of the first stanza in light of the implications of the body of the text:

> Hark! the poor are starving daily;
>   Gold is jingling, bayonets clank;
> Hark! the great are living gaily,
>   And corruption's smelling rank.
>
> But the sands of time are running;
>   Ever hope, and never fear!
> Oh! the people's hour is coming!
>   Oh! the people's hour is near!
>
> Then! exult with one another,
>   Then shall wrong and bloodshed cease;
> Man in man respect a brother,
>   And the world be won for peace! (ll. 113–24)

A millenarian reading is further encouraged by the poem's specific historical context, as it was published on the eve of nineteenth-century Europe's most politically cataclysmic year. As nation after nation succumbed to democratic and nationalist revolt across Europe in 1848, one of Jones's poetic responses was 'The March of Freedom', which engages in a Shelleyan personification of 'Freedom', characterized as an unstoppable female spirit making her way across Europe. Again, Jones lists sites of conflict, and there is some overlap with those featured in 'The Age of Peace'. But this time the emphasis is on these sites being celebrated as centres of a potential Europe-wide liberation, rather than being treated as evidence of imperial or economic decline:

> The nations are all calling
>> To and fro, from strand to strand;
> Uniting in one army
>> The slaves of every land.
>
> Lopsided thrones are creaking,
>> For 'loyalty' is dead;
> And commonsense is speaking
>> Of honesty instead.
>
> And coming Freedom whispers,
>> 'Mid the rushing of her wings,
> Of loyalty to nature,
>> Not loyalty to kings.

('The March of Freedom', ll. 1–12)

This emphatic feminine personification of freedom, though by no means a Jones innovation, introduces an important element to its author's relationship with his audience. By appropriating a feminine voice by proxy, Jones can use the female/male binary to oppose feminine 'commonsense' with the masculine Reason of industrial capitalism. Furthermore, the mythical Earth Mother is implicitly invoked when 'loyalty to nature' is chosen over 'loyalty to [masculine] kings'. Later in the poem the maternal elements of the female figure are employed as Freedom, after her infectious presence in European locations including Poland, Austria, Switzerland, and France, returns to what appears to be her home, Britain. Her scolding of the population of the perceived birthplace of political freedom represents an attempt by Jones to combine humiliation and reassurance in his address to his readership:

> Still onward Freedom wandered,
>> Till she touched the British soil;
> *Elysium of money*
>> And *Tartarus of toil!*
>
> And loudly here she chided;
>> 'My chosen people, ye!
> I gave ye many chances:
>> Why so long in growing free?
>
> 'Ye bend in resignation,
>> A tame and patient herd!

88 THE 'MIGHTY MIND' (1846–48)

> Union be the motto,
>   And onward! be the word!' (ll. 161–72)

The necessity of revolution is emphasized by the description of Britain as the Roman heaven ('Elysium') of capitalism, and the Greek hell ('Tartarus') of the workers. While these are characteristically hyperbolic depictions, their subtlety lies in their suggestion that the current domestic political state is essentially foreign in nature. By contrast, the strategy of maternalizing the catalyst of political destabilization effectively domesticates revolution. That the British are characterized as the 'chosen people' of Freedom further naturalizes the unfamiliar political turmoil that, as 'European', could so easily be thought of as 'un-British'. Through the symbolic aegis of the returning figure of Freedom, revolution is imbued with connotations of the warmth, safety, and inevitability traditionally associated with home. The unfamiliar becomes familiar, the unstable becomes stable, and the dangerous becomes safe. These radical transformations are made possible by Jones's poetic appropriation of feminine values.

Notes to Chapter 3

1. Ernest Jones, Diary, 8/10/1846, MCRO, MS. f281.89 J5/30.
2. Allen Davenport (1775–1846), a shoemaker by trade, was the president of the East London Democratic Association and a supporter of the Chartist Land Plan. His first poetry was published in 1819 but his *Northern Star* poetry page debut ('Repeal and the Charter') was on 5 August 1843. Benjamin Stott (1813–50) was a bookbinder active in local radical politics in Manchester. He was a relatively prolific contributor to the *Northern Star* poetry pages with over twenty pieces published from 1841, many of which were collected in the volume *Songs for the Millions and Other Poems* (1843). Thomas Cooper (1805–92), like Davenport a shoemaker by trade, was Jones's predecessor as unofficial Chartist Laureate before falling out with the Chartist leadership in 1846. His long work in Spenserian stanzas, *The Purgatory of Suicides* (1845), was composed during a two-year prison term and is considered a major achievement of Chartist poetics.
3. Anthony H. Harrison, *Victorian Poets and the Politics of Culture: Discourse and Ideology* (Charlottesville: University of Virginia, 1998), p. 1.
4. Ibid., p. 82.
5. George Poulet, 'Phenomenology of Reading', *New Literary History*, 1, (1969), 59.
6. Maidment, p. 37.
7. Review of *Chartist Poems*, NS 24/10/1846.
8. Francis O'Gorman, 'Matthew Arnold and Rereading', *Cambridge Quarterly*, 41, 2 (2012), 245–61 (p. 246).
9. Maidment, p. 38.
10. For further discussion of the complex relationship between Chartist poetry and politics see Sanders, pp. 6–37.
11. Andrew Franta, *Romanticism and the Rise of the Mass Public* (Cambridge: Cambridge University Press, 2007), p. 112.
12. For further discussion of Shelley's awareness of, and relationship with, his future readership, see Andrew Bennett, *Romantic Poets and the Culture of Posterity* (Cambridge: Cambridge University Press, 1999), pp. 158–78.
13. [Anon.], 'The Politics of Poets No. I', *The Chartist Circular*, 11 July 1840, cited in Kovalev, p. 295–96.
14. Sanders, p. 7. Harney was an influential radical Chartist and member of the London Working Men's Association, who went on to edit the *Northern Star* from 1845 until 1850. McDouall, a surgeon who joined the Chartist cause in 1838, was a popular lecturer and edited the periodical *McDouall's Chartist and Republican Journal*. He was imprisoned twice. Samuel Kydd was a lecturer

The 'Mighty Mind' (1846–48)   89

and agitator who argued from an anti-free trade Chartist position. He became a successful barrister.

15. Sanders, p. 21.
16. Ibid., pp. 76–77.
17. Matthew Reynolds, *The Realms of Verse 1830–1870: English Poetry in a Time of Nation-Building* (Oxford: Oxford University Press, 2001), p. 14.
18. Alfred Lord Tennyson, *Memoir*, ii, p. 127, cited in Reynolds, p. 11.
19. Ernest Jones, 'Our Summons', *NS* 16/5/1846 (in Kovalev, pp. 135–36); 'Our Warning', *NS* 1/8/1846 (in Kovalev, pp. 138–39); 'Our Cheer', *NS* 8/8/1846 (Kovalev, pp. 139–40).
20. Shelley, 'Ode to the West Wind', in *Shelley: Poetical Works,* pp. 577–79 (p. 577).
21. Taylor, p. 78.
22. Saville, p. 22.
23. Sanders, p. 172.
24. Maidment, p. 38.
25. Ibid., pp. 39 & 40, respectively.
26. Kenneth Burke, *Language as Symbolic Action: Essays on Life, Literature and Method* (Berkeley: University of California Press, 1968).
27. Chase, p. 260.
28. Taylor, p. 96.
29. Elizabeth Barrett Browning, 'The Cry of the Children', in *The Works of Elizabeth Barrett Browning*, ed. by Sara Donaldson and others, 5 vols (London: Pickering & Chatto, 2010), I, 442–43.
30. Ernest Jones, 'The Working-Man's Song', *NS* 1/5/1847.
31. *Bacup Times*, 10 February 1877, cited by Saville, p. 82.
32. Only just. According to Saville, Marx and Jones first met 'when the former came to England for the second congress of the Communist League in November 1847, for they both spoke at a meeting organised by the Fraternal Democrats and the Polish Committee to celebrate the anniversary of the 1830 Polish Revolution' (p. 27).
33. Tricia Lootens, 'Victorian Poetry and Patriotism', in *The Cambridge Companion to Victorian Poetry*, ed. by Joseph Bristow (Cambridge: Cambridge University Press, 2000), pp. 256–59.
34. Ernest Jones, 'The New Year's Song of Our Exile', *NS* 16/1/1847.
35. Ernest Jones, 'Poland's Hope', *NS* 27/2/1847.
36. Many older Chartists (in terms of both age and length of membership) were used to the stubbornness of the British government by now, but the general shift of the movement as the economic situation worsened through 1846 to 1848 towards a tacit acceptance of the principle of violence (at least in 'self-defence') saw some members resign. Jones's poetic predecessor, Thomas Cooper, was a high profile opponent of the principle of 'physical force'.
37. Ernest Jones, 'The Age of Peace', *NS* 4/12/1847.
38. Janowitz, *Lyric and Love in the Romantic Tradition*, p. 152.
39. Ibid., p. 144.

CHAPTER 4

Lyrical Prison Poetry
1848–50

In *Lyric and Labour in the Romantic Tradition*, Anne Janowitz suggests that the poetry Jones composed in prison saw a consolidation of his poetic voice that included an expression of increased identity with, and through, the Chartist body:

> Jones's poetry prior to his imprisonment in 1848 engages chiefly with the genres of the Chartist hymn and song, in which he aimed to imagine and lyricise the experience of the group struggle, modified by his own steeping in the lyricism of romantic solitude. His prison poetry moves towards defining a collective subjectivity and identity from an opposing source, his individual experience in jail.[1]

This move towards definition would suggest an integration of poetic themes, genres, and voices but Jones's post-prison poetry saw, if anything, a fragmentation of his poetic output into the constituent voices of lyric romanticism, collective hymnody, satirical social commentary, and visionary epic. Ronald Paul has noted that:

> One of the ironies of Jones's development is that, while his political ideas after his release from prison gravitated more and more towards socialism (influenced by his close co-operation at this time with Marx and Engels), his poetry began losing much of its immediate popular accessibility.[2]

Although Jones may have emerged from prison with his Chartist identity reinforced by experience and reputation, conversely, his poetry underwent a process of diffusion, so that, in comparison with the relative homogeneity of his *Northern Star* poetry (1846–48), it becomes increasingly difficult to describe Jones's post-1850 'poetic voice'. Apart from poetry composed immediately prior to his release which appears to represent a conscious return to his pre-prison poetic style, Jones's prison poetry suggests the influence of the overwhelming effects of isolation, and the plight of fellow Chartists, inside or outside prison, can scarcely be seen to figure at all. If Jones's most famous post-prison lyric 'The Song of the Low' (1852) can be viewed as the supreme example of his talent for 'defining a collective subjectivity', then there is little in his prison poetry that pre-figures it. Indeed, Jones's grasp of a 'collective subjectivity', his ability to express the needs and wants of the Chartist 'we', could already be said to exist fully-formed in *Northern Star* poems such as 'The Working-Man's Song' and 'Onward'. This chapter finds that, for the most part, prison represents a poetic interlude in Jones's career, with explorations of his own imagination and struggles with isolation taking precedence over the kind of public engagement that typified his poetry in the two years before his arrest. Jones made political capital from his experience in jail, and the presentation of his prison poetry was part of that process, but the poetry itself offers little evidence of an enhanced engagement with the Chartist body.

The Radical Imprisoned

The arrest of Ernest Jones, along with many other Chartist activists, should be seen in the context of the atmosphere of the spring and summer of 1848. With news or rumours of regimes across Europe falling in a series of democratic revolutions, the political mood in Great Britain was understandably nervous, and the Chartists were the focus of scrutiny. A *Times* editorial just a few days before Jones's arrest reflected the opinions of many British conservatives as it reacted to the sporadic violence that occurred in the aftermath of the march through the City of London on 29 May 1848 of more than 50,000 Chartists and Repealers calling for the release of John Mitchell (1815–75) of the Young Ireland movement.[3] Awareness of recent breakdowns of law and order, particularly in the Chartist heartlands of West Yorkshire, coloured the rhetoric:[4]

> So far they are beaten. Order and law are vindicated at the expense of some score broken heads and limbs. But is this the be-all and end-all here? We cannot expect this. The nature of things forbids us to expect it. It has been a failure. But who had guessed at the attempt? It was a failure, but of such an effort as would in some countries in Europe have made a revolution. What guarantee have we that the attempt will not be repeated, with the same secrecy, with the same organization, and even a more desperate struggle? How can we assure ourselves that the blood which boiled for a contest and a victory, will be cooled and tamed by such a defeat; or the animosities which it has ripened between antagonistic classes will speedily die away? Human nature and experience forbid us to indulge such a hope.[5]

The editorial continues by admitting that unemployment is causing real suffering including starvation on the streets of Britain, but suggests that Chartism uses such suffering to undermine the political system. It reserves particular ire for those whom it perceives 'are well paid, well fed, and well dressed, but who are equally discontented. *Their* grievances are sentimental ones; their purpose a dishonest purpose.'[6] The problem for Jones was that in the summer of 1848, he was viewed as one of the most prominent examples of this kind of affluent Chartist sympathizer.

Jones was sentenced to two years' imprisonment in July 1848 for sedition in relation to a speech he gave to a meeting of thousands of Chartist supporters at Bishop Bonner's Field in East London on June 4th.[7] During the trial particular attention was paid to these closing words of Jones's address to the crowd:

> Rest assured that I will be struggling in your cause in Bradford, in Halifax, in Manchester, and in the other places where storm and turbulence are now going on. Rest assured that I shall not preach a miserable, namby-pamby doctrine of non-resistance and passive obedience. But at the same time I shall preach a doctrine of manly firmness and not hot-headed impetuosity. If you mean to do anything, see well first if you have the power to do it; and then, having made up

your mind, do not let even death itself prevent you from carrying it into effect
[...] Only preparation — only organisation is wanted, and the Green Flag shall
float over Downing Street, and St. Stephen's. Only energy is wanted — only
determination — and what will be the result? Why? That John Mitchell, and
John Frost will be brought back, and Sir George Grey and Lord John Russell
will be sent to change places with them.[8]

In reality this speech was no more or less provocative than many speeches Jones had
given up and down the country. In a speech on the question of moral and physical
force at a public meeting in London on 28 March 1848 he had declared:

I advise physical organisation, because I know what the people are determined
to do, should moral means fail. If, then, they are compelled to have recourse to
extreme measures at last, is it not necessary that we must be prepared for them?
A pretty business it would be, when driven to that extreme to find ourselves
unprepared.[9]

As Miles Taylor has noted of the speech at Bishop Bonner's Fields:

Jones had said virtually nothing that day that he had not previously propounded
in meetings of the Chartist convention. However, for once someone was
listening to his every word. James White, a short-hand writer and itinerant
supplier of copy for some of the London dailies, was in attendance as a police
spy and recorded Jones's speech verbatim.[10]

Jones reportedly praised White's shorthand skills when he was arrested. After Jones
and his fellow speaker, Alexander Sharp, had left the scene there were clashes
between some of the crowd and members of the 'K' division of the Metropolitan
Police, who were discovered to have been secretly observing the meeting from a
nearby church. Jones was arrested in Manchester two days later. Although Jones
was convicted for the content of his rhetoric rather than his poetry, an interesting
analogue of the previous chapter's discussion of the poet–audience relationship
emerges from the legal interpretation of 'sedition and unlawful assembly' made
at the trial of another Chartist prisoner just a few days earlier. Taylor notes the
importance of this interpretation for the outcome of Jones's trial:

The trial of John Fussell at the beginning of July had set the tone. In Fussell's
trial Sir John Jervis, the attorney general, had insisted that sedition meant not
only the precise language used, but also the circumstances of the meeting at
which the words were uttered and the subsequent consequences of the speech.
These were markedly different criteria from previous prosecutions for sedition,
when the Crown had concentrated on determining the intentions of the
speakers and the precise wording of their utterances. Now the burden of proof
lay in determining the unforeseeable effects of such speeches.[11]

This legal focus on the context of the reception of language, and on language's
effect upon the listener, rather than merely an interpretation of its inherent or
intended meaning, was instrumental in Jones's conviction. The emphasis on a direct
causal link was an even more emphatic acknowledgement of the direct relationship
between Jones's use of language and the subsequent actions of his audience than
Jones's previous assertion that his poetry was 'forming the tone of the mighty mind
of people'. In a legalistic anticipation of reader-response theory, the true nature of

language is perceived not to be revealed until its effect on the audience has been fully analyzed; the active agency of language, at least in the form of rhetoric, is taken for granted.

From Jones's treatment in the first year of his term in the Westminster House of Correction (commonly known as Tothill Fields Prison and built in the then modern 'Panopticon' style), it would appear that the authorities continued to exercise caution with regard to the possible consequences of Jones's utterances. Before 1848 there had been a tendency to treat high-profile political prisoners, particularly those regarded as 'gentleman radicals', including William Cobbett (1763–1835), James Leigh Hunt (1784–1859), and even Feargus O'Connor when he was imprisoned at York Castle between 1840 and 1841, as almost under a form of house arrest. Hunt's imprisonment for defaming the Prince Regent in the pages of the *Examiner* in 1813 transformed him into a political and literary *cause célèbre* while he was still incarcerated in Surrey County Gaol. The testimony of his eldest son, Thornton Leigh Hunt, suggests that his prison accommodation became a combination of family home and literary salon:

> He had two rooms — a small one, with a high window, which the present writer still remembers entering while Leigh Hunt was in conversation with Henry Brougham; and a larger room, covered with a paper representing a trellis of roses, and having a door which opened upon a small enclosed garden. He also had liberty to walk in the kitchen-garden behind the governor's house. Amongst the furniture was a pianoforte.[12]

The experience of Ernest Jones a generation later could not have been in more marked contrast. For a large proportion of his prison term Jones was denied access to writing materials, his visits were severely restricted, and he was given no opportunity to communicate with the outside world. Beyond the aims of punishment, deterrence, or the setting of an example, the purpose of Jones's imprisonment was partly to silence him. Jones's effective isolation from the political and literary scene in which he had been immersed for two years was almost total, and he entered a world of hard labour, solitary confinement, and widespread disease.[13] The most bizarre treatment to which Jones was subjected was the literal silencing of prisoners, who were impelled during exercise periods to wear beak-like masks to enforce a complete lack of communication with fellow inmates.

The forced isolation that Jones underwent for periods of his sentence was also in contrast to the prison experiences of his Chartist poetic predecessor, Thomas Cooper, just five years before. Cooper was tried for seditious conspiracy in May 1843 and sent to Stafford Gaol for two years, where he formed a friendship with fellow Chartist, Arthur O'Neill (1819–96), which lasted almost fifty years. It is clear from Stephen Roberts's account that their friendship served to alleviate the effects of the privations of prison life:

> Although confined for twelve hours a day in cold cells and presented with off-putting food, Cooper and O'Neill seem to have had a less unpleasant time of it than many of their comrades. Both studious men, they were naturally drawn to each other and allowed to spend much of their time together. In their day cell they read and discussed eighteenth century religious texts by Humphrey

Prideaux and Joseph Milner — which seemingly Cooper had not been able to get his hands on as a young autodidact — and resolved to learn Hebrew — which Cooper, characteristically, overdid.[14]

Many years later, O'Neill was to describe Stafford Gaol as 'more like a home than a prison', which one imagines would not have been the case had he spent significant periods of his incarceration alone in enforced silence.[15] As it transpired, under these conditions of relative social and intellectual nourishment, Cooper was able to compose his epic poem in Spenserian stanzas, *The Purgatory of Suicides: A Prison Rhyme in Ten Books* (1845). This dense, intellectually ambitious work which cemented his poetic reputation beyond the bounds of Chartism begins with a poetic translation of the ten-hour speech he gave in his own defence at his trial.[16] It then details his prison experiences counterpointed with dream visions which encompass discussions of political theory with historical figures who have famously committed suicide (and are therefore suspended in Purgatory), including Sappho, Nero, Judas, and Lord Castlereagh. The personal experience of incarceration provides the focal point into which, and from which, the political ideas of the poem flow. Stephanie Kuduk recognizes that Cooper's broadening politicization of his own experience through his poetry represents an example of an important radical template: 'This effort to interpret individual narrative events through the lens of political theory is a centrepiece of radical argument, and can be understood as the central goal of radical working-class poetry'.[17] Through this poem Cooper, as Janowitz claims of Jones, 'poetically carves out a place for his lyrical singularity to become part of a larger collective subjectivity'.[18] Imprisonment as a concrete manifestation of political oppression concentrates the symbolic resonance of the writer's words both in the process and experience of production and the context of reception. As a physical representative of societal oppression the poet-prisoner is more easily able to universalize his experience to his fellow sufferers within and beyond the prison walls. For Jones, whose background lacked the class authenticity of the shoemaker Cooper, this process was achieved politically. But if it was achieved poetically, it was through the fact of the existence of his prison poetry, rather than through that poetry's content. Jones's prison poetry was testament to his own suffering; if this was then associated with the suffering of his fellow Chartists then it was a retrospective conferral.

Given his political and literary energies, it was inevitable that Jones would produce poetry while incarcerated if he could; uncertainty remains, however, as to when, and how, this poetry was produced. For many years, when the only people writing about Jones as a historical figure were those sympathetic to the historical narrative of working-class struggle, his own account was taken at face value. This account famously claims that some poetry, particularly parts of the early draft of the relatively long work in heroic couplets, 'The New World', was written using the medium of his own blood mixed with soot. When John Saville covered the period of Jones's imprisonment in the biographical introduction to his 1952 volume of Jones's political writings he was content to quote extensively and unquestioningly from the 1868 pamphlet *Ernest Jones: Who Is He? What Has He Done?* Because of the rather patchy biographical information the public received about Jones during his Chartist years (an ambiguity which enhanced his social mystique), this widely distributed publication provided the basis for most biographical accounts of Jones for the next century. The political and poetic martyrdom of its narrative is amplified by its subject's relative gentility:

> Ernest Jones in the second year of his imprisonment, was so broken in health, that he could no longer stand upright — he was found lying on the floor of his cell, and then, only, taken to the prison hospital. He was told that if he would petition for his release and promise to abjure politics for the future, the remainder of his sentence would be remitted — but *he refused his liberty on those conditions*, said the work he had once begun he would never turn from, and was accordingly reconsigned to his cell. [...]
>
> However, he had mental resources of his own. During his imprisonment, and before pen, ink, and paper were allowed, he *wrote* some of the finest poems in the English language. The devices by which he obtained writing materials are amusing. Pens he got by finding occasionally a feather from a rook's wing that had dropped in the prison yard. This quill he cut secretly with a razor, when brought to him twice a week to shave; an ink bottle he contrived to make from a piece of soap he got from the washing-shed, and this he filled with ink from the ink bottle when he was allowed to write his quarterly letters, the fly-leaves of a Bible, prayer-book and any books he was, as before stated, allowed to read. But one poem — The New World — was composed before he succeeded in securing ink, and this was written almost entirely *with his own blood*.[19]

Taylor's research suggests that this publication, which was produced by The Reform League to support Jones's Manchester election campaign of 1868,[20] was largely dictated by Jones himself, and that the poet's various accounts of his incarceration were more than a little inconsistent.[21] Taylor is not the only commentator to express scepticism over the sanguinary provenance of 'The New World'. But, even given Jones's known capacity for exaggeration and distortion, it is still feasible that the account was based in truth. It is incontestable that Jones was denied writing materials for some of the time he was incarcerated, and almost inconceivable that he should fail to compose poetry during this particularly inspired phase of his career when given ample cause and time to do so. The fact remains that, in such a situation, blood may have been the only available fluid with sufficient opacity for the job. While it is improbable that a poem the length of 'The New World' could have been written 'almost entirely' in blood, even over a period of two years, it is still possible that notes were taken as aides-memoire, or that it was begun using this method. Without physical evidence, the truth can never be known. The problem is the almost Eucharistic amplitude of the mythic resonance of the image of a prisoner writing poetry in his own blood. This is a narrative (employed in fiction by Charles Dickens and Alexandre Dumas) which is undermined by its own symbolic power.

As Jones's most recent and most thorough biographer, Taylor's greatest scepticism in this area concerns the provenance of the poems Jones claimed to have composed in prison. These consist of twenty-four lyric works and 'The New World' (which will be discussed in the next chapter). Although Taylor presents no supporting evidence for his thesis that they were written after Jones's release other than their author's unreliability, he writes that in prison 'he may or may not have written a hatful of poems', and refers to 'Jones's infamous prison poems' and to the 'so-called "prison poems"'.[22] Subsequently, he refers to 'Jones's "New World"', originally written "in blood" in prison in 1849 or, more likely, dashed off at the seaside in the summer of 1850'.[23] This work of over twelve hundred lines has been described by Paul as 'one of the most remarkable and elaborate examples of a poetic critique of imperialism produced in the whole of the Victorian period'.[24] Wherever it was composed or written, it was probably not 'dashed off'. It may be the case that poetry which was largely composed in prison on scraps of paper or memorized was revised on release, and that Jones's specification of the month and sometimes even the day (their apparent dates of composition run from July 1848 to July 1850 and so exactly parallel his imprisonment) for each piece in the *Notes to the People* newspaper refers to their original conception. In terms of rates of poetic production, twenty-four lyric pieces and one long work in two years seems, if anything, slightly sparse for Jones. Although it probably can never be established where or when Jones composed these poems, for the purposes of this study, the texts will be regarded as prison poems.

The Radical Released

On his release from prison Jones embarked on a number of editorships of radical periodicals, the first of which was the weekly newspaper of political poems and prose, *Notes to the People*. In effect, and with characteristic literary energy, Jones tended to write most, if not all of the copy for these publications. The fourth issue of *Notes to the People* was devoted to the lyric poetry that emerged from Jones's incarceration. The poems, which were presented in order of composition, were prefaced by a defiant and at times vitriolic introduction and dedication that conflated the suffering of their author with that of his fellow prisoners, and associated this suffering with the daily experience of the British working class in general:

> Ah! what are the sufferings we bore in prison — nothing for us to bear in the cause of humanity — nothing for us to bear — but *much for them to inflict!* And what are the sufferings of those IN prison, compared with the sufferings of those still OUT? Nay! All England is a prison for the poor, its keys are gold, its walls are ocean, and Vice, Prejudice, and Ignorance its jailors![25]

This blurring of the lines between the incarcerated and the nominally free serves the dual purpose of emphasizing the restrictions on political liberty in the country as a whole while consoling prisoners that their plight is merely an intensification of the experience of those beyond the prison walls. In an admittedly simplified form, this perception of the penal system as the constructive template of wider society prefigures Michel Foucault's concept of the 'carceral continuum':

> Prison continues, on those who are entrusted to it, a work begun elsewhere, which the whole of society pursues on each individual through innumerable mechanisms of discipline. By means of a carceral continuum, the authority that sentences infiltrates all those other authorities that supervise, transform, correct, improve.[26]

Importantly for Jones on his release, prison also blurred the lines between himself and working-class Chartists. His introduction continues with a perhaps deliberately indeterminate conflation of his personal prison experiences with those of his fellow Chartist detainees, many of whom received the same sentence — two years. The reader is left in no doubt as to the physical and psychological suffering inflicted by those years, and retributive action is projected:

> The Venetian of old opened an account of debtor and creditor between himself and foe: the debt is registered — the payment yet to come.
> Two years of separate confinement on the silent system.
> Two years of books withheld — and pen denied.
> Two years of separation from the living, and not allowed communion with the dead.
> Two years of illness in a plague-struck prison, till the body became a rack on which the soul was tortured.
> Two years of poverty and grief at home; two years insult and neglect to all.
> Day by day, and night by night, the eternal SAME — the bare walls our library — solitude our companion — and insolence our task master. Two years, and all as one great, endless day![27]

The reference to Venice is probably meant to suggest images of the infamous 'Leads' prison above the Doge's palace in that city, and the alleged arbitrary use of power by Venice's ruling 'Council of Ten' from 1310 to 1797. The repetition is clearly intended to convey personal bitterness, but at the same time the plural term 'our' is used to express a collective suffering that binds Jones to a Chartist cohort of political prisoners. The political outcome of this bond was considerable: Jones's confidence of his own place within the Chartist body became strong enough for him to assume the role of effective Chartist leader as Feargus O'Connor's health declined. Poetically, isolation brings the return of some pre-Chartist themes and styles. In his dedication to his fellow prisoners he explicitly links the progression of his poetic voice throughout his period of incarceration to his emotional and psychological mood:

> Brothers! these pages are dedicated to you — because you will best appreciate the gradual change of feeling, developed by two years of prison life. The heart is like a harp tuned by the hand of circumstance — but, I trust, though varied in tone, ever to the great key-note of principle. In these poems you will see the gradual change of mood, as in a psychological table — they were secretly written at the period named — now melancholy — now indignant — now the creation of fancy — at other times the echo of anger, but never once, I am proud to think, the voice of failing constancy or courage.
> Brothers! accept the offering of a fellow captive.[28]

The repetition of the exclamation mark after the term 'brothers', though characteristic of Jones's prose style, is self-consciously inclusive, and there is an almost palpable relief that collective suffering has cancelled out the residual stigma of his former social status and his relatively late entry into Chartism. Not only does imprisonment bring Jones an equivalent of the social status of working-class Chartists that his early *Northern Star* poetry seemed to reach for, but the political and personal extremity of prison experience now matches the occasional hyperbole and high drama of his poetic style. The poetic journey that follows the dedication is presented as a psycho-poetic template for the survival of the radical spirit under duress.

98   LYRICAL PRISON POETRY (1848–50)

'A Prisoner's Night-Thought', written in August 1848 and consisting of four quatrains in iambic pentameter, reads as an emotionally authentic vision of the prison experience.[29] Its title almost certainly refers to Edward Young's nine-part work in blank verse, *The Complaint, or Night Thoughts* (1742–45), with which Jones may have been familiar during his schooling in the German states — Young's poetry was particularly popular there and was known to have influenced the young Goethe.[30] Possibly reflecting a reaction to the cumulative effect of the relentless realities of the daily routine of prison life, the first stanza sets a register of resigned weariness that resists even the rather melodramatic conclusion of the work. With his characteristically explicit use of language, Jones does not shy away from the use of the term 'martyr', but an incipient sadness pervades this exploration of the heroic narrative arc. This is a lyrical exploration of a heroism which, though dramatic, appears rooted in the real and in the present:

> My life is but a toll of many woes,
>   And keen excitement, wearing to the core;
> And fervently I hope an hour's repose,
>   My duty done, and all my warfare o'er.
>
> Loud shouts have beaten on my tingling brain;
>   Lone prisons thrilled the fevered thread of life;
> The trophies perish — but the wrecks remain!
>   And burning scars survive the dizzy strife.
>
> Oh! 'tis a dreadful war, for *one* to wage,
>   Against deep-rooted prejudice and power;
> Crush, in one life, the seeds of many an age,
>   And blast black centuries in a single hour!
>
> Who dares it, throws his life into the scale, —
>   Redemption's voluntary sacrifice:
> His hope — to be a martyr, should he fail,
>   Or, at best, to conquer — as he dies!

('A Prisoner's Night-Thought', ll. 1–16)

Testing the dedication's insistence that these poems contain no example of 'failing constancy', this work seems suspended in a moment of negative anagnorisis, resisting the traditionally constructive nature of the protagonist's self-knowing phase in the Aristotelian narrative. By eschewing the optimism of Jones's earlier Chartist poetry, 'A Prisoner's Night-Thought' interrogates the nature of heroism and martyrdom with a previously unexplored psychological honesty. Indeed, the depth of the poem's pessimism is such that even the potentially uplifting conclusion offered by the conquest that features in the final line is counteracted by the spectre of accompanying death.

A sense of community is completely absent from this poem, and the italicization of '*one*' in the seventh line is suggestive not just of the intensely personal nature of the struggle of the speaker, but perhaps that, in the Chartist context, community itself is being destroyed by this series of custodial punishments. The absence of print, or even oral, culture in Tothill Fields prison has the effect of disrupting any sense of what Benedict Anderson terms an 'imagined community'. As Anderson writes of Biblical depictions of prison, 'they are never imagined as *typical* of this or that society. Each, like the one where Salome was bewitched by John the Baptist, is magically alone'.[31] This view of prison as a spatial and societal 'other' might seem to contradict Foucault's conception of the 'carceral continuum' which 'extends without interruption from the smallest coercions to the longest penal detention', but in life, as in poetry, the difference depends on the point of observation.[32] Foucault also suggests that prison is at the apex of a 'carceral pyramid'; perhaps the best view of a mountain is not from its peak.[33]

In a letter from prison to his literary executor, Robert Ross, which was originally intended to form a part of *De Profundis* (1905), Oscar Wilde, like Foucault and Jones in his introduction to the poems, appears to critique society by closely equating the experience of prison to life outside the cells: 'Of course, from one point of view, I know that on the day of my release I shall be merely passing from one prison to another, and there are times when the whole world seems to me no larger than my prison cell, and as full of terror for me'.[34] And yet Wilde's interpretation of this continuum is not figured through ideas of systems of economic or social control, but through a more Romantic, experiential perspective of opposing states of motion and stasis. Later in the letter he writes:

> Prison life makes one see people and things as they really are. That is why it turns one to stone. It is the people outside who are deceived by the illusions of a life in constant motion. They revolve with life and contribute to its unreality. We who are immobile both see and know.[35]

Despite the apparent inclusivity of Wilde's phrase 'we who are immobile', *De Profundis* is unlike *The Ballad of Reading Gaol* (which was written in 1897 after Wilde's release) in that it is an entirely personal piece of writing. The nature of Wilde's imprisonment clearly differed from that of Jones in that he lacked the potential for the consolation of the shared suffering of a community which, for Jones, despite the low-point perspective of 'A Prisoner's Night-Thought', might have extended through concentric layers of fellow Chartist prisoners, fellow Chartists, and the working class at large. However, like Jones, part of Wilde's coping strategy was, through his writing, to identify himself with historical and contemporary figures whom he perceived as having been unfairly imprisoned. *De Profundis* shares with Jones's prison poetry the varying functions of what Jones described as a 'psychological table' and a vehicle for consolatory self-mythologization. Norbert Kohl sees sections of *De Profundis* as performing an important transformative function:

> By identifying C.3.3. [Wilde's prison cell number] indirectly with Christ, and by building an analogy between his own life and that of Verlaine and Krop- otkin, he is erecting a monument to a self which, even if it is different from before, is at least as imposing and impressive: instead of the dandy falling from the pedestal, we now have the portrait of the artist as martyr. No humble, uncomplaining resignation to his fate, but instead its aesthetic elevation to the scale of an historic drama — this was how Wilde was able to adapt to his new situation.[36]

This process of 'aesthetic elevation' operated through the prison writing of both men, but, given the relative fates of Wilde and Jones on release from incarceration, it could be argued that Jones's use of the strategy was the more successful. This is largely because of the very different circumstances of the two criminal prosecutions. For Wilde, imprisonment 'meant the loss of his social position and also ultimately of his art'.[37] Conversely, prison, however degrading and physically damaging an experience, eventually consolidated Jones's identity within his chosen social group — working-class radicals — and had the further effect of retrospectively vindicating his art, especially in terms of its received function as an expression of personal and political defiance.

In 'A Prisoner's Night-Thought', isolation leads to a sense of bitterness and resignation, but personal resolve is ultimately not weakened. In effect, the individual prisoner, divided from the communal force of the Chartist body in the most literal and physical of ways, is made to feel the full weight of the political pressure ranged against him. And yet, conversely, if original self-identification as a Chartist involves an attainment of a level of political consciousness, then imprisonment also strips away any residual illusion that, as *The Times* leader put it, 'antagonistic classes' are not opposed to each other. As though to emphasize the total disruption that prison inflicts upon the prisoner's life there is a disruption of the rhythm of the poem through the use of polysyllabic terms in the fourteenth line. To describe imprisonment as 'redemption's voluntary sacrifice' operates at the wider political level in that it is a poetic reclamation of autonomy under conditions of extreme restraint; but the use of the term 'redemption' is perhaps autobiographical in Jones's case, referring to the residual guilt of a previous life of privilege. The poem itself is partially redeemed from its uncharacteristically dark vision of political martyrdom by being framed as a 'night-thought': a waking dream that exposes a perhaps untypical vulnerability.

'Prison Bars', a poem of sixteen lines in terse trimetric iambs composed in November 1848, contains one of Jones's most distinctive uses of poetic imagery, as the prison bars themselves are transformed into radical political ammunition:[38]

> Ye scowling prison bars
>   That compass me about,
> I'll forge ye into armour
>   To face the world without.
>
> Bold Aspiration's furnace
>   Shall fuse thee with its heat,
> And stern resolve shall fashion
>   With steady iron beat.
>
> Experience' solid anvil
>   The burning mass shall hold;
> And Patience' bony fingers
>   Each groove exactly mould.
>
> Then with my modern armour
>   Above my antient scars,
> I'll march upon my foemen
>   And strike with prison bars.
>
> ('Prison Bars', ll. 1–16)

In keeping with the repetitive rhythms suggested by its industrial imagery, the metre of this poem is regular and controlled, with no word, phrase, or line straying either semantically or rhythmically from the poem's single-minded approach to its conclusion. For such a short poem there is an extraordinary concentration of terms associated with Victorian ideals of masculinity: 'forge', 'bold', 'fuse', 'stern', 'resolve', 'steady', 'beat', 'solid', 'march', 'strike'. These terms are offset by the more circumspect nature of the capitalized triumvirate of terms which represent the transformative agents in the poem: 'Aspiration', 'Experience', and 'Patience'. These three terms all relate closely to temporality but in much more subtle and complex ways than the simple marking of time suggested by 'beat' or 'march'. It is perhaps fitting that when Jones found himself possessing nothing but time, he found ways to vary his approaches towards it.

The muscular imagery of 'Prison Bars' is neo-medievalist, with 'modern armour' protecting 'antient scars'. The technologically and socially reductive experience of prison life is in itself suggestive of a medieval squalor which plays into a stock of imagery which Jones already possessed. It is possible that a line from the previous poem may have originally referred to this chronologically regressive nature of the prison experience. There is a suspicion that the twelfth line of 'A Prisoner's Night-Thought' contains a typographical error. The semantically obscure 'And blast *black* centuries in a single hour!' perhaps should read 'And blast *back* centuries in a single hour!' (my emphasis), which would make more sense as a description of prison as a medievalization of modern experience. That the previous line reads, 'Crush, in one life, the seeds of many an age', would appear to support this contention. In the vision of 'Prison Bars', however, the speaker, using the driving rhythms echoed in the poem's metre, transforms the medievally emblematic prison bars into modern political weaponry. The repetitive rhythms of prison life, the 'eternal SAME' of the introduction, become, through the image of the blacksmith, constructive agents to build weapons that will be used against the gaolers themselves once the prisoner is released. Although the poem ultimately concerns actions that will be carried out on release of the prisoner, its promise is clearly intended to strengthen the resolve of the speaker whilst undergoing incarceration. In an environment of interminable sameness, forms of poetic transformation become especially appropriate, even necessary tools of survival.

'Excursion in Imagination'

'The Garden Seat' (composed on 5 July 1849) continues the Romantic, lyrical tenor of the prison poems by creating from the speaker's imagination a poetic vision of place, panorama, and history.[39] In self-conscious reference to the imaginative construction of the scene of the poem, the first two stanzas prescribe the conditions for the poem's invocation of historical and geographical juxtapositions:

> When the sea is still as glass,
> And the whispering breezes pass
> On messages from zone to zone, or waft from pole to pole,
> A dewdrop of Savannah sweet —
> A particle of Arab heat,
> Commingling Nature's essences in one harmonious whole.

When the bright, magnetic stars
　　Seem leaning from their cars,
As drawn by some kind influence from clear familiar skies;
　　And thoughts, as dreams misprized,
　　Great truths, unrecognised!
Strike sudden chords from out the world's eternal harmonies.

('The Garden Seat', ll. 1–12)

The anapaestic beginnings of the first two lines and the irregular rhythm of the third disrupt an essentially iambic metre. This effect combines with the enjambment between the second and third lines to give the beginning of the poem a natural, conversational rhythm — the reader is initially encouraged to disregard the metre of the poem and read it prosaically. When the first stanza concludes with the rhythmic regularity of a long line constructed as a strictly iambic heptameter (the longest iambic line commonly used in English poetry) a pitch is established somewhere between conversation and invocation. The poem is addressed to a friend, but it is also a dream vision, framed as such by its geographically expansive imagery. The third stanza narrows the focus of the imagery to a specific point of observation:

When the sun sets in the sea,
　　Like Time in Eternity;
And space beyond horizon seems stretching without end:
　　Then come to an arbour still,
　　Halfway up a western hill,
That I destined for such an hour, and planted for such a friend.
　　(ll. 13–18)

As a poem written halfway through a prison term, it is possible to read into the themes of predestination and construction a compensatory wielding of power through the flexing of the poetic imagination. The spatial reach described by the poem is internalized, brought under authorial jurisdiction, and its effects are concentrated on a fictitious location of the speaker's construction. The figures of imaginative expansion become agents of literary control. As a formal emphasis of creative faculty the iteration of the speaker's agency is effectively doubled by the caesura in the eighteenth line. Yet while many of the verbs in the poem emphasize motion or transformation — 'pass on', 'commingling', 'leaning', 'drawn', 'striking', 'setting', 'stretching' — the arbour, like the sea in the first line, is 'still'; it is, like an observatory, a place of relative stasis from which to view a constantly changing universe.

　　The vegetation of the arbour described in the fourth stanza appears based on the heterogeneous botanical curiosities of Kew Gardens or the Botanic Gardens in Oxford. There is a 'cedar from Assyria' (l. 19), a 'willow from St. Helena' (l. 20), and a 'lily-rose from Mexico' (l. 22), which create a sense of carefully deliberated artifice and juxtaposition. But the geographically disparate origins of the specimens also reveal references to historical eras, the qualities of which are intended to be present by association. A vine, which emblematically 'intertwines' other plants, is from 'classic Tusculum' (l. 21) — one of the ancient Roman cities in the Alban hills; a pine from Norway is described as 'scaldic' (l. 24), which is a reference to the Scandinavian medieval poetic tradition. In the fifth stanza the historical theme is elaborated on when the garden seat of the title is revealed to be a composite, made from fragments of ancient stone taken from famous historical sites including Babylon, Carthage, Aztec ruins, and even from the 'heartless breast' of the 'Theban sphinx' (l. 28). This melding of artefacts from antiquity into the central image of the poem figures the present as a direct culmination of a vast and varied past, a historical continuum that extends to, and is symbolically 'seated' in, the perspective of the observers.

In the final two stanzas that cumulative present is visually confronted. An image of the earth as a site of urban and technological expansion is revealed to be the object viewed from the arbour:

> And thence you may behold
> A map of earth unrolled,
> With the steamers on the ocean, and the railways on the land;
> And hear the city's hum
> Up the hillside deadened come,
> Like the last ebb of the waters on a far-receding strand.
>
> Oh! there, methinks, 'twere sweet
> To sit in converse meet,
> With palpable progression before our vision spread;
> And trace the mighty plan
> Of the destinies of man,
> Measuring the living by the stature of the dead. (ll. 31–42)

The introduction of images of modernity comes as a surprise to the reader after the cosmic and historical expansiveness of the preceding stanzas. This poetic effect mirrors the social and political effects of the acceleration of historical change brought about by the Industrial Revolution. It is significant that Jones wrote this poem less than a decade after considerable advances in the technology of photography had been made by various inventors including Louis Daguerre (1787–1851) and William Henry Fox Talbot (1800–77).[40] The emergence of reliable fixing of light-derived images probably inspires the conflation of image and reality inherent in the phrasing of the lines, 'And there you may behold | A map of earth unrolled', and the sense of technological control and visual enclosure contained in 'palpable progression before our vision spread'. But, as Scott Hess suggests, it is possible to detect in some poetry a link between the concept of the Romantic self and the photographic viewer, based on a fundamental realignment of the individual identity:

> Romantic subjectivity and the modern technology of the photograph are not opposed, but in a broader sense complement and even produce one another. The objective world of the photographic image and the 'deep' autonomous subjectivity of the viewer come into being together, in a single complementary relationship in which subject and object, mind and body, immaterial consciousness and material world, are coupled together by their formal separation. There can be no photograph without this implied autonomous subject or consciousness, looking on from outside the world of the image; but by the same token, the autonomous subject depends on the pictorial perspective and stability of this objective world in order to construct its own sense of unity and interiority.[41]

Beyond expressing a desire to have the freedom to view such landscapes, or the consolation of an imaginative [re]construction of visual stimuli, 'The Garden Seat' resists the dehumanizing experience of prison through its defining of a subjective identity via a particular perspectival relationship with a stable image of philosophical significance. In an analogy of the photographic process, the viewer, by framing, 'owns' the image viewed, and the subjective self is defined and enhanced by association with the process; the static observer creates the image and is reciprocally altered by its existence. In the wider poetic sense this poem perhaps marks the beginning of Jones's growing awareness of the social and philosophical possibilities of technological advancement.

Morally, the detachment afforded the viewers by the elevated location of the arbour in 'The Garden Seat' is reflected in the relatively neutral language used to describe the scene of industrial and urban expansion. In contrast to the well-defined opposites of previous poems by Jones whose subject is industrialization such as 'The Cornfield and the Factory', it is merely stated that progression exists, it is 'palpable', and that it is part of a 'mighty plan'. Indeed, it might be noted that the term 'progression', with no qualifying adjective attached, is generally thought of as positive. The conclusion reached by the act of 'measuring the living by the stature of the dead' is left open — no judgement is passed. The strongest contrast in the last stanza of the poem is between the air of pleasurable companionship suggested by its first two lines and the philosophical weight of the subject of its last three lines. This relaxed attitude to the discussion of issues of philosophical, and by extension political, magnitude, suggests a depth of consideration and political long-sightedness that may have existed in Jones before his imprisonment, but was rarely communicated in his poetry. 'The Garden Seat' feels like the beginning of a process of contemplation and discussion; as though a forced detachment from the daily life of politics has engendered a deeper consideration of the philosophies that lie behind.

On initial consideration, it might appear that the elements of high culture contained in 'The Garden Seat' run counter to the suggestion that Jones's prison experience ultimately drew him closer to his working-class Chartist readership. However, the cultural aspirations of the Chartist movement had produced a pre-existing tension between the traditions of demotic poetic forms and high cultural poetics which texts such as Cooper's *The Purgatory of Suicides* had already attempted to negotiate. The existence of this seminal Chartist prison work permitted Jones's inclusion of references to classical culture, and both writers were integral in the middle years of Chartism to the emerging ideas of working-class education which eventually became much more important to the movement in the 1850s. This is not to say that the initial functions of these literary forms were necessarily altruistic or didactic. In Jones's prison work, and indeed Cooper's, it is possible to discern a resistance to the degradation of prison life (which in Jones's case must have involved exposure to elements of society with which he was experientially unfamiliar) centred on the embrace of high cultural forms. Literary engagement with high culture re-affirms the *individual* identity of the writer as 'special' within the prison milieu, even as the writer identifies commonalities between himself and his fellow prisoners, and nominally addresses his work to 'the people'.

In content, if not form, 'The Garden Seat' shares similarities with the group of Romantic works often referred to as 'conversation poems'. The originator and poet most closely associated with this poetic form is Samuel Taylor Coleridge, and it is his 'This Lime-Tree Bower My Prison' (1797) that 'The Garden Seat' most resembles in its themes and narrative structure.[42] Considering the very different circumstances of their origins, the poems are drawn closer together by the fact that Jones does not refer to his confinement and Coleridge exaggerates his — in both works confinement leads to a freeing of the imagination. In Coleridge's work the speaker is prevented from joining a walk through natural scenery with his friends William and Dorothy Wordsworth and Charles Lamb by an injury to his foot, and rests under the branches of the lime-tree, imagining the scenes that his friends are viewing in reality. The poem is affectionately addressed to Charles Lamb, and while the addressee of 'The Garden Seat' is not revealed, it is reasonable to assume that 'such a friend' existed. An apparent similarity between the two poems lies in the self-conscious nature of the 'excursion in imagination', as Paul Magnuson describes it, that both works employ. Magnuson sees Coleridge's poem, and the (mostly imaginative) actions within it, as essentially consolatory:

> Within the formal pattern of these [conversation] poems, a reader may construe the relation of the mind to nature philosophically or theologically, but the movement of the speaker's imagination may also be read psychologically. The poems have been called crisis lyrics in which Coleridge confronts a loss, overcomes that loss through an excursion in imagination to nature and to sympathy with other minds, and often utters a blessing on the person addressed. 'This Lime-Tree Bower My Prison' begins with Coleridge's loss of 'Beauties and feelings, such as would have been / Most sweet' (3–4). What is lost to the bodily eye is gained by the spiritual eye of imagination as it follows Charles Lamb and the Wordsworths on their walk down into the dell and up to view the scene over the Bristol Channel. At the end of the poem, his bower is no longer a prison, but a natural scene in which the sunlight on the tree mirrors both the dell and the 'glorious Sun'. Coleridge's conclusion is that
>
> > 'Tis well to be bereft of promis'd good,
> > That we may lift the soul, and contemplate
> > With lively joy the joys we cannot share. (65–67)
>
> The poem is not only an imaginative apprehension of nature's joy but also an escape from loss, an act of imagination's self-recognition.[43]

Though Jones's incarceration is real rather than metaphorical (Coleridge could have escaped from his arboreal 'prison', however slowly), and his landscape is wholly imagined rather than imaginatively reconstructed, both poems serve the function of consolation through the observations of the inner eye. In both poems an inaccessible place is accessed through the mind, and the description of the process is addressed to a dear friend. These friends can be seen as avatars of the speakers, whose experience of the landscape is initially only by proxy. This mechanism is obvious in 'This Lime-Tree Bower My Prison', where Coleridge effectively sees through the eyes of Lamb until he is reconciled to his confinement and begins to see nature's beauty in his own garden:

> Yet still the solitary humble-bee
> Sings in the bean-flower! Henceforth I shall know
> That Nature ne'er deserts the wise and pure;
> No plot so narrow, but Nature there,
> No waste so vacant, but may well employ
> Each faculty of sense, and keep the heart
> Awake to Love and Beauty!
>   ('This Lime-Tree Bower My Prison', ll. 58–64)

This consolatory effect of an engagement with nature is more apparent in a Jones poem discussed later in this chapter ('The Prisoner's Dream'), but in 'The Garden Seat' the same initial vicarious perspective through a friend's eyes leads to an equivalent experience for the speaker. The relative freedom of the friend in Jones's poem is hinted at in the lines 'And thence you may behold | A map of earth unrolled'. Only in the last stanza, when the actions are framed by a conjecturally indicative 'methinks', does the speaker refer to his own projected presence in the arbour.

One question regarding both poems is to what extent these 'excursions in imagination' are reliant on the written descriptions of them? Jones's confinement may be of a much more serious nature, but both men describe an imaginative 'escape' in detail that seems unlikely to have emerged purely from the wanderings of directionless reverie. If the writing of these poems retrospectively created the imaginative experiences they describe (even if only partially) then the distinction between the pre- and post-composition states of vision can be related to Coleridge's own distinction between 'fancy' and 'Imagination' as described in his *Biographia Literaria* (1817):

> The fancy brings together images that have no connexion natural or moral, but are yoked together by the poet by means of some accidental coincidence [...] The Imagination modifies images, and gives unity to variety: it sees all things in one, *il più nell' uno*.[44]

In this sense the construction of a poem from its conceptual beginnings is a result of the imagination working on the fancy: that which appears to have no connection is made to connect. The artificial nature of Jones's arbour is a good analogy of this effect in operation. The thought processes that lead the poet to choose a 'cedar from Assyria' may be, in Coleridgean terms, 'fanciful', but the choice to search in the first place, and to bring disparate objects together to express a meaningful whole, relies on the constructive imagination. In 'The Garden Seat' the arbour represents, in its geographical exoticism and illustrious historical heritage, a kind of implied perfection. Jones's expression of an imagined event at an imagined location can be viewed as the consolidation of a daydream; the poem that results becomes a codified entry into a place of emotional and psychological comfort. Indeed, the philosophical magnitude of the questions posed by the view of an industrialized world laid before the viewers from the arbour, and the avenues of contemplation and discussion their confrontation entails, is itself a psychological escape route from the mental distress caused by periods of solitary and silent confinement.

It was stated near the beginning of this chapter that part of the purpose of Jones's imprisonment was to silence him. Christopher Hill, in his study *A Turbu-*

lent, Seditious, and Factious People: John Bunyan and his Church, has suggested that for dedicated political prisoners as historically disparate as Bunyan (1628–88) and Antonio Gramsci (1891–1937), such judicial ambitions are often doomed to failure:[45]

> He [Bunyan] was charged under the 1593 act for holding 'unlawful meetings and conventicles', 'calling together the people'. But both he and his accusers knew that he was being penalised for his *preaching*: this is what both sides emphasise. Preaching was not in itself an offence under that act, nor under any other, though it was soon to be made illegal. Bunyan ironically offered to preach in public if private meetings were objected to, or to hand over notes of all his sermons. But it was the *act* of preaching, as well as the content, that offended. Mussolini's prosecutor said of Gramsci in 1928: 'For twenty years we must stop that brain from working.' So with Bunyan: it was necessary to silence him. In neither case was the objective achieved.[46]

It was in prison that Bunyan conceived and largely wrote *The Pilgrim's Progress from This World to That Which is to Come* (1678). Beyond the judicial attempt to silence a notorious orator, there are similarities between Jones's treatment and that of Bunyan's in terms of the circumstances and charges brought. It was the crowd context of Jones's speech that led to his arrest, and his official charge of 'sedition' was often referred to as 'seditious speech-making'. There is also the parallel of Bunyan's ironic offer to preach in public with Jones's ironic compliment of the shorthand skills of the government spy who notated his speech. Antonio Gramsci, the Italian philosopher and leader of the Communist Party, was effectively silenced during the eleven-year imprisonment which led to his death in 1937, but the letters he wrote from prison formed the basis of an influential political philosophy. Indeed, it is possible to argue that, without the experience of imprisonment, Gramsci would not have been able to produce the depth of philosophy contained in his *Prison Notebooks* (1947). Lynne Lawner suggests the importance of the circumstantial origins of Gramsci's 'major contribution to post-Leninist Marxist philosophy' when she writes, 'Gramsci was cut off from the immediate political battle and had to turn his attention to general questions of revolutionary theory and strategy in the modern world'.[47] Although by no means as well-known or influential, Jones's long poem 'The New World', with its theories of historical progression and critique of Victorian colonialism, appears to have benefitted from a similar shift towards general questions of theory which emerged from isolation. In a letter from prison to his wife Julia, Gramsci describes the unwanted attainment of the focus that enabled his writings, '[M]y own existence was brusquely, brutally channelled in one direction by external pressures; liberty grew possible only for the inner life, and my will became only the will to resist'.[48] The monoculture of prison paradoxically produces the conditions for some writers eventually to broaden and enrich the cultures from which they are isolated. From the union of silence and imagination emerges the most eloquent discourse.

The next poem in Jones's series, 'The Silent Cell', deals directly with issues of silence and imagination.[49] It is introduced by the statement that it was 'composed, on the sixth day of my incarceration, in a solitary cell, on bread and water, and without books, — August 1849'. The poem links the declaration of defiance in

Jones's introduction less with political or spiritual determination than with the ability of the imagination to resist the atrophy that isolation can engender:

> They told me 'twas a fearful thing
>   To pine in prison lone
> The brain became a shrivelled scroll,
>   The heart a living stone.
>
> Nor solitude, nor silent cell
>   The teeming mind can tame:
> No tribute needs the granite well;
>   No food the planet-flame.
>
> Denied the fruit of others' thought,
>   To write my own denied,
> Sweet sisters, Hope and Memory, brought
>   Bright volumes to my side.
>
> And oft we trace, with airy pen,
>   Full many a word of worth;
> For Time will pass, and Freedom then
>   Shall flash them on the earth.

('The Silent Cell', ll. 1–16)

These first four stanzas progress from pitting the 'teeming mind' against the ossifying effects of solitary confinement to a description of the process of composition when denied books or writing materials. It is reasonable to assume that Jones's legal training, and his recent experiences as an orator repeating long political speeches in different locations across the country, contributed to the capacity of his memory. However, given similar circumstances, it is difficult to imagine any writer failing to exercise their 'airy pen' and attempting to commit their words to memory. It is possible that Jones derived this phrase from memories of Shakespeare's *A Midsummer Night's Dream*:

> And as imagination bodies forth
> The forms of things unknown: the Poet's pen
> Turns them to shapes and gives to airy nothing
> A local habitation, and a name. (5.1.14–18)

In the next three stanzas Jones compares the inevitability of this process of imaginative creation with the imperative of his own bloodstream, which symbolically becomes both the source and conduit of his 'Fancy':

> They told me that my veins would flag,
>   My ardour would decay;
> And heavily their fetters drag
>   My blood's young strength away.
>
> Like conquerors bounding to the goal,
>   Where cold, white marble gleams,
> Magnificent red rivers! roll! —
>   Roll! all you thousand streams!

Oft, to passion's stormy gale,
  When sleep I seek in vain,
Fleets of Fancy up them sail,
  And anchor in my brain.

('The Silent Cell', ll. 17–28)

This exploded view of the physical body, a Swiftian magnification of scale, is particularly appropriate to poetry composed when the body in question is virtually the only object in the room. Denied external stimuli, the imagination turns inwards and narrates the body's natural processes. Presumably, the goal of the bloodstream, the 'cold, white marble', refers to the brain, whose coldness and whiteness denotes a sterility that is overcome by the arrival of 'Fancy'. That 'Fancy' is 'anchored' or fixed in the brain would seem to suggest that it becomes imagination in the Coleridgean sense by a conscious process. Janowitz quotes the first stanza and the sixth stanza of this poem in isolation to support her contention that 'Jones draws on the resources of the group to find solace and overcome his sense of personal isolation: his very body becomes the scene of a drawing together of multitudes'.[50] This interpretation could emerge from reading 'magnificent red rivers' (l. 23) as referring to the mobilizing mass of the Chartist body, but although some of the terms in the poem are militaristic ('conquerors', l. 21, 'proud marches', l. 32), the identification in the subsequent stanza of 'fleets of Fancy' as the active agents in the poem suggests that the focus of the work is lyrical, subjective, and inward-looking.

This subjectivity remains even as the poem ends on a defiant note which could suggest retention of the radical spirit. The claims that prison will reduce the individual brain to a 'shrivelled scroll' (l. 3) are refuted — the speaker has not been broken by the prison experience. There is also a magnanimity towards the gaolers that subverts their moral position:

But never a wish for base retreat,
  Or thought of a recreant part,
While yet a single pulse shall beat
  Proud marches in my heart.

They'll find me still unchanged and strong,
  When breaks their puny thrall:
With hate — for not one living soul —
  And pity — for them all. (ll. 29–36)

The use of oppositional terms with both corporeal and moral connotations, including 'strong' and 'puny', and 'proud' and 'pity', points to an expansion of the self which encompasses both the physical and spiritual being. The poem's figuring of the body, and of the imagination through the body, transforms the prisoner into the dominant party in the detainer/detainee relationship by suggesting a spiritual, intellectual, and even physical superiority. To describe the gaolers' hold on him as 'their puny thrall' wilfully minimizes the effect of prison as the prisoner-martyr, from his morally elevated position, feels nothing but pity for his tormentors. Between the almost magical agency attributed to the imagination (the 'airy pen', the conjuring up of 'bright volumes'), the imagistic magnification of the prisoner-body, and the moral reduction of the gaolers implied by the emotion of pity, the poem enables the prisoner to assert control over a situation of extreme restriction, and through his imagination the function of the silence of the cell is transformed from punitive to creative.

Jones's most detailed exploration of the workings of his own imagination while in prison is found in 'The Prisoner's Dream' (composed in September 1849).[51] This longest of the twenty-four lyric poem series is also the most varied in its form: its rhyme schemes and stanza shapes shift to adjust to the mood and subject of each section. It begins by using the wind as a vehicle for the speaker's imagination to retrace its path across an idyllic country landscape:

> The wind! the wind plays o'er the prison bar,
>   Still fresh from kissing the green forest-leaves;
> Bending the wheat-fields in the country far;
>   Shaking the woodbine round the cottage eaves;
>   Wreathing the buds and bells
>   In sweet, secluded dells;
> Ruffling the milky down upon the breast
> Of soft swans sitting on their humid nest;
> And the large pond's silvery dappled edge
> Brushing the cool drops from the rustling sedge.
>   ('The Prisoner's Dream', ll. 1–10)

There is a similarity between this figuring of the wind as a conveyor of imaginative escape for the inmate and Emily Brontë's 'The Prisoner: A Fragment', which, having been published in 1846, Jones may well have read.[52] The prisoner in Brontë's poem also equates imagination with a vicarious liberty that provides discrete periods of solace which can be translated into a defiant nullification of the degradation of prison:

> Still, let my tyrants know, I am not doomed to wear
> Year after year in gloom, and desolate despair;
> A messenger of Hope, comes every night to me,
> And offers for short life, eternal liberty.
>
> He comes with western winds, with evening's wandering airs,
> With that clear dusk of heaven that brings the thickest stars.
> Winds take a pensive tone, and stars a tender fire,
> And visions rise, and change, that kill me with desire.
>
>   ('The Prisoner: A Fragment', ll. 33–40)

The antithetical linking of 'short life' and 'eternal liberty' are echoed in Jones's use of imagination as a seemingly limitless font of transcendental experience in 'The Prisoner's Dream' and, to a lesser extent, in 'The Garden Seat' and 'The Silent Cell'. The life of the mind is pitched against reality and is always victorious because of its lack of reliance on temporality and existing sensory stimuli. The final couplet of Brontë's poem has the original speaker of the poem, presumably the prison governor, note in the prisoner an awareness of a higher jurisdiction which invalidates the earthly sentence conferred on her: 'Her cheek, her gleaming eye, declared that man had given | A sentence, unapproved, and overruled by heaven' (ll. 63–64). The prisoners of Jones and Brontë, in their absolute belief in their innocence by the codes of true morality, have access to a world of imagination unsullied by associations of guilt.

The brevity of the reference to prison in the first line of Jones's poem is striking when compared with the richness of the rural imagery of which the stanza mostly consists. This appears at first a return to the idealization of the countryside that typified Jones's Land Plan-themed poetry, but after a similarly brief reminder that the speaker of the poem is actually located in a prison cell, the second stanza's anaphoric listing of varied natural imagery begins to suggest that an increasing self-consciousness lies behind the portrayal of the idyll:

> And as I list the sound
> His broad wings make the prison roof around,
>   At times I close my eyes,
> And visions of the beautiful arise:
> The heathery highland stained with purpling hue,
> And water lilies dripping rich with dew,
> And evening sunbeams on white cottage-walls,
> And cawing rookeries round ancestral halls,
> And rural mills by sprightly river-falls
>   And with the music blent,
>   Full many a sound and scent
>   Come pouring, like a dream,
>   From hill, and plain, and stream.
>   ('The Prisoner's Dream', ll. 11–23)

The arbitrary nature of the images denotes the working of the 'Fancy' rather than constructive imagination. In his *Biographia Literaria*, Coleridge suggests that the uncontrolled 'Fancy' is related to 'delirium', while the unfettered 'Imagination' would lead to an intensification of focus more properly equated with 'mania'.[53] While Coleridge would appear to assign an inferior status to the 'Fancy' relative to the 'Imagination', Jeffrey C. Robinson finds in the former a closer relation to true poetry, and a concomitant alignment with the radical spirit:

> Of course, proponents of the Fancy view these 'failings' as the essential poetic faculty precisely because they engage domains of existence beyond the familiar, because they court elements of chance (thus acknowledging that the mind does not control all events), and because they recognise the body's role in perception and understanding, all of which awaken the conscious mind to a 'de-familiarised' and therefore truer version of the world. And it is this realization, this freedom of the mind, that social and political organizations seeking ideological control often suppress.[54]

The title of the poem, 'The Prisoner's Dream', suggests an embrace of the Fancy, and the hallucinatory visitations of 'vision', 'sound', and 'scent', coupled with the apparently random shifts from image to image, bring a delirious quality to the beginning of this work. The ephemeral nature of the images is referred to as the long second stanza links with the third, much shorter one:

> And many feathery-footed thoughts arise,
> Of sorrows past, and past prosperities,
> And scenes where Recollection's treasury lies:

> The old Elm-avenue that to the door
> On summer evenings brought the smiling poor,
> While round the stately trees that lined the way
> Their merry children ran in rose-enkindling play:
> For in that land, where half my youth was spent,
> The rich had not yet crushed their young content. (ll. 29–37)

That the thoughts are 'feathery-footed' suggests lightness which may connote not just their ephemeral nature but a philosophical lack of weight; however, the images coalesce into something close to narrative when 'Recollection' is brought into play. In the third stanza Jones appears to be referring to his childhood in Holstein ('that land, where half my youth was spent'), which is nostalgically presented as a Romantic idyll. Although a political point is made about the relative quality of life of the 'smiling poor' in a pre-industrial society, the focus of the stanza is on nostalgia, and the ability of memory to console. The next stanza brings a sharp volta as the speaker is aroused from his reverie:

> Ha! faithless Fancy! there I wake again!
> The narrow walls oppress my swelling brain,
> Big with great thoughts, that seek a vent in vain,
> Still let me dream! for, while the world's half seeming,
> And men are false, and villains are scheming,
> There lives a true philosophy in dreaming. (ll. 38–43)

Again, images of expansion are present in the characterization of the 'swelling brain | Big with great thoughts', and the inconsistent nature of 'Fancy' is highlighted by its description as 'faithless'. But prison's effect of making the world 'half seeming' balances the unreality of dream-life with the apparent unreality caused by the artificial and repetitive nature of the life of the prisoner. The blurring of the actual makes the unreal seem real. The dream serves as an escape from a morally corrupt world of schemes and falsification, but its 'true philosophy' also suggests a solution to these moral problems. This stanza begins by noting the fragility of 'Fancy', but reaffirms its importance to the speaker as a place of refuge and development.

The next four stanzas describe an 'excursion in imagination' which arguably shifts the focus of the poem from 'faithless' Fancy to the more constructive mode of imagination. Mirroring the speaker's greater control over the workings of his own mind the emphasis shifts towards pastoral images of humanity in harmony with nature. As in 'The Garden Seat', a hill provides an elevated perspective, but in this poem the objects viewed vary in focus. The speaker seems to be able to view the landscape not just as a panorama, but as a detailed topography, as the perspective of the mind's eye narrows or broadens. This section of the poem begins with 'Methinks', the archaic framing term that Jones used to begin the last stanza of 'The Garden Seat' and can be used to denote a conscious willing of thought, a 'thinking of thinking':

> Methinks, by some clear day's departing light
> I mount that old tradition haunted height
> And feel the cool breeze sweeping up from far,
> Pure, as if wafted from yon evening star.

> One pine or two, with tingling branches spread,
> Make soft, Eolian music over head;
> Before me, tillage rich outruns the eyes,
> Till field and cottage melt in vague surmise;
> Behind, dark pinewoods loom like mysteries;
> And, far below, the grey hall wrapped in shade;
> And clustering hamlet in the homely glade;
> And bridge, and stream, and island, and the mill
> And church low-nestling by the nether hill. (ll. 44–56)

The term 'methinks', rather than introducing a suggestion or opinion, denotes the first step on an imaginary journey. The scene is set with the familiar sensory tropes of the 'cool breeze' and the 'Eolian music' that results from the breeze's interaction with the 'tingling branches'. The latter term is especially appropriate to the poem because of its association with Coleridge's 'The Eolian Harp' (1796), and that poem's figuring of the order of music emerging from the apparently random actions of the wind. Indeed, the first line of 'The Prisoner's Dream', 'The wind! the wind plays o'er the prison-bar', could be taken as an ironic reference to Coleridge's poem and its discussion of the relationship between harmony, nature, and the human observer. It might be noted that prison bars and the metal strings of an Aeolian harp differ in scale and relative plasticity, but in shape and substance they are largely the same.

The following three lines contain verbs which relate to perspective and imagination — 'out-run', 'melt', and 'loom'. The image of the 'tillage rich' which 'out-runs the eyes' serves the dual purpose of denoting the scale of the scene before the speaker, but also suggests the continuation of the scene beyond visual limits. The importance of this image as an analogy for the freedom that is associated with imagination is indicated by its similarity to l. 15 of 'The Garden Seat': 'And space beyond horizon seems stretching without end'. The imagination is spatially situated as operating both *behind* vision and *beyond* vision. In 'The Prisoner's Dream' this stretching of perspective leads the 'field and cottage' to 'melt in vague surmise', highlighting the dream-like nature of the image. That the 'pinewoods loom like mysteries' *behind* the speaker emphasizes the extra-visual nature of the speaker's perspective and imagination, but also adds a sense of menace that tempers the idealism of the poem's imagery. However, the formal regularity of the anaphoric final four lines brings human order back to the scene and the man-made structures of 'hall', 'hamlet', 'bridge', 'mill', and 'church' suggest a reassuring familiarity to counter the lack of control that might be associated with 'wild' nature. The hunkering imagery of the church 'low-nestling by the nether hill' enhances the sense of insulation by suggesting the protective aegis of a Christian community.

The description of pastoral scenes continues in the next three stanzas with subjects shifting from aural sensory experience (the noises of farm animals and the sound of the village clock) to descriptions of the inhabitants of the village (the 'labourer', l. 65, the 'shepherd', l. 67, the 'angler', l. 70, and the 'pastor', l. 73) going about their daily business as the sun begins to set. The eighth stanza marks a drawn-out close to the 'excursion in imagination' as the speaker descends from his elevated viewing point to return home:

And so I mark the sleepy world grow dim,
Till twilight makes the dull horizon swim;
Then down thread the pinewood's labyrinth green,
Till the grey postern of the house is seen;
But shun the brook, for, by its reedy brink,
The shy deer from the covert come to drink;
And, since to us they leave the garish light,
'Twere pity, sure! to scare their genial night. (ll. 76–83)

The first three lines of this stanza again indicate a preoccupation with perspective and perception. The 'sleepy world' is both the pastoral world described and the more general dream world of the speaker, and as both 'grow dim' perception is blurred as 'twilight makes the dull horizon dim'. That the speaker emerges from a forest path which is described as a 'labyrinth' suggests a return from a place of spatial and perspectival indeterminacy. The timidity of the deer is significant as a symbol of the fragility of the imagined scene, and can be linked to the description of 'thoughts' in l. 29 as 'feathery-footed'. The speaker's decision to divert his path in order not to disturb the deer indicates a wish to leave this fragile dream-world intact even as he returns to reality.

The ninth and penultimate stanza of 'The Prisoner's Dream' describes the speaker retiring to his bed and begins to explore the mechanisms and effects of the imagination's capacity to transport:

And now, to give the eve a fitting crown,
Quaff one long draft of crystal rhenish down —
    And so to bed —
While moonlight hangs around the silent room
Its shadowy arms from ethereal loom,
    With tracery fancy-led;
And sighing winds the boughs quick shadow send
Across the wind's white, moon-marbled bend;
    Or thro' the dappled sky,
The passing clouds their silken banners furl
As o'er their path some hushing meteor streams;
    Then let Imagination's alchemy
The fine material of its memories blend,
In the rich crucible of midnight dreams,
To some transparent palace of pure pearl —
And wake next morn a Poet! (ll. 83–99)

As this stanza distinguishes itself conceptually from those preceding it, so its rhyme scheme differs and becomes more complex. Although the rhyme scheme varies throughout the work, nothing more complicated than rhyming couplets, triplets, or alternating rhymes occur up to this point in the poem. The above stanza formally echoes its themes of weaving and blending with a rhyme scheme (AABCCBDDEFGEDGFE) which departs from the standard as the stanza progresses and becomes more ode-like in its complexity.[55] In its imagery, the stanza begins with a reference to the land of Jones's youth with the speaker taking a 'long draft of crystal rhenish' before bed. That this gives the 'eve a fitting crown' suggests that the previous imagined scenes are more Germanic in Jones's imagination than English, and relate to 'that land, where half my youth was spent' (l. 36). The description of the bedroom where the speaker notes the effects of moonlight and wind as 'silent' would appear to reclaim silence as a benevolent quality in contrast to the silence of prison being an enforced punishment that suppresses expression. Here, silence is the gateway to another world as the speaker enters a dream within a dream, where 'Imagination's alchemy' creates experience from memory, and that experience is transformed into poetry. The last line of the stanza describes a willed metamorphosis which is really an affirmation of self-identity; a declaration of creative power through control of perception.

The final stanza is a paean not to 'Imagination' but to 'Poesy'. The focus of the poem returns to the prisoner in his cell and the process of creating poetry is praised for its restorative qualities:

> Poesy!
> Thro' thee I've felt my failing heart again,
> And life re-thrilling thro' each flaccid vein,
> And saved an hour from sleep, and snatched an hour from pain!
> And borne upon thy wings as on a wind,
> Soared up — up to the pinnacles of thought!
> How care, pain, prison, dwindled far behind!
> Oh! little cares! Oh! visions glory-fraught!
> There *is* — there *is* an empire in the mind! (ll. 100–08)

In a self-reflexive gesture, the poem is held to be proof of its own hypothesis — that 'Poesy', the process of composing poetry, is the agency which restores the prisoner to emotional and psychological health in the face of daily deprivations. Within this thinking, poetry is the fixative, the alchemical preservative in 'Imagination's alchemy' which prevents the visions of memory and imagination from being merely fleeting glimpses of another world. During the process of poetic composition, that world is made 'real' and accessible, and the poem itself preserves like amber the products of the imagination. Through poetry, the imagination can be unfettered but what emerges can be retained, and, to a prisoner, that level of control over the only un-caged aspect of their being is of vital importance. In the letter to Robert Ross which prefaces *De Profundis*, Wilde states: 'I need not remind you that mere expression is to an artist the supreme and only mode of life. It is by utterance that we live'.[56] For the artist in prison, that imperative is intensified not only by being isolated and therefore magnified by circumstance, but expression and utterance acquire a transformative function that reifies the products of the prisoner's imagination, restores the prisoner's spirit, and consolidates their sense of self-identification.

The importance of memory to the process of self-identification is as evident in 'The Prisoner's Dream' as it is in the work of William Wordsworth, who, from 'Lines Written a Few Miles Above Tintern Abbey' (1798) to 'The Excursion' (1814), explored memory's capacity to define and redefine the self, often in relation to remembered landscapes. For Christopher Salvesen, memory in Wordsworth's work provides a link between physicality and the moral sense through its reconfiguring of identity:

> The workings of memory seem, in Wordsworth, to be closely bound up with the senses — with the visual sense, and perhaps most completely with what he sometimes called 'the bodily sense'. It is this kind of total sensuousness, partly an amalgam of all the senses, but further involving the sense of 'being', of existing physically in time, which will help us to understand Wordsworth's sense of the past: it is, paradoxically enough, through this physical sense that the underlying moral use of all Wordsworth's poetry and remembering can be demonstrated.[57]

Jones's detailed re-creation of physical sensations in 'The Prisoner's Dream' similarly invokes a reiterated presence of the spirit of the writer in the remembered location and eventually leads to a self-identification as the morally idealized figure of the poet. Memory becomes a process of consolidation, not just of that which is remembered, but, through its importance to the mechanisms of 'Poesy', of the individual for whom memory, for the large part, creates subjectivity.

Reading Jones's prison poems as a sequence, with their shifts from expressions of something close to despair, through declarations of defiance, to explorations of the workings of the imagination, it becomes possible to understand their author's claim that some were written in blood, even if this is an exaggeration or a mythologization of the circumstances in which they were written. In 'The Silent Cell', 'fleets of Fancy' (l. 27) sail through the bloodstream to supply the brain; at the end of 'The Prisoner's Dream', 'Fancy' brings back to life 'each flaccid vein' (l. 102). The ingredients of poetry are dependent on mechanisms of the body and the body is revived by the ingredients of poetry. Poetry becomes part of a self-sustaining cycle of survival which, ultimately, gives the prisoner agency in the outside world. Jones's sanguinary imagery takes that which is most personal to the self, the body, and externalizes the effects of its mechanisms through modes of expression which will eventually be received by the population beyond the prison walls. But the process of creating poetry, 'Poesy', simultaneously sustains the body — the artistic imperative, which is at least partly social in its function, creates a mutually beneficial feedback loop between the prisoner and wider society. Within this nexus of relationships the poems themselves become more than just forms of expression, they are bridges which cross the divides between three very different worlds: the world of the imagination; the reality of the prison cell; and the world outside prison. The poems, as artefacts or objects, as written texts or memorized thought structures, assume an enhanced significance and are in a sense fetishized by the prisoner; they become symbols of a process which confers power on their creator. That memories of the outside world inform or instigate acts of imaginative creation from which the poems emerge completes a cycle of which the reality of imprisonment is just a part. The prisoner, through the act of writing, reduces prison to a functional aspect of a process over which he has the greater share of control.

Within the poems, the relationship between the speaker and the prison, and by extension the corrupt government that prison represents, alters according to the relative activity or passivity of the prisoner. In 'A Prisoner's Night-Thought' a weariness or even depression engenders an overwhelmingly pessimistic view of life ('trophies perish — but the wrecks remain', l. 7) which results in a passive reception of prison's effects. Prison isolates the prisoner to the extent where even ties to the community of Chartist prisoners are severed. In 'Prison Bars' the speaker confronts the 'scowling prison bars' (l. 1) in an active defiance which insists on a future of transformation. The direction of aggression is reversed and it becomes an agent of change. While this can be seen as an acknowledgement that the bridges between the different worlds which the poems represent can carry two-way traffic, it is also an acceptance that the prison space is a location of contestation, and that the prisoner at least has the status of being one of the contestants. Although in 'Prison Bars' Jones is writing of a future act of revenge or retribution, the act of transformation occurs as he writes — the prison bars, the boundaries between his world and the world outside, are transformed into agents of their own destruction. Ioan Davies, in his sociological study *Writers in Prison*, notes in prison writing an inherent equivalence between the prison and the prisoner:

> It is not so much that the public sphere (the prison) dictates the private (the personal everyday sense of ourselves), though it appears to do so, but that in the organization of space the centripetal and the centrifugal coexist, so that the exits and entrances are contiguous, and while there is the illusion of total power there is, in fact, the two-way mirror of total mistrust by each of all.
> The language of prison space is therefore one in which eyes, voices, limbs interact in a moving out from the cell with its definite physical contours and back into the cell from the more obvious dimensions of the power/ideology that attempts to control.[58]

Within the context of this characterization of the prison cell as a site of social osmosis, 'A Prisoner's Night-Thought' could be seen as 'centripetal', or inwardly flowing in its motion, while 'Prison Bars' is 'centrifugal', and yet, as Jones's poetic prison voice develops, both directions of flow could be said to be in operation in 'The Garden Seat' and 'The Prisoner's Dream'. In 'The Garden Seat' the 'excursion in imagination' results in a philosophical consideration of the external world, while 'The Prisoner's Dream' describes movement into realms of the imagination which eventually lead to the self-identification of the speaker as a 'Poet', the capitalization suggesting an emphasis on the public role of such a figure.

The Centrifugal Epilogue

The poems Jones produced in the few months leading up to his release in July 1850 appear to represent a conscious shift towards the purely centrifugal, with their concern being outward-looking subjects. The speaking voice in these poems returns to the mask of cynicism and political fervour which characterized many of the *Northern Star* poems, largely leaving behind the personal, subjective 'I' of some of the earlier prison works which would usually be associated with the Romantic self.[59] 'St. Coutts's', which from the order it appears in the sequence would seem to have been composed sometime in late April 1850, works as a fitting bridge between prison and political poetry in that its subject concerns, as an explanatory note states at the beginning of the poem, 'THE CHARITY CHURCH REARED OPPOSITE THE PRISON GATE'.[60] This serves as a spatial gateway between the insularity of Jones's prison life and the outside world which he is soon to rejoin. The poem begins with a satirical parody of Anglican attitudes to charity, before Jones's familiar political, dissenting voice exposes the perceived hypocrisy of the economic and religious implications of the established Church's charity system:

> 'Glory to God! the fane is raised!
> And they who the most have given
> Will rank far over the niggard souls,
> On the seats of a higher heaven!'
>
> The seats in heaven are for the just,
> And neither bought nor sold:
> God is not bribed with granite-dust,
> As men are bribed with gold.
>
> Tho' soar the dome, and spread the wall
> In pillared glory dight —
> They weigh not, should you sum them all
> The Jewish widow's mite.
>
> ('St. Coutt's', ll. 1–12)

Using the Bible story from Mark 12:42 of the widow's donation of a few coins to charity and the relative generosity that Jesus notes in the gesture, Jones admonishes the church for its apparent linking of the material with the spiritual, citing not just the equation of donations with heavenly reward, but the use of these donations for the needless building of impressive edifices. In the next stanzas Jones assumes the attitude of Jesus to this modern situation, a poetic device which prefigures the more explicit linking of the principles of Christianity with those of democracy which characterize some of his later oratory and poetry:

> Were Christ to pass your pompous pile,
> He'd spurn it where it stands,
> And say: 'my father dwelleth not
> 'In houses made of hands.'
>
> 'Do justice! — help the poor and weak! —
> 'And let the oppressed go free!
> 'In lowly, loving hearts I seek
> 'The temples fit for me!'
>
> With feet, not minds, that move to God,
> And prayer from lip alone,
> The modern Pharisees make bread
> Phylacteries of stone. (ll. 13–24)

This call for a re-prioritization of church values is clearly a political statement, but it also expresses an alignment with dissenting attitudes towards perceived religious materialism which hark back to the Reformation. Jones's form of Christian democracy was rooted in the Nonconformist tradition but was also more politically radical than the tenets of the emerging Christian Socialist movement, whose first journal appeared in July 1851, just two months after the first issue of *Notes to the People*. Needless to say, Jones kept a close eye on what he saw as an essentially middle-class movement which, crucially, did not support the call for the Charter.[61]

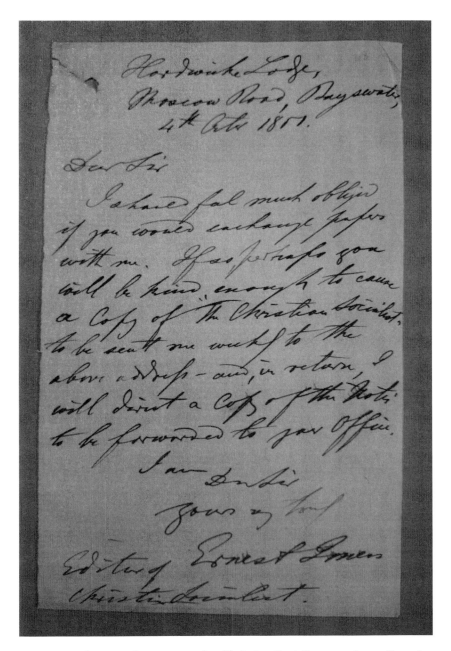

Fig 4.1. Jones keeps a close eye on the Christian Socialists — a letter from Jones dated 4 October 1851 to the editor of the movement's journal, suggesting they regularly swap publications. (Letter in Author's possession)

The final two stanzas of 'St. Coutts's' reiterate the opinion that it is the intention of the giver which is the important element in an act of charity, and that the relief of the suffering of human beings should always take precedence over the raising of new churches:

> But, when are balanced act and thought
>   Attesting saints shall read,
> How oft against each other brought
>   The motive blots the deed!
>
> More righteous far shall then appear,
>   Before the judgement-throne,
> The holiness of flesh and blood,
>   Than holiness of stone. (ll. 25–32)

From this poem what seems to offend Jones about the raising of a new charity church is not just the politically emollient effect of charity given from the wealthy to the poor, but the ostentation with which its generosity is proclaimed by the Church. The weighing of a balance between 'act and thought' suggests that self-serving charitable acts undermine the Christian integrity of the whole process. The poem finishes with an accusation of idolatry which again aligns itself with a dissenting tradition, recalling Milton's attack on Roman Catholicism, or those whom he considers to worship 'stocks and stones', in his sonnet 'On the Late Massacre in Piedmont' (1655).

If, by taking a building just outside Tothill Fields as its subject, 'St. Coutts's' serves as a poetic stepping-stone between prison poetry and a return to politically-engaged poetry with collective concerns, then 'Hymn for Lammas-Day' reads as Jones preparing fully to re-enter the political fray.[62] Composed in the month of his release, July 1850, the poem, along with the two works ('Easter Hymn' and 'Hymn for Ascension-Day') which immediately precede it in the series, represents a conscious return to the collective nature of Chartist verse in its hymnal form. There is no formal or thematic continuity between these poems and the larger body of prison poems, the collective voice seems to appear only in anticipation of release, and to differ little from the voice of the majority of the pre-prison *Northern Star* poems. Indeed 'Hymn for Lammas-Day' shares its metre and line length with 'The Working-Man's Song', as its framing as a hymn intends communal recitation or singing. The title of the work refers to a festival associated with the harvesting of wheat which, though nominally Christian in the English-speaking countries where it is celebrated, may have its origins in Pagan rites:

> Sharpen the sickle, the fields are white;
>   'Tis the time of the harvest at last.
> Reapers, be up with the morning light,
>   Ere the blush of its youth be past.
> Why stand on the highway and lounge at the gate,
>   With a summer day's work to perform?
> If you wait for the hiring 'tis long you may wait —
>   Till the hour of the night and the storm.
>   ('Hymn for Lammas-Day', ll. 1–8)

We are clearly back on familiar territory here. Jones's prison poetry has shifted from the lyrical to the collective, from the centripetal to the centrifugal, and this is now poetry at its most public, intended even to be sung by the public. The ambiguity of the first words allows either for an interpretation based on an agricultural metaphor, or an implicit threat of armed rebellion. This is an intensification of a similar use of imagery involving a sickle in 'The Working-Man's Song' where the ambiguity is also present and there is a more explicit reference to confrontation, but the absence of the verb 'sharpen' renders it slightly more benign: 'And the sickle shall baffle the lance' (l. 45). A similarly implicit threat involving bladed agricultural equipment is contained in the final lines of 'The March of Freedom': 'Now, scythemen! to the harvest! |Reap! you who sowed the seed' (ll. 199–200). Such imagery reveals Jones's broadly anti-industrial instincts by imaging a nominally rural mobilization of radical force in support of the Charter.

There is also a return to the admonishing tenor of early Chartist poems including 'Our Cheer', where the use of the related verb 'languish' (l. 1) prefigures the characterization of an un-mobilized working class which, in 'Hymn for Lammas-Day', 'lounge[s] at the gate'. The two remaining stanzas of the poem reinforce the analogy between agriculture and militarization by extending the arable field metaphor to encompass battlefield imagery. The repeat of 'Sharpen the sickle' as an opening refrain for each stanza maintains the sense of threat carried by the poem:

> Sharpen the sickle; how proud they stand,
>   In the pomp of their golden grain!
> But, I'm thinking, ere noon 'neath the sweep of my hand
>   How many will lie on the plain.
> Though the ditch be wide, the fence be high,
>   There's a spirit to carry us o'er;
> For God never meant his people to die,
>   In sight of so rich a store.
>
> Sharpen the sickle; how full the ears!
>   While our children are crying for bread;
> And the field has been watered with orphans' tears
>   And enriched with their fathers dead.
> And hopes that are buried, and hearts that broke,
>   Lie deep in the treasuring sod:
> Then sweep down the grain with a thunder-stroke,
>   In the name of humanity's God! (ll. 9–24)

The appearance of the speaker through the term 'I' in the eleventh line represents a personal subjective voice which, apart from in the essentially lyrical, loosely autobiographical 'The Better Hope', is relatively unusual in Jones's Chartist poetry. Jones's assumption that his Chartist credentials have been enhanced by his imprisonment has given rise to an increased confidence that a closer association between his poetic voice and his Chartist persona would be possible and profitable. Although Jones's poetry rarely appears to lack confidence, it has been demonstrated in the previous chapter that, whether consciously or unconsciously, his poetry is careful to negotiate the shifts in relationship that his poetic discourse tracks as his Chartist career develops.

122 LYRICAL PRISON POETRY (1848–50)

As ever with Jones's Chartist poetry, 'Hymn for Lammas-Day' contains an implicit message to its readers which relates to the progress of the struggle for the Charter. The fact that the field is 'enriched with their fathers dead' and the 'sod' is described as 'treasuring', suggests that past failures of the Chartist movement, or even working-class struggle generally, merely lay the ground for future success. The regenerative associations of rural imagery are used to encourage the Chartist body not to relinquish the battle for the Charter in the face of the obvious failures of 1848. In this sense, the poem can be seen as Jones laying down a marker for the efforts he will make to revive the Chartist movement over the next eight years.

Despite Jones's claims in his introduction that the works he presents contain no 'voice of failing constancy' it is possible to detect evidence of a crisis of identity in the poems. His imprisonment, the event which should have cemented his Chartist reputation, paradoxically separated him physically and socially from the Chartist body, and he was to bear the suffering of his experience alone. In 'A Prisoner's Night-Thought' he speaks of a 'wearing to the core' (l. 2), 'the fevered threads of life' (l. 6), and 'burning scars' (l. 8). Even the indefinite article of the title suggests isolation or a loss of identity. The poems which express defiance and resolve, 'Prison Bars' and 'The Silent Cell', utilize prison as a weapon turned against itself. In the former this is done explicitly through potent symbols of incarceration, while the latter transforms silent punishment into an imaginative revivification of the body and spirit. Neither of these poems suggests that the speaker takes comfort from fellow sufferers or from well-wishers beyond the prison gates. There is no evidence that 'Jones draws on the resources of the group to find solace and overcome his sense of personal isolation'.[63] In 'The Garden Seat' and 'The Prisoner's Dream' imagination becomes the vehicle for a psychic freedom which can be used to consider broad-ranging philosophical questions, or merely to entertain and console. In the latter poem, through 'Imagination's alchemy' (l. 95), it is possible for the speaker to reach an epiphany of self-identification and 'wake next morn a Poet' (l. 99). The recovery of identity comes from within, not from without; from the imagination and its consolidation through the act, and products, of writing. Jones's revival is primarily through poetry, not political resolve, although the two may be concomitant on his release from prison. Denied the transformation of moral redemption open to prisoners who confront their own wrongdoing, Jones transforms and consolidates the self through poetry's fixing of an identity drawn from silence, memory, and imagination.

Notes to Chapter 4

1. Janowitz, *Lyric and Love in the Romantic Tradition*, p. 185.
2. Paul, p. 192.
3. R. G. Gammage's relatively contemporary account, *History of the Chartist Movement 1837–1854* (first published in 1854), describes the context and aftermath of the march in these terms: 'Almost as soon as convicted, Mitchell was hurried out of the country. Intense excitement reigned in Ireland, the manufacture of pikes going on briskly. Physical force still appeared to be organizing too in England. At a Chartist delegate meeting for Lancashire and Yorkshire, held on the 28th of May, a resolution was passed in favour of the formation of a National Guard. Meetings in London for the Charter and Repeal, and to sympathize with Mitchell, were held

on the 29th and 30th, on Clerkenwell Green. The first meeting was addressed by Messrs. Beezer, Jones, McCrae, M'Douall and others. It afterwards formed a procession, and traversed several streets of the metropolis. A collision took place in Redcross-street between the people and the police, and a proclamation was issued against the processions. The second meeting was addressed by Messrs. Williams, Sharp, and Daly. Just as the people were dispersing, the police interfered, and drove them from the ground. Another meeting was held on Wednesday night; a disturbance was anticipated. Specials, police, and military were in attendance, and the meeting was dispersed by force' (Gammage, p. 332).

4. In *Chartism: A New History* Malcolm Chase makes it clear that the uniting of Chartists and Repealers in northern towns with large Irish populations proved a dangerous combination for the authorities: 'Bradford's large Irish population was represented disproportionately in the declining trade of woolcombing. There, and in the wider region, 'Chartist scouts' watched police and troops, and National Guards drilled with pikes on the adjacent moors by night. On 19 May Bradford magistrates reported that police had effectively lost control of Adelaide Street, a Chartist stronghold in the heart of the town's Irish quarter. Four days later, when McDouall visited the town for a mass rally, 2,000 marched from Halifax to join Bradford's 10,000 in an extraordinary quasi-military display, with tricolours flying from pikestaffs and bands playing'. (Chase, p. 318). Gammage adds: 'Not the slightest interference took place by the authorities. Bradford was that day in possession of the Chartists' (p. 332).

5. 'Editorial', *The Times*, 2 June 1848.

6. Ibid.

7. Even more than usual for Chartist meetings, reports of the size of the crowd that Jones addressed on 4 June 1848 at Bishop Bonner's Fields vary considerably. Writing in 1854 Gammage merely stated that the crowd was 'large and excited' (p. 334). Taylor variously numbers the crowd at 300,000 (which one assumes is a typographical error given the relatively small size of the park in question) and 3,000 (Taylor, pp. 110, 118, & 122). Chase maintains that 'the number of demonstrators involved in the main gathering was small — at most 8,000 — but its mood was confrontational' (p. 319).

8. Saville, p. 105. John Mitchell (1815–75) was a prominent Irish Nationalist who wrote extensively for the *Nation* and was the first editor of the *United Irishman*. Legal proceedings for seditious speeches were begun against him on 15 April 1848. John Frost (1784–1877) was one of the leaders of the Chartist Newport Uprising of 1839. He was deported to Van Diemen's Land (Tasmania) in 1840. In 1848 Sir John Grey, 2nd Baronet (1799–1892) was Home Secretary and Lord John Russell (1892–78) Prime Minister.

9. Saville, p. 98.

10. Taylor, p. 113.

11. Ibid., p. 117.

12. Thornton Leigh Hunt (ed.), *The Correspondence of Leigh Hunt*, 2 vols (London: Smith, Elder & Co., 1862), I, 82.

13. Jones's fellow speaker at the Bishop Bonner's Field meeting, Alexander Sharp, was one of twelve Tothill prisoners who died in a cholera outbreak in the autumn of 1849.

14. Stephen Roberts, *The Chartist Prisoners: The Radical Lives of Thomas Cooper (1805–1892) and Arthur O'Neill (1819–1896)* (Oxford: Lang, 2008) p. 26.

15. *Birmingham Daily Mail*, 9 December 1890.

16. John Alfred Langford, in his *Prison Books and Their Authors* (London: Tegg, 1861) included Cooper and *The Purgatory of Suicides* as a subject alongside writers including Boëthius, Cervantes, Bunyan, and Leigh Hunt.

17. Stephanie Kuduk, 'Sedition, Chartism, and Epic Poetry in Thomas Cooper's The Purgatory of Suicides', *Victorian Poetry*, 39, II (Summer 2001), 165–86 (p. 166).

18. Janowitz, *Lyric and Love in the Romantic Tradition*, p. 166.

19. *Ernest Jones: Who Is He? What Has He Done?*, cited by Saville, p. 34.

20. The Reform League was an influential political organization active from 1865 to 1869 that campaigned for universal male suffrage. They numbered Liberal Members of Parliament among their supporters and their membership included a higher proportion of the middle classes than the by then defunct National Charter Association. Their major achievement was their influence

on the 1867 Reform Act which substantially widened the franchise. For wider reading on the subject see *The Era of the Reform League: English Labour and Radical Politics 1857–1872*, ed. by John Breuilly, Gottfried Niedhart, and Antony Taylor (Mannheim: Palatium, 1995).

21. Taylor, pp. 18 & 133–36.

22. Ibid., pp. 135 & 151.

23. Ibid., p. 182.

24. Paul, p. 202.

25. *NP* (1851), I, 62.

26. Michel Foucault, *Discipline and Punish: The Birth of the Prison*, trans. by Alan Sheridan (London: Penguin, 1991), pp. 302–03.

27. *NP* (1851), I, 62.

28. Ibid., I, 63.

29. Ernest Jones, 'A Prisoner's Night Thought', in *NP* (1851), I, 63.

30. Derek Van Abbé, *Goethe: New Perspectives on a Writer and his Times* (London: Allen and Unwin, 1972), p. 44.

31. Benedict Anderson, *Imagined Communities: Reflections on the Origins and Spread of Nationalism* (London: Verso, 1983), p. 30.

32. Foucault, p. 303.

33. Ibid., p. 302.

34. Oscar Wilde, *De Profundis*, ed. by Robert Ross (London: Methuen & Co., 1919), p. vi.

35. Ibid., p. vii-viii.

36. Norbert Kohl, *Oscar Wilde: The Works of a Conformist Rebel*, trans. by David Henry Wilson (Cambridge: Cambridge University Press, 1989), p. 287.

37. Ibid., p. 275.

38. Ernest Jones, 'Prison Bars', in *NP* (1851), I, 64 (in Kovalev, p. 162).

39. Ernest Jones, 'The Garden Seat', in *NP* (1851), I, 66.

40. The French government released the technology of the 'daguerreotype' into the public domain on 19 August 1839.

41. Scott Hess, 'William Wordsworth and Photographic Subjectivity', *Nineteenth-Century Literature*, 63, 3 (December 2008), 283–320 (p. 294).

42. Samuel Taylor Coleridge, 'This Lime-Tree Bower My Prison', in *Coleridge: Selected Poems*, ed. by Richard Holmes (London: HarperCollins, 1996), pp. 43–45.

43. Paul Magnuson, 'The "Conversation" Poems', in *The Cambridge Companion to Coleridge*, ed. by Lucy Newlyn (Cambridge: Cambridge University Press, 2002), pp. 32–44 (pp. 38–39).

44. Samuel Taylor Coleridge, *Biographia Literaria: Or, Biographical Sketches of My Literary Life and Opinions*, 2 vols (New York: Putnam, 1848), I, 205n.

45. Bunyan may have described himself as a religious prisoner; his prosecutors were certainly concerned by the political ramifications of his preaching. For further reading on this matter, see Christopher Hill, *A Turbulent, Seditious, and Factious People: John Bunyan and his Church* (Oxford: Oxford University Press, 1988), Chapter Ten, 'Preaching and Imprisonment'.

46. Ibid., pp. 106–07.

47. Lynne Lawner, 'Introduction', in Antonio Gramsci, *Letters from Prison* (London: Jonathan Cape, 1974), pp. 4 & 5.

48. Antonio Gramsci, letter to Julia Gramsci, 25 January 1936, in *Letters from Prison*, p. 262.

49. Ernest Jones, 'The Silent Cell', in *NP* (1851), I, 66–67 (in Kovalev, pp. 163–64).

50. Janowitz, *Lyric and Love in the Romantic Tradition*, p. 185.

51. Ernest Jones, 'The Prisoner's Dream', in *NP* (1851), I, 67–68.

52. Emily Brontë, 'The Prisoner: A Fragment', in *The Poems of Emily Brontë*, ed. by Derek Roper and Edward Chitham (Oxford: Clarendon, 1995), pp. 181–83.

53. Coleridge, *Biographia Literaria*, p. 205n.

54. Jeffrey C. Robinson, *Unfettering Poetry: Fancy in British Romanticism* (Basingstoke: Palgrave, 2006), p. 5.

55. This poem employs another trope borrowed from the ode when the word that completes this stanza's rhyme scheme, 'Poesy!', is formally delayed and becomes the first word of the next stanza (see next page). This is indicated by line spacing.

LYRICAL PRISON POETRY (1848–50)   125

56. Wilde, p. viii.
57. Christopher Salvesen, *The Landscape of Memory: A Study of Wordsworth's Poetry* (London: Edward Arnold, 1965), p. 76.
58. Ioan Davies, *Writers in Prison* (Oxford: Blackwell, 1990), p. 60.
59. Within the twenty-four short poems Jones produced in prison the term 'I' and its variants, used as referring to the speaker of the poem, occur thirty-six times. In forty *Northern Star* poems it occurs hardly at all.
60. Ernest Jones, 'St. Coutt's', in *NP* (1851), I, 69.
61. A letter from Jones to the editor of the *Christian Socialist Journal* from October 1851 requesting that the two men weekly swap copies of their respective papers is in the possession of the author.
62. Ernest Jones, 'Hymn for Lammas-Day', in *NP* (1851), I, 70 (in Kovalev, pp. 164–65).
63. Janowitz, *Lyric and Love in the Romantic Tradition*, p. 185.

CHAPTER 5

'The New World, a Democratic Poem'
1851

Although 'The New World' might be regarded as Jones's magnum opus, its provenance and its structure have frequently been misinterpreted.[1] Gregory Claeys, in *Imperial Sceptics: British Critics of Empire 1850–1920*, suggests that as a reaction to the Indian Uprising of 1857 Jones 'wrote a lengthy poem, 'The Revolt of Hindostan', in its defence'.[2] In fact, the poem was republished and renamed as such in response to the uprising, and had been completed at least six years before. The first canto celebrates America's democracy and introduces the poem's class, economic, and geo-political themes; it is the only part of the poem which explicitly deals with actual historical events (although even this section ends with a prediction of an American civil war associated with the slave trade). Apart from some of the first lines of Canto II which Anne Janowitz has suggested may represent events in the Afghan wars of 1842, the subsequent seven cantos are all predictive of a future which occasionally closely resembles the past, thus underlining the poem's sequential view of a history perceived through a refracted, analogical poetic frame.[3]

The second canto describes the Indian expulsion of British forces from their nation, but the third details the growth of an Indian empire which eventually becomes corrupt and succumbs to a civil war in which a monarch is overthrown. The subject of the fourth canto is the rise of a merchant and middle class which undermines the aristocracy and exploits the workers. Jones uses an imagined Indian future as a lens through which to view an English past and present. When Edward Royle quotes a section from the fourth canto in his book *Chartism* he is only partially correct when he claims that it is 'treating the middle-class betrayal of 1832'.[4] Like some previous observers, he has failed to note the complex chronological structure of 'The New World', which is almost entirely prophetic, though its subject is history. It is possible these confusions arise from the widespread publication of discrete sections of poem, and the close similarities their events sometimes bear to actual national histories.[5] As an example of the poem's temporal and geographical distortions, India is the actual subject of the fourth canto though contemporary England is clearly the metaphorical subject when Ireland is poetically transfigured into Ceylon (Sri Lanka), a 'neighbouring isle' where 'a million died' (IV, 263), 'reaped by famine's scythe' (IV, 265). Janowitz has noted that 'the history of British capitalism and imperialism, and the possibility of its reiteration in the United States is [...] displaced into the projected history of the now emancipated Hindostan'.[6] The substantial Indian section of the poem, which comprises four of the poem's eight cantos, represents an historical survey through which the past, the present, and future of Britain are perceived through a rigidly structured political frame.

The fifth canto of 'The New World' relates the overthrow of capitalism in the Indian state, and it is significant that the victory is achieved bloodlessly. Just as in the Chartist dream, moral force backed by numerical advantage is sufficient agency for revolution. But if this is the point where the metaphorical Indian future narrative meets Jones's hoped-for near-future of Britain, the scene then shifts in the sixth canto to a Europe about to be besieged by the nations of Africa in revenge for the abuses of slavery and colonialism. The securing of freedom for the oppressed nations of Africa as Europe is overrun triggers a miraculous surge of groundwater into the Sahara, which becomes a fertile land. The seventh canto predicts the Jews returning to Israel in a peaceful mass emigration blessed by other nations, but it is the eighth canto that contains some of the most famous predictions in the poem, as an unnamed Pacific republic is formed and technology starts to become a force for good in the world.

The conclusion of the poem predicts a social, political, and scientific idyll which, quite apart from its remarkable technological predictions, goes far beyond the ambitions of Chartism and bears closer similarities to the ideas of Marx and Engels than to those of Henri Saint-Simon (1760–1825), Robert Owen (1771–1858), and Charles Fourier (1772–1837), who Vincent Geoghegan identifies as early-nineteenth-century proponents of 'utopian socialism'. And yet 'The New World' is a utopian text, and its title's double meaning refers to both the United States and to a paradisiacal future which is global in its effect. Geoghegan's description of the functions of utopia is easily mapped onto Jones's text:

> By playing fast and loose with time and space, logic and morality, and by thinking the unthinkable, a utopia asks the most embarrassing questions. As an imaginative construction of a whole society, the utopia can bring into play the rich critical apparatus of the literary form and a sensitivity to the holistic nature of society, enabling it to mock, satirize, reduce the prominent parts, to illuminate and emphasize the neglected, shadowy, hidden parts — and to show the inter-relatedness — of the existing system.[7]

Jones's geographical and temporal inversions and distortions enable the poem to comment on the past and the present, and to predict a future which grows out of the contemporary political reality. But the progression of history is ultimately towards the greater good, as humanity learns lessons about its conduct from history, and increasing social sophistication and technological ability inevitably begin to work for the benefit of humankind.

Critical Receptions

Read as a prison poem, 'The New World' can be seen as a literary response to Thomas Cooper's *The Purgatory of Suicides* in its thematic breadth and historical range, and both poems build on the democratic, epic legacy of Leigh Hunt's *The Story of Rimini* (1816), which was composed during its author's imprisonment for defaming the Prince Regent. The example of Hunt's stoicism in the face of his incarceration (no doubt aided by the relative comfort of his conditions), and his continued production and advocacy of democratic literature must have served as a model to Cooper and Jones. However, Jones's poem reflects its author's interest in what he sees as the necessarily international nature of a move towards democracy, which Janowitz recognizes as a reflection of more general Chartist trends of the period:

> The globalism of the poem and its analysis of British imperialism is part of the internationalism which began to permeate the Chartist movement in the period beginning with the revolutions of 1848, and modifying some of the older rhetoric patterns of domestic oppositional patriotism.[8]

Just as Jones's steeping in the medieval/mythic narratives of German Romanticism was adapted to address the anti-industrial agrarian idealisms of the Land Plan in his pre-prison poetry, so his German heritage became an essential element of his vocal internationalism in the poetry he produced after prison. However, Jones never fails to link domestic political concerns with his broader view of the progression of geo-political trends. Isobel Armstrong notes a particular example of the consistent thematic duality of 'The New World': 'Colonial exploitation mirrors exploitation at home — hence the logic of emigration, where the state displaces its poor into the colonies'.[9] It is this integration of international and domestic radical perspectives, coupled with the treatment of history as a succession of distinct phases linked by causality, which has led some observers to associate 'The New World' with Marxist historical materialism. It is certainly true that Marx's *Communist Manifesto* had been serialized in German in a newspaper with which Jones was more than familiar, the *Deutsche Londoner Zeitung*, in the spring of 1848: this was the publication which carried some of Jones's last pre-Chartist, German-language poetry. In an introduction to his volume of Jones's political speeches and writings, John Saville emphasizes the influence of Marx and Engels on the young Chartist in the two years leading up to his imprisonment:

> The influence of Marx and Engels in the development of his understanding was to be decisive. At the outset, that influence was communicated indirectly through [George Julian] Harney, with whom Jones was associated from his first days in the movement. [...] Marx he first met when the former came to England for the second congress of the Communist League in November 1847, for they both spoke on the same platform at a meeting organised by the Fraternal Democrats and the Polish Committee to celebrate the anniversary of the 1830 Polish Revolution.[10]

There is also evidence that Marx was in close cooperation with Jones during his writing of the material contained in *Notes to the People* (whose first issue opened with 'The New World'). This evidence comes from Marx himself, whom Saville quotes writing to Engels on 4 November 1864:

> By chance a few numbers of E. Jones's *Notes to the People* (1851, 1852) have come into my hands again; these, so far as the main points of the economic articles are concerned, were written under my immediate guidance and partly also with my direct cooperation.[11]

This close association has led some literary critics to conclude that 'The New World' was influenced by the theories of Marx and Engels. In his article '"In Louring Hindostan"', Ronald Paul writes:

> Indeed, in the course of the poetic narrative, Jones provides no less than a dialectical survey of almost the whole history of class society from feudalism and the decline of the aristocracy, to capitalism and the rise of the bourgeoisie — a process which in turn culminates in the revolt of the working classes. In such an antithetical view of the past, one can see the influence of a text like the *Communist Manifesto*, the first English translation of which appeared in November 1850 in *The Red Republican*, Harney's Chartist journal with which Jones was also closely associated.[12]

However, there has been some critical disagreement over the extent to which Marx and Engels influenced Jones's day-to-day politics. G. D. H. Cole, in *Socialist Thought: The Forerunners 1789–1850*, closely identifies Jones's political philosophy with that of his German friend:

> The Socialism of Ernest Jones, as it developed after 1848, was in its essentials that of Marx. Its central dogma was that of the class-struggle as the necessary form of social development; and with this went an insistence on the doctrine of surplus value and on the historical tendency towards a concentration of capital.[13]

But, in her review of Taylor's biography of Jones, 'Ernest Jones: Who Is He? What Has He Done?' (which takes its title from the 1868 Reform League pamphlet of that name), Janowitz questions the tendency of Saville (whose collection of Jones's writing was published the year before Cole's historical survey) and other writers to jump to conclusions regarding the true nature of Jones's politics at this time:

> In the past, socialists such as John Saville have considered Jones to be the first genuine Chartist/Marxist (particularly in his friendship with Engels), though if there is a strain of European socialism in Jones, it is probably less coherent than Saville might have wished.[14]

Interestingly, Saville qualifies his own claims for Jones's Marxist credentials with the following statement, 'Jones himself was no theorist, but a superb populariser, and he absorbed easily and readily the philosophy and the ideas of the authors of the *Communist Manifesto*'.[15] The key statement here is that Jones was no theorist, and whilst there appears a weight of circumstantial evidence to support the claim that 'The New World' is in effect the first poem to deal with Marxist historical materialism, careful reading reveals that the text falls some way short of this. Although there is recognition of the importance of economic forces in shaping society, there is little evidence of a sophisticated Marxist critique of the capitalist system in the text, and its historical phases are not explicitly linked to the control of means of production. By far the most coherent political elements of Jones's epic lie in its treatment of imperialism and its call for a collective internationalism. The cycles of ascendancy and decadence in 'The New World' (and its implicit critique of contemporary society through an historical prism) relate just as easily to Edward Gibbon's *Decline and Fall of the Roman Empire* (1776–89) as any other text. And as we shall see, the technologically advanced, utopian future that the poem describes emerges more from a defeat of imperialism than of capitalism, and is not characterized as an authentically Marxist socialist or communist society.

In his substantial prose introduction to 'The New World' Jones likens Great Britain to 'the plague-stricken hull of a stately wreck', some of whose inhabitants must to flee to America's 'new Atlantis'.[16] Jones's condemnation of the organization of British society in this introduction is wide-ranging, encompassing industry, trade, empire, and religion within a critique that portrays these as interdependent arms of a controlling hegemony:

> On its colonies the sun never sets, but the blood never dries. In mechanical power it has outstripped the world, but that power it employs to displace labour and starve unwilling idlers. Every factory is more corrupt than a barrack, more painful than a prison, and more fatal than a battle-field. Its commerce touches every shore, but their ports have been opened by artillery, and are held with murder. [...] It has been increasing its wealth, but corrupting its manhood; trebling its churches, but losing its Christianity; sending forth missionaries, but rendering their faith hated by its professors; building charities, but making more poor than it relieved — stealing a pound, and asking gratitude for giving back a farthing! — and, withal, it dazzles the world by its attitude of quiescent grandeur. But that grandeur is decaying.[17]

As an example of the continuing influence of Jones's use of language, the rhetorically balanced first sentence of this quotation provides the title of John Newsinger's book *The Blood Never Dried: A People's History of the British Empire.*[18] This broad survey of imperial conflict from the mid-nineteenth century to the present day sets itself in opposition to those it considers 'contemporary apologists for empire', a trend seen to be most potently represented by the commercial success of Niall Ferguson's *Empire: How Britain Made The Modern World* (2003). Interestingly, the epigraph to Newsinger's work confirms Janowitz's characterization of modern socialist views of Jones by attributing the quoted phrase to 'Ernest Jones, Chartist and socialist, 1851'.

Jones's message to America in the introduction to 'The New World' is to guard against the complacency which has led Great Britain to the present state of affairs, and not to take its democracy for granted. Indeed, he uses the historical example of Venice to point out that 'the mere republican form secures neither prosperity nor freedom, though essential for their existence'.[19] The cultural state of America is explicitly linked with its own self-image, and Jones suggests that, in its youthful phase, it is susceptible to the corrupting influence of the 'quiescent grandeur' of British cultural productions. Jones calls on American writers to stop emulating the British, and urges the creation of a home-grown literature which is essential to the consolidation of a national democracy:

> With the exception of some goodly veterans, stern old republican penmen, your literature flutters in silks, velvets, and ostrich feathers. Your authors come over here, and go into ecstasies about a royal procession and a court-ball — they are inoculating your mind with the old venom of Europe: look to it, young talents of the west — better write in rough numbers and on homely themes, than emulate the lines of Pope and Tennyson, if tuned to the servility of the courts.[20]

Jones may be partly referring here to the literary argument between Henry Wadsworth Longfellow (1807–82) and Edgar Allan Poe (1809–49), which had been partly centred on Poe's perception of the elder poet's Euro-centrism. It was in an introduction to Poe's inclusion in a series entitled 'Poets of America' in *Notes to the People* that Jones elaborated on his call for the creation of an independent American literature:

> The Americans are a shrewd and far-seeing people, but they are somewhat too material; they must not believe that a nation can long exist without men of thought, as well as men of action. The salvation of America lies in the possession of a Republican literature. The literature of England is slowly sapping the foundation of her institutions. England does all her thinking, and if this system continues, the action of this great nation will be in accordance with the will of the old country.[21]

A direct causal relationship between 'will' and 'action' is identified, and, in national and political terms, literature, which both reflects and creates the cultural life of a people, is figured as an important formative element of 'will'. This insistence on an independent literature as a prerequisite component of political self-reliance echoes the cultural critique of Chartist commentators in newspapers including the *Northern Star*, the *Red Republican*, and Jones's own *Labourer*. In this respect 'The New World', with its explicitly definitive subtitle, 'A Democratic Poem', can be seen not just as an anti-imperialist critique, but as an attempted template for the creation of an English democratic poetics. In an open letter addressed to 'the British Democracy', published in George Julian Harney's *Friend of the People* magazine on 24 May 1851,[22] Jones suggested that the present low point in Chartist history was 'the point in which democratic literature is needed'.[23] In Janowitz's opinion:

> *The New World* authorises Jones to take up fully his place as the new Laureate of Labour. It aspires to the level of the public poem, with its global sweep, and its provenance in prison demonstrates the poet's suffering.[24]

Jones's epic diverges from his earlier Chartist work in its self-conscious address to a wider audience whilst remaining ideologically attuned to Chartist ambitions.

Although the development of the tradition of the mock-epic in the eighteenth century might have appeared to sound the death-knell for more conventional approaches to the genre, the scope and depth of recent critical works including Herbert Tucker's *Epic Britain's Heroic Muse 1790–1910* (which describes 'The New World' as a 'probably sincere [...] couplet screed'),[25] and Simon Dentith's *Epic and Empire in Nineteenth-Century Britain*, would suggest otherwise. The latter writer begins his work by quoting the following 1857 statement by Marx on the fundamentally anachronistic nature of the epic genre:

> Is Achilles possible with powder and lead? Or the *Iliad* with the printing press, not to mention the printing machine? Do not the song and the saga and the muse necessarily come to an end with the printer's bar, hence do not the necessary conditions for epic poetry vanish.[26]

Dentith's explanation of how nineteenth-century epics negotiate this apparent paradox concerning their existence is centred on the idea of 'epic primitivism', whereby 'ideas of modernity current in the nineteenth century, though established in the eighteenth, are predicated upon an engagement with the sense of historical distance carried by primary epics, especially those of Homer'.[27] In his explicitly radical text, Jones's use of the epic genre as an instrument of political demystification of the imperialist project is situated within this interpretation even as it attempts to subvert not just the genre, but the society within which the text is published. In this sense it has much in common with twentieth-century epic critiques of empire including Derek Walcott's *Omeros* (1990), even though that work is structurally based on Homer's *Iliad*, in contrast with Jones's radically innovative chronological structure.

When Jones uses the heroic couplet, the poetic form most closely associated with one of the courtly targets of his introduction, Alexander Pope (1688–1744), he is following a Romantic tradition established by similar uses of the form by Keats in 'Endymion' (1818), or Shelley in 'Julian and Maddalo' (1819). Jones had already used heroic couplets in some of his longer *Northern Star* poems including 'The Cornfield and the Factory', 'England's Greatness', and 'Britannia'; the latter two anticipating 'The New World''s themes of empire and oppression.[28] The familiarity of the iambic pentameter and the relative ease of composition of the coupled rhymes aid the construction of stanzas of variable length and allow the poet to concentrate on the larger shifts of theme that the epic genre demands. Focusing on the prophetic, technology-themed later sections of the poem, Timothy Randall notes that Jones's chosen poetic form reflects the equilibrium he finds in his theories: 'Such audacious prophesying into the future may appear incongruously juxtaposed with Jones's use of the traditional heroic couplet. Yet the confident symmetrical balance of these couplets perfectly harmonizes with Jones's rational conception of science'.[29] It might also be noted that a poem whose approach to all of its major themes is markedly deterministic finds apt expression in the rhyme scheme with the most rapid resolve and the highest predictability.

Canto 1

The first of the eight cantos which comprise 'The New World' acts as an introduction to the poem, establishing its broad geopolitical scope as it celebrates America's development and political promise, relating the latter to its geographical variety and isolation:

> From freedom born to Time, transcendent birth!
> Colossus destined to bestride the earth,
> While heaved old empires with unwonted throes,
> Man's sanctuary, America, arose.
>
> Dull Europe, startled by thy first wild tones,
> Propped up thy cradle with her crumbling thrones;
> And France, sad nurse of thy rude infant days,
> Lulled thy first slumber with her 'Marseillaise.'
>
> Nations have passed, and kingdoms flown away —
> But history bids thee hope a longer day,
> Wise witness of an ancient world's decay:

> No common guards before thy barriers stand —
> The elements themselves defend thy land. (1, 1–13)

America's national potential is contrasted with the negative terms used in association with Europe: 'dull', 'crumbling', 'decay'. America is 'transcendent', both a 'Colossus' and 'Man's sanctuary', suggesting its status as an unassailable new beginning for humanity. However, possible seeds of the new country's degeneration are identified in its continued reliance on the slave trade and the potentially corrupting influence of too great an emphasis on commerce and industry, which are poetically represented by the terms 'gold' and 'steel':

> Ah! that the wisdom here so dearly bought
> Would sanctify thy wild, luxuriant thought,
> And righteously efface the stripes of slaves
> From that proud flag where heaven's high splendour waves!
> But not the black alone the wrong shall feel,
> The white man sinks the prey of gold and steel. (1, 57–62)

The regular equation of Great Britain's working class with slaves in Jones's *Northern Star* poetry is more strongly stated by reference to America's actual slave population, and the suggestion is that the workers of America will eventually be reduced to a state of slavery by the adoption of a British economic system.[30] Effective enslavement of a large body of the population is presented as an inevitable consequence of economic reliance on the capitalist system. Although the success of the British abolitionist movement is positively contrasted with the debasement of the American flag through the association with slavery (the dark pun on 'stripes' is emblematic of the whipped bodies of slaves), the focus of the stanza is still very much on the plea for a rejection of British-style imperialism and industrial capitalism. Jones predicts America as a future imperial power, driven by the same goals as the British Empire, and experiencing the same eventual social degeneration. But he sees Asia as the probable site of this imperial advancement, as America looks to its un-colonized West for its direction of expansion:

> But when, thy natural limits once possessed,
> Thou, too, shalt seek to colonise a West;
> Round coral-girt Japan thy ships shall fly,
> And China's plains behold thine armies die: —
> Unequal burdens press the exhausted land,
> Till richer states petition, rise, withstand. (1, 69–74)

Although America's relative lack of history means that it is to some degree exempt from the historical phases of the past that Jones identifies in other countries, he confidently predicts an imperial future for the republic unless it resists the determining force of industrial capitalism. It is this force which will place 'unequal burdens' upon the 'exhausted land' and lead to imperialist expansion into Asian territory. The claim in l. 74 that 'richer states petition, rise, withstand' identifies inevitable nationalist rebellions against colonizers as a central fault-line in imperialist ideology.

The final lines of the first canto of 'The New World' predict a slave uprising against America, but suggest that the inevitability of this event is part of an ineluctable historical progression towards a state of universal harmony:

> Then where the South sits throned in flame, above
> The hearts as fervid as the land they love,
> Swift sinks the white, and towering o'er the rest
> The hot mulatto rears his fiery crest: —
> Awhile the jarring elements contend,
> Till mingling lines with softening passions blend:
> Thus wrong's avenged, and Afric's burning stain
> Darkens her torturer's brow, and floods his vein,
> And, in the children, brands the father-Cain.
> The giant fragments slowly break away, —
> Ripe fruit of ages men misname decay;
> But from the change no rival powers shall soar,
> And freedom's friendly union fight no more. (1, 83–95)

Paul suggests that Jones's figures and use of terms to describe different ethnicities in the poem owe much to the prevailing literary orientalism that to a large extent was inherited from the Romantic works of Lord Byron and Robert Southey. However, he claims in mitigation that Jones 'also reveals an unusual awareness of the predicament facing indigenous peoples who were on the receiving end of oppressive European colonial policies'.[31] Although there are elements of Victorian taboos regarding miscegenation in the lines 'Thus wrong's avenged, and Afric's burning stain | Darkens her torturer's brow, and floods his vein', the speaker is clearly in favour of the actions of the slaves, and their rebellion precipitates a progression towards the general good. The final couplet of the canto reiterates the oft-stated opinion that political freedom for all removes the necessity of war.

Jones's rigidly sequential view of the causes and mechanisms of empire — 'The New World' is essentially an historical survey that extends its account into the future — appears to run counter to some recent writing on the development of the British Empire, particularly that of John Darwin. Darwin suggests that what seemed to be a cohesive 'world-system' by the early twentieth century was formed almost haphazardly from a 'sprawling legacy of war and mercantilism'.[32] Far from empire being subject to a governmental master-plan, 'Victorian imperialists were drawn from different interests and classes. They were driven by motives that were at times contradictory. Rival visions of empire pulled them in different directions'.[33] Interestingly, with respect to the prophetic ambitions of 'The New World', Darwin subsequently states: 'however clear-sighted the prophet, it would not have been easy to foresee the path followed by British expansion between 1830 and 1880'.[34] But it is important to recognize that Jones's sense of historical progression includes elements of indeterminate, or even autonomous, agency, which have their poetic precedent in Shelley's 'Ode to the West Wind'. It is perhaps going too far to suggest that Jones had any conception of a 'political unconscious' in the sense that modern Marxist theorists including Fredric Jameson might identify, but it can be seen in Jones's early Chartist poetry that political agency is sometimes an elusive, numinous element. Although the actions of individuals and the consciously assembled collective can influence the course of history, the economic system and political institutions often appear to operate autonomously, independent of the consciousnesses of which they

'THE NEW WORLD, A DEMOCRATIC POEM' (1851)   135

are comprised. Where Jones and Darwin fully converge is in their conceptions of Britain's sometimes tenuous military hold on its colonies. The latter writes:

> Victorian Britain was a powerful state, but it was not all-powerful, and much nonsense is talked of Victorian 'hegemony'. Even a minister as aggressive as Lord Palmerston, whose belligerent rhetoric is sometimes naively equated with his conduct of policy, was always acutely aware that British strength had its limits, especially on land. Victorian statesmen avoided confrontation with other strong powers whenever they could.[35]

Jones's recognition of Britain's military vulnerability informs subsequent sections of 'The New World', both in terms of its moral implications for the British soldiers stationed overseas, and for what it suggests about the wisdom of British expansion into other territories when colonized nations are inevitably going to react at some point to the exploitation of their populations and natural resources.

Canto II

The second canto of 'The New World', which at two hundred and seventy-four lines is almost three times the length of the first canto, takes the form of a narrative concerning an imagined rebellion by the Indian people against their British colonizers. Though presumably a prediction of future events, the action is narrated in the past tense, and the first lines make it clear that Jones envisages this rebellion occurring before America's own colonial expansion:

> When erst the West its warrior-march began,
> The eyes of earth were drawn to Hindostan:
> Long time the clouds stood gathering, tier on tier,
> And thickening thunders, muttering, growled more near.
> Thro' plain and valley pressed uneasy heat,
> That burnt volcanic under English feet.
> Fierce and more fierce from Himmalayah's height
> Fresh flash on flash keeps heralding the fight, —
> The border-feuds a deeper hue assume,
> And all the northern skies are wrapt in gloom. (II, 1–10)

Jones's use of the past tense for a future narrative, which is largely continued through to the end of the poem, serves the dual purpose of making the reading of the text less linguistically cumbersome and reducing the prophetic tone of the piece, presenting the whole as more politically relevant and apparently factual. That the 'eyes of the world' are focused on 'Hindostan' suggests not only the growing influence of means of mass communication (the technology of the electrical telegraph was beginning to be commercially applied as Jones wrote the poem), but that observers could themselves predict the ensuing political events. The heavy use of figures associated with the pathetic fallacy — gathering clouds, 'thickening thunders', 'uneasy heat' — presage the coming political upheaval through metaphor but also suggest the 'natural' qualities of the revolutionary actions with which the narrative is concerned. Very similar terms and figures used to presage military action were employed by Tennyson almost a decade later in his patriotic poem 'The War', which was published in *The Times* on 9 May 1859 at a time of British anxieties about invasion caused by the rise of Napoleon III:

> There is a sound of thunder afar,
>   Storm in the South that darkens the day,
> Storm of battle and thunder of war,
>   Well, if it do not come our way.
>   Form! form! Riflemen form!
>   Ready, be ready to meet the storm!
>   Riflemen, riflemen, riflemen form!
>   ('The War', ll. 1–7)[36]

Despite the similarity of the martial themes in these two poems their ideological stances could not be more opposed. In the third stanza of 'The War', Tennyson sees the issue of political reform as an unwelcome distraction from the more serious matter of the military defence of the realm:

> Let your Reforms for the moment go,
>   Look to your butts and take good aims.
> Better a rotten borough or so,
>   Than a rotten fleet or a city in flames!
>   ('The War', ll. 15–18)

Although published anonymously, it might be argued that, as Poet Laureate, Tennyson's defensive poetic stance more effectively reflected the opinions of the majority of his readers. It is also the case that, beginning with the militaristic nostalgia occasioned by the death of the Duke of Wellington in 1852, the decade after Jones's writing of 'The New World' saw the British public's attitude to war shift as it reacted to the events of the Crimean War (1853–56) and the Indian Rebellion (1857–58).[37] Edward M. Spiers notes the difficulties faced by Richard Cobden (1804–65) and John Bright (1811–89) as representatives of a broad-based peace movement of the time:

> After Russophobia gripped much of the nation in 1854, and the peace movement tried to intercede by sending a deputation to meet the Tsar in St Petersburg, the public response was incandescent. [...] By the outbreak of the Indian Mutiny in 1857, neither Cobden nor Bright was willing to champion the cause of peace.[38]

The military precedent for Jones's vision of a future Indian rebellion had been set by the first Anglo-Afghan War of 1839–42, culminating in the humiliating 'Retreat from Kabul', in which over 16,000 British and Indian troops and civilians were massacred by Afghan forces. It is in the context of this military set-back that Jones frames his warnings about the safety of British troops in India, playing on fears arising from the Afghan conflict regarding the availability and loyalty of allied imperial forces and the quality of British military leadership:

> A host's defeated! — and the succour sped
> With doubtful fortune makes uncertain head.
> Sudden, the rising South new force demands,
> But Affghan swords recall distracted bands.
> The generals see their scanty legions yield,
> But dare not bring the Sepoy to the field. (II, 11–16)

Jones then imagines the debate in Parliament, figuring the hawkish supporters of British oppression as 'Moloch', the Ammonite god associated with sacrifice: 'There, Moloch calls, though gorged beyond his fill, | For "Fleets and armies! Fleets and armies!" still' (ll. 25–26). The debate is presented satirically and parliamentary opposition to the sending of more forces to crush the rebellion is centred on the hypocrisy of the supposed Christian justification for colonization, identifying the 'civilizing' mission of the British Empire as a largely commercial operation. The speech of the unidentified opposing Member of Parliament is unequivocal in its condemnation of the imperial exercise, questioning not just its morality, but its ultimate wisdom:

> 'You urged — 'We civilise, reform, redeem!'
> 'In proof of which' — a smile escaped his lips,
> 'You sent out bishops in your battle-ships;
> 'Excused each deed of death, each lack of ruth,
> 'By boasting, 'How we spread the Gospel-truth!'
> 'Let not earth say, 'The blood you never weighed
> 'While gold was plentiful and profit made:
> 'But now the cost absorbs the larger share,
> 'Truth, Arts, and Faith may of themselves take care!' (II, 34–42)

The moral, cultural, and even the eventual economic costs of imperial expansion are deemed to outweigh the benefits. The speaker's suggestion that 'the cost absorbs the larger share' strikes at the heart of what Jones sees as the prime, and partially ulterior, motive for imperialism beyond any claims for modernization or Christian mission. The inevitable financial burden of military enforcement means that imperialism fails to work even on its own terms.

Jones's use of dialogue to articulate his politics in this passage is more extensive than in any of his *Northern Star* poetry, and later in this canto he introduces another relatively new poetic element: a defined dramatic character around whom the narrative unfolds. The British army's commission purchase system and its tendency to draw its officer class from a narrow band of wealthy families (an issue which would later come to prominence following the disastrous 'Charge of the Light Brigade' of 1854) both led to perceptions of military incompetence, which Jones satirizes by introducing an aged, experienced general whose rise through the ranks from relatively low beginnings is meritocratic. Just as imperialism sows the seeds of its own defeat, so the largely class-based system of military promotion is shown to have failed Britain when, as the Indian rebellion threatens to defeat British and allied forces, the military is forced by desperate pragmatism to choose a middle-class general to lead its army:

> This Britain felt, till pride of wealth and birth
> Were forced by danger to give way to worth:
> A veteran soldier for her leader chose,
> By public service worn, and private woes;
> But, where one, quick, strong will alone could save,
> A timid council's guiding thraldom gave. (II, 76–81)

The British army's purchase system had been in place for centuries, but Jones suggests that the goal of a large and efficient army to police an expanded empire is undermined by the systematic exclusion of all but the wealthiest from the officer ranks. Jones's argument was not new. In 1833, Arthur Wellesley, 1st Duke of Wellington (1769–52), felt compelled by critics of the army's system of promotion to defend its inherent wisdom:

> It is promotion by purchase which brings into the service men of fortune and education; men who have some connection with the interests and fortunes of the country, besides the commission which they hold from His Majesty. It is this circumstance which exempts the British Army from the character of being a 'mercenary army' and has rendered its employment, for nearly a century and a half, not only not inconsistent with the constitutional privileges of the country, but safe and beneficial.[39]

This argument that the closer military command is to the ruling class the less likely the army is to be subverted during an attempted military coup was based on a comparison between the British military and the more 'professionalized' armies of some European countries. However, the main thrust of many arguments in support of the system was based on simple discipline. Anthony Bruce writes:

> The fact that officers and the rank and file originated from opposite ends of the social scale contributed towards the maintenance of military discipline, since the deference generally shown in civilian life, particularly in rural society, to the upper classes was transferred to the army. In other words, the artificial differences of military rank corresponded with real social differences of birth and breeding.[40]

But within four years of the publication of 'The New World', as the Crimean War inflicted huge losses on a disorganized British army, the clamour for army reform was widespread. *The Times* of 23 December 1854 was unequivocal in its condemnation of contemporary army hierarchy:

> We echo the opinion of almost every experienced soldier or well-informed gentleman, when we say that the noblest army England ever sent from these shores has been sacrificed to the grossest mismanagement. Incompetency, lethargy, aristocratic hauteur, official indifference, favour, routine, perverseness and stupidity reign level and riot in the camp before Sebastopol, in the harbour of Balaklava, in the hospitals of Scutari, and how much nearer to home we do not venture to say.[41]

After a Royal Commission and the failure of those calling for incremental reform to mollify a public horrified by the disasters of Crimea, the purchase system in the British army was eventually abolished in 1871.

The sympathetic portrait of the old soldier in this section of 'The New World' can be read as a veiled tribute to Jones's own late father, who served as a captain in the 15th Hussars, was severely injured in the Peninsular Campaign at Sahagun in 1809, and was recalled to fight at the Battle of Waterloo in 1815, where he was temporarily upgraded to brigade major.[42] Although Captain Charles Jones came from gentry stock, elements of class anxiety emerge from his biography — his twenty-year service as aide-de-camp to the Duke of Cumberland (who later became King Ernst of Hanover) ended in a bitter dispute over pay. It is reasonable to assume that some of Jones's later antipathy towards the aristocracy might partly have emerged from the experiences of his father. The aged general in 'The New World' ('that good old trusty blade', l. 102) fights a campaign that is doomed from the start, partly because of the meddling of his aristocratic fellow officers ('tent loungers', l. 137), but mostly because his soldiers are unmotivated, gaining neither freedom nor financial reward for their efforts:

> But his no host to face the glorious might
> Of hearts that liberty inspires to fight.
> What gain they, save they, by the deathful strife?
> What meed have they to balance risk of life?
> They conquer empires: not a single rood
> Is their's — not even the ground whereon they stood,
> When victory drenched it with their gallant blood!
> Think ye that men will still the patriot play,
> Bleed, starve, and murder for four pence per day —
> And when the live machine is worn to nought,
> Be left to rot as things unworth a thought? (II, 103–14)

As well as presenting the military holding of an unwilling colony as an almost impossible task, Jones deconstructs the *casus belli* of the individual soldier on both sides of the conflict, contrasting the 'glorious might' of those who fight for their own liberty with the 'live machine[s]' of the British army. This depiction of the systematic dehumanization of subjects for military purposes can be directly related to Jones's critiques of the industrial system in his pre-prison *Northern Star* poetry, where factory workers are described as 'machines cast to neglect' ('Our Summons', l. 7), 'cheap machines' ('England's Greatness', l. 71), and 'nothing but — machines' ('The Factory Town', l. 40). The relationship between the soldier and the army is based on exploitation in the same way, and for much the same reasons, as the relationship between the industrial worker and the employer.

In Jones's imagined battle between the British colonial forces and Indian troops, motivation becomes the deciding factor despite the technological advantage of guns over swords and spears. As a determining agent, the potency of the motivation of the Indian troops, born of the knowledge of centuries of oppression, is analogous to the potential power of the will of the working class in Jones's *Northern Star* poetry. In 'The Song of the Starving' it is simply stated that 'the people have the power, | if only they had the will!' (ll. 15–16).[43] In 'The New World', the will of the Indian troops, and their success in battle, is similarly related to divinely-ordained morality and the inevitable progression of history:

> Here crashed the shot — there swept the Indian spear,
> And death won grandeur from an English cheer:
> Devotion vain! vain science deadliest pride!
> God, hope, and history take the Hindhû side!
> Here, but a host in misused courage strong:
> A nation there, with centuries of wrong! (II, 189–94)

Although the British soldiers are courageous, that courage is 'misused', presumably both morally and militarily, and bravery generated merely by an 'army's fame' is deemed no match for its patriotic equivalent which the Indian forces possess. Against the triumvirate of abstract elements supporting the Indian cause — 'God, hope, and history' — the British military is characterized by 'devotion vain', 'pride', and 'vain science'. 'Science', although it effectively becomes the saviour of mankind in the later sections of the poem, is presented negatively when pitched against freedom and the human spirit.

When the decisive battle is fought the vanity and fame of the British army is figured through reference to British victories on the Indian subcontinent, but the success of the more highly motivated and numerous Indian forces is inevitable:

> The crest-fallen armies, scattered and worn down,
> Give one last rally for their old renown;
> And where the blue sea meets their longing eyes,
> Turn yet again to face their enemies.
> Once more the famous flags parading see:
> 'Sobraon' — 'Aliwal' — and 'Meeanee' —
> Poor war-worn banners 'mid sulphureous gloom,
> Like ghosts of victories round an empire's tomb.
>
> The thunder died to calm — the day was done —
> And England conquered 'neath a setting sun! (II, 243–52)

'Sobraon' and 'Aliwal' refer to battles won in 1846 by the British in the Punjab in the First Anglo-Sikh War (1845–46), whereas 'Meeanee' refers to the Battle of Miani (February 1843) in which forces led by Sir Charles Napier secured the area of Sindh (now in Pakistan) for British rule. The ephemeral nature of these military successes ('ghosts of victories round an empire's tomb') is indicative of the instability of empire, which proves incapable of resisting what Jones termed in a poem title shortly before his imprisonment 'The March of Freedom'. The moment of defeat for British forces is presented formally through an isolated couplet, which, by slowing the reader's progress and placing increased emphasis on its statements, echoes the enormous implications of the post-battle calm it figures. There is an oblique and ironic allusion to the phrase 'the sun never sets on the British Empire' (which was actually first used in the sixteenth century in reference to the Spanish Empire) as 'England [is] conquered 'neath a setting sun'.

The canto ends with the old general apparently considering a counter-attack as his forces are driven to the coast and naval support which could act either as reinforcements or as a rescue party arrives. But the way that this stanza is worded suggests that a collective failure of appetite for battle amongst the rank and file of the British forces precludes the possibility of a counter-attack:

> At break of dawn the leader left his tent,
> And walked the mountain's craggy battlement.
> Far stretched the inland — not a foe seemed there —
> Lorn lay the Ghaut beneath the untroubled air,
> And, close in shore the strong, obedient fleet,
> Arrived, alike for succour or retreat, —
> The electric thought like lightning kindling came:
> 'Renew the war, and dare the glorious game!
> 'Swoop on each straggling band, that singly hies

'THE NEW WORLD, A DEMOCRATIC POEM' (1851) 141

> 'To hoped-for havoc of a host that flies!' —
> Hark! thrilling cheers from rock to harbour run:
> Alas they shout but for their safety won!
>
> A mighty shadow, deep, and stern, and still
> Threw o'er the fleet and flood each Indian hill;
> The encampment's flag just reached the rising light,
> Like lingering glory of the evening's fight:
> One hour its last farewell majestic waved
> Old England's pride, unchallenged and unbraved;
> But a soft wind at sunrise, like God's hand,
> Quietly bent it homeward from that land! —
> Sad wound the weary numbers to the sea,
> The signal's up, and Hindostan is free! (II, 253–74)

The defeat of imperial ambition is represented by the emotions of the old general, whose hopes are momentarily raised by the shouts of his troops, only to realize they are celebrating their escape from battle. Jones treads a fine line throughout this canto as he attempts to question the motivation of the British troops without appearing to accuse them of cowardice, but it is significant that he ends his battle narrative with what can only be interpreted as an ignominious retreat by the British army. There is a return to the pathetic fallacy featured at the beginning of the canto as 'a mighty shadow, deep, and stern, and still | threw o'er the fleet and flood each Indian hill' and a 'soft wind' points the Union flag ('Old England's pride') towards Britain 'like God's hand'. But the ultimate sympathies of the poet are revealed by the celebratory register of the concluding phrase, 'Hindostan is free!'

Canto III

The third canto of 'The New World' details the consolidation, development, and upheavals of an Indian imperial state after the expulsion of British forces. Through this narrative Jones deconstructs the nature of imperial culture as a self-sustaining, mythologizing force which builds on past glories to ensure military successes in the future:

> Then spread as grand an empire to the view
> As History, time's untiring scribe, e'er knew;
> At simpler faith its purer worship aims,
> And Vishnu yields in part what knowledge claims.
> Then Chivalry his proudest flag unrolled,
> And Superstition crowned her kings with gold.
> Then solemn priests through awful temples past,
> Whose now God excommunicates the last.
> Then bannered towers with wild romances rung,
> And bards their harps to love and glory strung;
> Like moonlight's magic upon sculptures rare,
> They showed the true, but made it seem too fair. (III, 1–12)

Various religions are consolidated into a state Church which, in allusion to Jones's perception of English history, is associated with 'Chivalry' and 'Superstition'. The

142 'The New World, a Democratic Poem' (1851)

God of this centralized religion 'excommunicates the last' and a mythologizing culture is established which, with 'bannered towers', 'wild romances', and 'bards their harps to love and glory strung', idealizes a national narrative in order to reinforce patriotic feeling amongst the populace. It is at this point of relative prosperity and national unity that Jones identifies the critical transition to an imperialist state, as patriotism leads to a perception of national superiority and a sense of entitlement that justifies expansion:

> Nations, like men, too oft are given to roam,
> And seek abroad what they could find at home.
> They send their armies out on ventures far;
> Their halt is — havoc, and their journey — war;
> Destruction's traders! who, to start their trade,
> Steal, for the bayonet, metal from the spade.
> The interest's — blood; the capital is — life;
> The debt — is vengeance; the instalment — strife;
> The payment's — death; and wounds are the receipt;
> The market's — battle; and the whole — a cheat. (III, 15–24)

Jones's deconstruction of the prime causes of imperial expansion is figured through a mass of economic terms that emphasize the mercantile function of empire: 'trade', 'interest', 'capital', 'debt', 'instalment', 'payment', 'receipt', and 'market'. This materialistic policy of acquisition not only belies the mythical cultural basis of imperialism — to which religion is party — but betrays its own people by undermining its productive base, stealing 'metal from the spade' and seeking 'what they could find at home'. The accusation that the imperial system is 'a cheat' relates more to a betrayal of the population of the conquering state than to the peoples it conquers.

This newly founded Indian empire then invades China, threatening American interests, and the two nations become embroiled in a battle fought on Chinese soil:

> As tho' ambition baffled nature's laws,
> A consequence without apparent cause!
> When Seric bounds the Hindhû ranks invade,
> America must hurl a mad crusade,
> And in that hour the seed began to sow,
> Which ripened to the Union's overthrow.
> Encountering hosts, in plains of rich Cathay,
> At once their quarrel, battle-field, and prey,
> Gallantly burn, heroically slay!
> But each, of course, would help the poor Chinese:
> Those kill to civilise — to save them, these.
> The Hindhû masters of the land remain,
> In battle vanquished, victors in campaign. (III, 24–37)

The first couplet of this quotation satirizes the kind of faux naivety which is surprised that imperial wars must so often be fought. But this is no war of liberation; it is a conflict between empires, similar to the one the world would witness two years after 'The New World' was published when the Crimean War would involve the British, the French, the Ottoman, and the Russian Empires.[44] Jones also satirizes the ostensible military missions of the two imperial powers, who both claim to be aiding

'THE NEW WORLD, A DEMOCRATIC POEM' (1851)   143

the 'poor Chinese'. The American forces score a victory over the Indians but are unable to oust them from China. Ultimately, India retains possession of its Chinese territories and while the conflict weakens America and leaves it vulnerable to the slave rebellion detailed in Canto I, the Indian empire is apparently further consolidated by the victory and 'spread[s] east and west their vast dominion wide' (III, 38).

However, the Indian defeat in battle to American forces is likened to the Roman experiences at Capua and Cannae in the Second Punic War in the third century BC, when defeats inflicted by Hannibal's forces weakened Rome. Externally, the Indian empire becomes stretched to the point where its hold on territories becomes tenuous, 'diluted laws with weakened pulses act' (III, 46), and within India, political manoeuvrings by ambitious nobles begin to encourage sedition. As outlying territories sense India's weakness, they gather around its border readying for invasion:

> Around the expiring realm the vultures wait;
> The North knocks loudly at its Alpine gate;
> Siberian tribes and Tahta nations come, —
> The Goths and Huns of Oriental Rome, —
> And westward, rising like the unruly Frank,
> Impatient Persia presses at its flank. (III, 54–59)

The effect of these threats of invasion foment political instability within the realm, which has seen a succession of monarchs fail to control the destabilizing machinations of a self-seeking class of nobles and courtiers: 'Full long on mischief and rebellion bent, | Those faithless lords had harboured discontent' (III, 64–65). After a sustained period of treachery, espionage, and religious persecution enforced by the established Church ('Thus churchcraft guards pollution's foulest shrine', II, 92), a long-reigning, despised monarch dies and is succeeded by his weak, but good-hearted son ('Nature denied him health and strength, but gave | A generous spirit, and a patience brave', II, 104–05). This youthful king attempts to liberalize the laws of the nation, and for a time becomes popular amongst the people, and thus gains tacit support from the nobles. But as the economy starts to falter, the nobles seize their chance to undermine the monarch and blame his policies for the widespread unemployment and poverty that blights the nation:

> 'If burdens crush ye, and if bread is high,
> 'It is the King — the King's to blame!' they cry.
> 'If famine threats, work lacks, and wages fall,
> 'The King, the King alone, is cause of all!'
> Thus prejudice allots their several shares, —
> Whatever's wrong is his, what's right is theirs.
> Hard fate of those who overstep the times!
> His very virtues are imputed crimes. (III, 50–57)

In Jones's sympathy for this king it is possible to detect vestiges of his former monarchism colouring the republicanism that the poem as a whole appears to espouse. The fact that the figure of a benevolent monarch intrudes into what declares itself to be a 'democratic poem' might be excused as highlighting the random governmental results of aristocratic primogeniture, but the narrative of this young 'gentle-hearted' king has even more prominence in the poem than that of the old general. A biographical interpretation of this section of the poem might conclude that Jones's own anxieties regarding political leadership inform its narrative. Jones was certainly very young to hold the political responsibilities of Chartist leadership which became even more concentrated after his release from prison in 1850. The final couplet of the above stanza might also be read as referring to the Chartist defeat following the Kennington Common mass meeting of 10 April 1848, after which Jones became acutely aware that the effect of political action is largely dependent on its timing. Indeed, almost the final message of the prose introduction of 'The New World' is for those who seek freedom to avoid the temptation to 'overstep the times'. The typographical framing of his key phrase in this statement is emphatic:

> A stage on the road to freedom was never yet overleaped with impunity. The secret of victory is —
>
> NOTHING BEFORE ITS TIME.
>
> The test of the statesman is to know when that time has come — the duty of the people is, never to let it pass.[45]

Jones's historical purview insists on the properly ordered occurrence of prescribed political phases before the eventual achievement of equality and liberty. Although this part of the future Indian national narrative is intended loosely to represent the events of the English Civil War (1642–51) — Charles I ascended the English throne in 1625 at the age of twenty-four and his reign was beset by religious and economic arguments — the sequential nature of Jones's view of history imbues the text with multiple layers of meaning.

When the decisive battle of the inevitable civil war approaches, the nobles who seek to overthrow the king assemble their army from the poorest sections of society and emphasize to their troops the social difference between themselves and their aristocratic enemy:

> Then grimly smiled those traitors, to behold
> The glittering vestures and the burnished gold,
> The pampered chargers, and the riders proud —
> And pressed the contrast on the famished crowd. (III, 241–44)

However closely these events are modelled on the events of the English Civil War, Jones's obvious sympathy for the monarch in this narrative is remarkable given his avowed republicanism at this stage of his career. The loyalty of the king's forces in the face of their defeat provides an interesting contrast to the eventual capitulation of the British forces described in the previous canto:

> In vain his gallant few their utmost dare:
> His farewell sign commands them to forbear.
> In sad submission droops each fated head,
> They sheathe their swords, and die by law instead. (III, 274–77)

Although he condemns the institution of monarchy ('For every king is a rebel to his God', III, 297), Jones appears to retain an affection for the kind of benevolent nobility which also features in 'The Two Races', even as he recognizes its unsuit-

'The New World, a Democratic Poem' (1851) 145

ability as a system of governance ('Virtue on thrones is like a pearl misplaced', III, 295). Jones's message seems to be that while monarchy is a system which must be overthrown, such an action is counter-productive if the system of government replacing it is not for the greater good. Although the path of history will, through the relentless march of social progression, generally ascend towards greater freedoms and prosperity, this particular *coup d'état* is an unfortunate occurrence which appears to be almost instantly regretted by the bulk of the population:

> Still with the millions shall the right abide,
> The living interest on the victim's side —
> Strange balance, that, 'twixt sympathy and fate,
> Atones in pity what it wronged in hate!
> The self-same king, in different times of men,
> Had been, their martyr now, their idol then;
> And History, as the record sad she keeps,
> Traces the mournful truth, and writing weeps. (III, 302–09)

The wording of this quotation again throws into question the true extent of Jones's republicanism as he suggests that, within a different set of political circumstances, the king would have been the people's 'idol'. Indeed, the liberalizing policies of the king which initially gained him popular support prove to be the historical basis of real freedoms gained for the nation in subsequent sections of the poem. The final lines of this canto present the king as a martyr, whose unknowing reward is the eventual benefit his legacy bestows on his people:

> Then not in vain that gallant life has flown;
> A glorious seed that gentle hand has sown:
> Bread on those troubled waters, dark and dim,
> Fruit for long years — tho' not returned to him. (III, 314–17)

Canto IV

The fourth canto deals with the transition to a constitutional monarchy and the rise of a new economic class based on commerce and industry. The 'peasants' find that the overthrow of monarchic feudalism brings no increase in freedom or wealth. Living conditions for the bulk of the population do not improve and an attempt at further rebellion leads to the restoration of a weakened monarchy which accelerates the growth of a new social strata:

> Wondering they wake to find in trust betrayed,
> 'Tis but a change of tyrants they have made.
> Indignant fury drives the half-armed throng —
> The hour has passed — the nobles prove too strong:
> Their steel-clad phalanx rides the peasant down,
> And haughty lords restore a tinsel crown.
>
> For once their feudal pride mistook its course:
> Kings find in cunning what they lose in force,
> And, liberal grown, their ounce of freedom sell
> To all who can — afford to pay them well:
> On golden stilts above the trampled mass
> From royal weakness rose THE MIDDLE-CLASS. (IV, 17–28)

While the political upheavals of a future Indian state related here bear strong similarities to the events of the English Restoration of Charles II in 1660, and the subsequent Glorious Revolution of 1688, it should be recognized that Jones leaves himself enough narrative leeway to indicate a universal trend of historical progression based on the tensions between economic classes. Any attempt to read this as an accurate analogue of English history would be hampered by the omission of an adequate emphasis on the part played in these narratives by religion. Although the formation of a state Church is indicated near the beginning of the third canto (III, 3–8) there is no representation of equivalent trends of Puritanism, Dissent, or the part that the tensions between Roman Catholicism and Protestantism played in the tumultuous years of the English seventeenth century. Organized religion is largely relegated to the role of an ideologically manipulative supporter of whichever economic institution holds sway at any given historical point. Almost all of the action in 'The New World' is rooted in the oppositions between economic classes, whether those classes are created by social development within societies or — as in the case of American slaves, Indian and African colonial subjects, or Jews — racial difference. In the language used in 'The New World' Paul identifies 'a more independent ideological stance on Jones's part in relation to the anti-colonial struggle than that of other Chartist radicals and even of Marx himself, who saw indigenous peoples mainly as victims of imperialism'.[46] But despite the absence of an explicitly Marxist economic critique, it is Jones's identification of the economic basis of all human relations regardless of ethnicity — indicated by his loose mapping of English historical cycles onto what would be regarded contemporaneously as a racial 'other' — which is one of the most notable features of the poem.

Jones characterizes the triumvirate of the monarchy, the landed aristocracy, and the mercantile class as a 'three headed hydra' (IV, 31) of which only the first head has been destroyed. The remaining two factions begin a battle for political and economic supremacy in which the rest of the population become pawns and victims:

> Between the hydra-heads contention rose,
> And landed idlers feared their monied foes.
> Each strikes at each — but every blow that parts
> Is aimed with poor men's arms thro' poor men's hearts.
> Those claim protection from their ill-won store;
> These seek full liberty to plunder more;
> Those drive up rents and bread, while these fore-stall,
> And pare the wages when the markets fall.
> Those throw down cottages, and clear a space
> For grazing-farm, and pleasure-park, and chase;
> These to the rattling mill the throng entice,
> And labour's surfeit brings down labour's price. (IV, 37–48)

The phrase 'the rattling mill' denotes the first appearance in the narrative of the Industrial Revolution as the peasants and members of the working class find themselves caught between twin monopolies over agriculture and industry. The moral equivalence suggested here between the aristocracy and the middle class provides an interesting contrast to Jones's explicit appeal to the aristocracy for help in defeating the capitalist hegemony in 'The Two Races'. It is significant that the latter poem was written in the first months of Jones's Chartist involvement, when he was still trading on the mystique of his aristocratic connections, and before the experience of prison and political developments including the failure of the Land Plan drove him further to the left within the Chartist movement.

The eventual middle-class victory enacted through legislation rather than physical battle is justified to the suffering working class in purely economic terms:

> 'If burdens crush ye, and if bread is high,
> 'The landlords — landlords are to blame!' they cry.
> 'Their vile monopolies, that feudal wreck!
> 'Restrict our trade, and thus your labour check.' (IV, 55–58)

Within this representation of the early- to mid-nineteenth-century political debates between the Tory party and the Whigs regarding free trade Jones characterizes the prevailing Whig argument as a 'dangerous half-truth' (IV, 61), indicating the complexity of contemporary economic debate with regard to the creation of employment. However, the end of the age of aristocracy ('Down sinks the noble! — down the scutcheons fall! | Death strikes the castle — ruin wraps the hall!', IV, 65–66) brings no economic relief to the poor and mass agitation brings a tightening of legal constraints against all forms of protest:

> The judge decides, from high judicial seat,
> The right to speak, petition, and to meet:
> 'To meet — in every public space, no doubt!
> 'If the police don't choose to keep you out.
> 'If at such meeting you may chance to be,
> 'And some one something says to somebody,
> 'Tho' not one syllable you may have heard,
> 'You're guilty, all the same, of every word!
> 'You may petition, if you like, the Throne —
> 'But then the ministers decide alone;
> 'Or Parliament — and, if they won't attend,
> 'What would you more? — the matter's at an end! (IV, 141–52)

Of course, in relation to recent political events involving the Chartists in Great Britain and Jones in particular these lines have special resonance, but as a representation of increased judicial control over working-class democratic movements they have relevance across Europe. There are long sections of 'The New World' where Jones fails to specify the location of the action, and references to governmental institutions including 'Parliament' make it easy to forget that this is still a projected Indian state that Jones is writing about. This lack of specificity creates a spatial and temporal indeterminacy similar to that employed in Shelley's visionary poems 'The Mask of Anarchy' (1819) and 'The Triumph of Life' (1822), although in the former, the Romantic poet figures real contemporary characters such as Lord Eldon (1751–1838) and Lord Castlereagh (1769–1822) through personified abstractions of, respectively, 'Fraud' and 'Murder'.

It is through the device of personified abstraction that Jones gives air to the voice of 'Economy'. Given that Jones has now ostensibly reached the 'present' in his alternative future history, it is little surprise that he finds material enough for more detailed descriptions of the economic and political landscape he portrays. In this section his target is laissez-faire economics and what would in twentieth-century America be termed 'the trickle-down effect':

> From shallow premise inference false would wrench,
> And spouts Economy from solemn bench:
> 'I drink champagne — that gives the poor man bread —
> 'The grower takes our calico instead.
> 'I keep my hunter — why that brow of gloom?
> 'Does not my hunter also keep his groom?' (IV, 171–76)

Jones, who had once shared O'Connor's Land Plan vision of the working class as smallholders effectively opting out of the economic system, has now developed a more sophisticated conception of the relation between production and consumption, and questions the idea that the financial well-being of the working class depends on the relative wealth of the middle class. He suggests that part of the problem of faltering production relates to the maintenance of an artificial service economy created by the wealthy:

> That idle luxury turns, in evil hour,
> To unproductive toil productive power;
> And coachmaker and lacquey, horse and groom,
> Impair production while they still consume. (IV, 197–200)

This satellite economy based on servility and acquiescence distorts the true relationship between production and consumption and contributes to the instability of a system in which the working class is always the victim. It is not long before the ruling class attempt to rectify an untenable economic system by means of a Malthusian solution:

> Then cried those subtle gold kings, one and all;
> 'The cure is found! THE COUNTRY is too small!
> 'Here's not enough your greedy maws to sate:
> 'TO SHIP! TO SHIP! you Paupers: emigrate!
> 'We'll grant free passage! aye! We'll even pay!
> 'So that you'll but be still — and go away!' (IV, 205–10)

Jones was consistently sceptical about the benefits of emigration and deportation on both economic and moral grounds. His prose articles in *Notes to the People* reveal an explicit link made between emigration policies, the economic health of Great Britain, and the disastrous results of exporting to the colonies the nation's 'most dangerous and discontented spirits'.[47] In an article entitled 'Our Colonies' Jones also argues that those who can afford to emigrate without economic incentive from government are often those who comprise the economic lifeblood of the country:

> If it is to be done by individual enterprise then it cannot be the poor who emigrate. Those cannot emigrate who cannot pay their passage out! It is those who still possess something worth saving from the general wreck, who emigrate. It is the so-called bone, marrow, and sinew of the country, it is the small floating capital that emigrates — it is those who still have something left, flying away from responsibility of supporting those who have nothing at all.[48]

'The New World, a Democratic Poem' (1851)   149

By encouraging the exportation of the most morally degraded, and the most economically productive, emigration damages the health of both of the nations involved
and contributes to general economic decline. Jones extends this analysis to a
general critique of the British colonial system, and argues the case for what partially
developed in the twentieth century — an economic commonwealth of nations:

> The entire system of colonial government is an error. Some nations think, if
> they were to lose their colonies, those colonies being great and flourishing,
> they would lose some tangible advantage. Nothing of the sort. Every
> advantage derived from a colony would be derived from a free state — be it
> commercial or otherwise — and the disadvantages, the expense, risk, anxiety
> and responsibility attaching to colonial and distant dependencies, would be
> removed. England would derive more benefit from a free state of Hindostan, a
> free Republic of Australia, than she does from abject, crouching, or rebelling
> nations — and she would no longer stand before the world as a sanctimonious
> murderess, painting the profaned cross with the blood of every nation she is
> strong enough to massacre.[49]

In the future Indian state of 'The New World' these economic and moral
arguments are expressed by a working class which, hearing tales of unproductive
soil and economic deprivation from those who have emigrated, refuses to leave
the country. Jones then details how the social unrest caused by economic decline
is controlled by a judicial system which closely resembles Foucault's conception
of a 'carceral continuum'. The ruling class, employing increasingly sophisticated
methods of social control, hold back from deploying troops ('Their power is girt by
no preventive show', IV, 151) and rely on increased judicial powers and a complex
system of human management and containment to do the work of the military:

> With humble names their strongholds they conceal:
> Jail, prison, work house, barrack, and bastile.
> Beggar and vagrant there they hold secure,
> Thro' that long battle of the rich and poor. (IV, 257–60)

The trigger for the eventual breaking-point in this class confrontation is the spectre
of mass starvation, and Jones's figuring of Ireland through the representation of
Ceylon as a large island off the coast of the Indian subcontinent is used as an
extreme example of the immoral nature of the capitalist economic system. Jones
provides an accurate analogue to English attitudes to the Irish Famine when
he describes the Indian state's shock at the scale of the human tragedy on its
geographical doorstep:

> In Ceylon's neighbouring isle a million died!
> Unburied corpses choked the charnel-side.
> One year's death-harvest, reaped by Famine's scythe,
> While Mammon laughed, and Moloch's heart was blithe.
> For once their very murderers stand aghast!
> They die too openly, and fall too fast.
> As vultures round the quivering carcase draw,
> More thick they pour the carrion-birds of war. (IV, 263–70)

There is a hint of Jones's awareness of the partially autonomous nature of the economic system which produces the famine in the contrast between the relative reactions of the personified abstractions he invokes and the actual human agents responsible. 'Mammon' (materialism) may laugh, and the heart of 'Moloch' (sacrifice) may be 'blithe', but the 'very murderers stand aghast'. This representation serves to highlight the fact that the capitalist system, once set in train, is capable of operating without conscious human agency — it is essentially out of control — and indicates that Jones believes the ruling class are not fully aware of the moral implications of their actions. Nevertheless, after its initial shock the Indian government sends troops to Ceylon to quell the rebellion caused by the famine: 'Their stalwart few, well-armed, and better trained, | Crushed the emaciate million that remained' (IV, 281–82). In the aftermath of the disaster, the millenarian soul-searching in the English press that followed in the wake of the Irish Famine is reflected as the Indian government searches for a scapegoat on which to blame its mismanagement. The canto ends with a denial of responsibility on the part of the government as divine will is cited as the cause of the famine:

> If famine scourges, and if bread is high,
> 'Tis God! 'tis God Himself's the cause!' they cry.
> 'Made we the land too little, or too bare?'
> 'Did we create you, or confine you there?'
> 'Did we the harvest blight? the increase stay?
> 'To church! to church! you sinners ! fast and pray!' (IV, 293–98)

In *The Times* of 9 January 1847 it was reported that two days before, at a meeting of Cavan landlords in central Ireland, Lord Farnham had stated that:

> It has pleased Divine Providence, by destroying the potato crop (the main support not only of the labouring classes, but also of most of the tenant-farmers), to plunge the population of Ireland into the most dreadful state of destitution and want and (in many parts of the kingdom) of actual famine; which, though it presses most in the first instances upon the lower orders, must inevitably affect every class of the community.[50]

Because the initial cause of the Famine was a potato blight that occurred Europe-wide, this attitude of divine causality was not confined to the ruling class, but it was nevertheless used to deflect attention away from the British government's financial and commercial mismanagement which contributed to the severity of the disaster and the inadequacy of subsequent relief policies. Jones's darkly satirical treatment of such attitudes through transfiguration from Ireland to Ceylon is mirrored by the work of his Irish contemporary, James Clarence Mangan. Mangan's 'Siberia' (1846) transposes the experience of Ireland to the wastelands of Northern Russian territories in order to defamiliarize the horror of starvation for his readers. The poetic device of geographical displacement provides an element of detachment that can serve as an emotional buffer — enabling the author to approach the issues of a tragedy which was then still unfolding — and as an illuminating alternative perspective:

> In Siberia's wastes
> The ice-wind's breath
> Woundeth like the toothéd steel;

'The New World, a Democratic Poem' (1851)   151

> Lost Siberia doth reveal
> Only blight and death.
>
> Blight and death alone.
> No Summer shines.
> Night is interblent with Day.
> In Siberia's wastes alway
> The blood blackens, the heart pines. (ll. 1–10)[51]

Mangan died of causes including malnutrition in 1849, while Jones was still in prison, but both poets shared the sense that domestic political issues could be viewed profitably through the perspective of another country. Mangan's poetic vision, while more opaque and metaphorical than that of Jones, nevertheless reaches for the same illumination through distortion, and both turned time and again in their poetry to the tragedy afflicting Ireland around the middle of the century.

Canto v

At seventy-six lines, the fifth canto of 'The New World' is just over a quarter of the length of its predecessor, and its detailing of a peaceful working-class revolution in the imagined future Indian state might be considered something of an anti-climax in dramatic terms. However, it is Jones's intention to show that the 'people' need only have the will to assemble as one body in order to take control of the country. This was an argument he iterated many times in his *Northern Star* poetry and which was consistently referred to in Shelley's later, popular verse. The canto begins with the natural imagery associated with the pathetic fallacy which has been used previously in the poem, but the coming political transformation is here attributed to a divine power:

> On that dread eve, ere God His deluge hurled,
> Unnatural stillness wrapped the wondering world.
> The Almighty threat could take no fuller form;
> Unearthly calm foretold unearthly storm. (v, 1–4)

The 'unnatural stillness' and the 'unearthly calm' relate to the identification of divine agency, raising the origins of the political upheaval to a transcendental level. Like the expulsion of the British from India, this political action is sanctioned or even instigated by God, and its poetic approach is markedly different from the accounts of political machinations which characterize the narratives of the civil war and the political defeat of the aristocracy by the middle class. In this tense, pre-revolutionary phase, while the rich arrogantly assume that the poor have been successfully repressed ('those who live most guilty prove most blind', v, 22), the voice of the state Church is given its longest speech in the whole poem. A religious justification for political quiescence is expressed, which is clearly intended as a satirical representation of Anglican attitudes to mid-nineteenth-century radical agitation:

> The Priest, more timid, pours fresh floods of lies,
> And doubly liberal grows, — of Paradise!
> 'In pain and poverty contented rest!

152 'The New World, a Democratic Poem' (1851)

> 'Whom God chastises most, he loves the best.
> 'Nor envy those to worldly treasures given:
> 'Leave earth to them, and take your share — in heaven!
> ''Tis true, the Scriptures of the poor man speak —
> 'Of lands, goods, freedom, ravished from the weak —
> 'Of tyrants crushed — and peoples' fetters rent —
> 'But all that's only spiritually meant!' (v, 29–38)

Despite this intensification of religious propaganda, the revolution occurs, and its organization is presented as self-generating and autonomous. Although the revolutionary force is described as 'generalled of God', which might indicate divine intervention rather than mere moral sanction, read in the context of the structure of the whole poem, the actions of the revolutionaries play out a defining scene representing an epiphany of class consciousness:

> At last, when least expected friends and foes,
> Grandly and silently the People rose!
> None gave the word! — they came, together brought
> By full maturity of ripened thought.
> Truth sought expression: — there the masses stood,
> In living characters of flesh and blood!
> Each foot at once the destined pathway trod; —
> An army raised and generalled of God! (v, 43–50)

Situated somewhere between conscious actors, pawns in an historical chess game, and foot-soldiers of a divine army, the nature of the revolutionaries' agency is difficult to define accurately. It is significant that no leader is identified and that they are not represented in this canto by any poetic voice. Their vocal silence is counterbalanced, however, by the basis of language in their appearance as 'living characters', perhaps indicating a greater awareness of the potency of literary culture as an instigator of revolution. The fact that they are brought together by the 'full maturity of ripened thought' suggests that a self-generated sophistication of culture has resulted in increased agency.

As an analogue of Jones's attempts within the Chartist movement and through his poetry to engage with the issue of Ireland, and the Irish populations in England and Ireland, the oppressed and decimated people of Ceylon play a decisive role in the Indian proletarian revolution. They are characterized as a ghostly presence which connotes both the impossibility of fully suppressing a nation and the inevitability of political vengeance for historical wrongs:

> Then erst was shown how vain embattled might,
> Whene'er the People will — and will the Right!
> They marched unarmed — yet no one dared resist:
> Camps, Courts, and Councils melted like a mist,
> And when amid their multitudes were seen
> The saddening bands of Ceylon's island green,
> Then from those kings of gold the courage fled,
> Like murder's when it thinks it meets the dead!
> 'Have spectres risen from the grave?' they cried,
> 'A nation comes — and yet a nation died!' (v, 51–60)

The fact that the multitude marches unarmed clearly echoes Shelley's vision of a successful passive resistance in 'The Mask of Anarchy', and the reference to 'Camps, Courts and Councils melt[ing] like a mist' owes much to the decisive moment in Shelley's poem:

> 'With folded arms and steady eyes
> And little fear, and less surprise
> Look upon them as they slay
> Till their rage has died away.'
>
> 'Then they will return with shame
> To the place from which they came,
> And the blood thus shed will speak
> In hot blushes on their cheek.' (ll. 337–44)[52]

Though perhaps for fear of discouraging the use of passive resistance in his own followers, the antagonists in Jones's poem do not 'slay', and the revolution is entirely peaceful, both sides' actions driven by the inevitability of historical progression:

> Nor cheered, nor shouted that majestic force;
> It moved, it acted, like a thing of course;
> No blood, no clamour, no tumultuous hate;
> As death invincible, and calm as fate! (v, 61–64)

And in keeping with Jones's increasing awareness of the need to define the nature of the aftermath of revolution, there are no retributive acts carried out by the victorious multitude. Far from the actions of an unruly mob, the revolutionaries are portrayed as capable of forgiving historical wrongdoing, confident in their ability to take control of their own republic without interference:

> While prostrate mercy raised her drooping head,
> Thus came the People, thus the gold-kings fled;
> None fought for them — none spoke: they slunk away,
> Like guilty shadows at appearing day;
> They were not persecuted — but forgot;
> Their place was vacant, and men missed them not.
> And Royalty, that dull and outworn tool!
> Bedizened doll upon a gilded stool —
> The seal that Party used to stamp an Act,
> Vanished in form, as it had long in fact.
> All wondered 'twas so easy, when 'twas o'er, —
> And marvelled it had not been done before. (v, 65–76)

The revolution is conducted peacefully and its aftermath is characterized by a lack of retribution which not only reflects the moral rectitude of the actors, but the naturalness of their actions. The former capitalist ruling class is simply forgotten and, significantly, its 'place was vacant': the sequence of succession of controlling hegemonies through the ages of feudalism, mercantilism, and industrialization is finally broken. This breaking of the chains of history is symbolized by the final disappearance of the aristocratic vestige, which Jones recognizes as a remaining element of ideological influence even as its actual power diminishes through the ages. The last lines' iteration of the ease of the political transformation once more implies that only the will of the people is wanting if they wish to attain representation and power.

Canto VI

The sixth canto begins by characterizing Europe at this point in history as 'free', presumably as a result of the kind of social upheavals experienced by India, but suggests that the continent's expansionist past has returned to haunt it in the shape of an African invasion:

> Free Europe, placid in her later day,
> While changing empires round her fleet away,
> Marks these enact, in sober pity's mood,
> The same career of folly site pursued.
> Nations buy wisdom with the coin of years,
> And write the book of history with their tears.
> Smarting no more from olden error's stings,
> That worse than Egypt's plagues, the plague of kings,
> Now had she dwelt for aye. secure from ill,
> But an old curse was cleaving to her still. (VI, 1–10)

A 'placid', republican Europe is visited by the 'old curse' of its slave-trading past despite having bought 'wisdom with the coin of years'. In this stanza Jones diverts from the rest of the poem's economic determinism in favour of an historical karmic balance — the pan-African invasion of Europe appears to have no political motive other than vengeance:

> Deep in the burning south a cloud appears,
> The smouldering wrath of full four thousand years,
> Whatever name caprice of history gave,
> Moor, Afrit, Ethiop, Negro, still meant slave!
> But from the gathering evil springs redress,
> And sin is punished by its own excess.
> Algeria's Frank, and boor of Table-rock, —
> The grafts of science on the savage stock
> The ravished slave of Egypt's Nubian host;
> And fierce bloodtraders of the golden coast,
> In East and West that thirst for vengeance wake,
> Which North and South instruct them how to slake;
> Their barbarous strength with Europe's lore recruit,
> The seed of future power, and fatal fruit. (VI, 11–24)

In contrast to the doubling of India with Britain in the earlier sections of the poem (which might be seen, at the very least, as an admittance of political equivalence), Africans are represented here as a racial 'other'. Jones is sympathetic to their historical plight, but represents their political actions through conventional Victorian orientalist tropes which deny them a coherent political agency. In marked contrast to the political sophistication of the projected process of Indian democratization in the previous canto, the action detailed in the sixth canto appears to be simply a violent uprising against centuries of oppression, devoid of the intellectual justification of class consciousness. And yet although some of the terms employed in this section ('savage stock', 'barbarous strength') are at the least enlightened end of the stereotypical spectrum, Jones still hints at an incisive deconstruction of Western nomenclature in the lines 'Whatever name caprice of history gave | Moor, Afrit, Ethiop, Negro, still meant slave!'. Recognition that the meaning of names in these circumstances is largely a European construction leads to a homogenization that paradoxically highlights the experience of the individual through the emphasis on the word 'slave'.

Even while taking account of the obvious difference between mid-nineteenth-century and twenty-first-century conceptions of ethnic representation, Jones's treatment of Africa and Africans in this canto might be characterized as oscillating between prejudice and enlightenment. While implied political solidarity between African subjects and the European working class is indicated in the lines 'Thro' mine, and field, and factory, dragged by turns, — | Misfortune's colleges where misery learns' (VI, 29–30), the dehumanizing trope of the individual white subject enveloped by the 'dark continent' is used to lend dramatic weight to the impending invasion of Europe:

> Pale rose an anxious face from Niger's wave,
> And murdered Park one groan of anguish gave;
> While distant ocean, starting at the knell,
> Washed from its sands, the letters L.E.L. (VI, 37–40)

References to Mungo Park (1771–1806), the Scottish explorer who died on the River Niger, and the writer Letitia Elizabeth Landon (1802–38), who died of suspected suicide just two months after arriving on the Cape Coast with her new husband, serve to reinforce contemporary mystifications of Africa and present it as inherently dangerous to Europeans. The African invasion of Europe becomes a nightmarish inversion of Europe's colonization and enslavement of its neighbouring continent.

Reflecting the epic nature of the poem, but also highlighting the historical exploitation of Africa by Europeans, the African invasion sweeps through histori-cally significant locations including Carthage, Sidon, and Rome. When it reaches Spain, that country's role in South and Central American exploitation is evoked and vicarious revenge is wreaked by the invaders:

> Now, dreadful ravage! from the bubbling main
> Bursts the black horror on the coasts of Spain.
> Laugh Mexico! and clap thy hands, Peru!
> Old Montezuma! break thy charnel through.
> Relight your lamps, poor Vestals of the Sun!
> That you may see Pizarro's work outdone! (VI, 65–70)

Paul has seized on phrases including 'the black horror' and 'the sable legions' (VI, 74) as indicative of a stereotypical figuring that taints what is otherwise a largely 'radically innovative' text.[53] And yet he also insists that despite this evidence of conventional Victorian orientalism, Jones exhibits a more 'ideologically independent stance' with regard to colonial subjects than many other nineteenth-century observers. While Jones's language occasionally appears to indicate a restricting awareness of racial otherness, the narrative direction of his epic and its treatment of Africans and also of Indians suggests a global inclusivity that overrides issues of ethnicity and national difference. This overall effect pervades despite the insidiously hierarchical racial determinism hinted at by the relative political maturity of different ethnicities in the poem.

The African invasion of Europe effectively peters out when it reaches Germany, whose relative lack of involvement in the slave trade as a nation appears to be a contributory factor in the cessation of hostilities. Other factors seem to be the finite nature of vengeance as a motive, a recognition on Africa's part that it has won liberty, and the mysterious intervention of divine will:

> White Europe gasps before the o'erwhelming blaze,
> But guiltless Germany the torrent stays,
> Compelled beneath the Eternal will Divine,
> To spend its force at Danube, Alps, and Rhine.
> As some volcano's once o'erflowing fires,
> Mid inward turbalence their wrath expires;
> On Afric's altered shores the thunders cease,
> For freedom, Heaven's firstborn, still heralds peace. (VI, 89–96)

Jones's depiction of a revenge-motivated war between Africa and Europe contradicts the rest of the poem's insistence on economic causes as the determining factor in political relations. And in keeping with this canto's divergence from previous themes in the work the apparently arbitrary end to the invasion instigates the first appearance in the poem of what might be thought of as a miraculous occurrence. The canto ends as the advent of peace is accompanied by a divinely sanctioned surge of Saharan groundwater that transforms North Africa's desert wastes into a fertile plain:

> The thick branched waters, beating from below,
> Throb to the surface, and resume their flow.
> Bound thro' Saharan sand creative springs,
> The sheltering palm its fruitful shadow flings,
> Teems with green life the rich luxuriant sod,
> And happy millions hymn the grace of God. (VI, 101–06)

Canto VII

The seventh canto, at sixty-eight lines the shortest of the poem, amplifies the poem's message of political redress, maturity, and fulfilment by predicting the return of the Jews to Israel. This commonly-cited Biblical trope is envisaged as occurring in a peaceful manner and with multilateral international approval:

> Now to the seat of David's royal muse
> Traditionary instinct draws the Jews.
> Two thousand years recall the exiles home,
> From each new Egypt, Babylon, and Rome.
> Needs but a march — Jerusalem is won!
> Bequeathed by History to Misfortune's son.
> No prior owners claim the invader's sword,
> The bride awaits her long-expected lord. (VII, 1–8)

'The New World, a Democratic Poem' (1851)   157

The marital metaphor involving the physical land and its estranged people contains within it the promise of repopulation not just by emigration but by a celebratory conception. By feminizing Israel and comparing the return of the Jews to marital consummation Jones suggests the legal sanctioning of the rebuilding of the Jewish nation in defiance of Islam's own claims to Jerusalem's sanctity, which he dismisses with the phrase 'no prior owners'. This is a typological appropriation of a Biblical promise finding its fulfilment through an ostensibly political process. Political actions receive the seal of approval from natural divinity and a conflation of political and religious narrative emerges. Rejecting the violent imagery of the Old Testament, or the apocalyptic visions of Revelations, Jones depicts the return of the Jews to Israel in much the same manner as he describes the peaceful proletarian Indian revolution in Canto v. The inevitability of the event precludes any protest or resistance to its process:

> No crimes revolting now their reign prepare —
> A heritage, and not a spoil, to share.
> No prophet host, with borrowed jewels left,
> Learn from their priest that God Commands a theft
> No wonder-works surpassing sorcerers' tricks,
> A barbarous tribe's untamed obedience fix.
> No Moses, with tired arms, and bated breath,
> Sits praying to his God for blood and death.
> No tarrying sun prolongs unnatural stay,
> That murders work may win in added day.
> Gladly and calmly comes, in solemn mirth,
> The great procession from the ends of earth.
> From town to town still swells the gathering mass,
> And wondering nations bless them as they pass. (VII, 9–22)

The representation of the reversal of the diasporic process avoids a messianic tone by insisting on the serene nature of the return, and yet the sense that this is a fulfilment of an ancient prophecy is never lost. The presence of a prophet-figure such as Moses may be deemed unnecessary, but in the particular mythopoeic frame that Jones has constructed, the fact that a largely political anti-type has emerged from a largely religious type is an entirely natural outcome.

The return of the Jews becomes the inspiration for a fundamental shift in human relations that reaches into the sphere of gender politics. Although equal political rights for women was stated as a philosophically desirable goal by some Chartists, its potential complication of the goal of the 'one man, one vote' platform precluded its insertion in the original Charter drawn up by the London Working Men's Association in 1837. Here Jones predicts the achievement of equal rights by women as a natural consequence of a worldwide move towards greater equality and political justice:

> The blushing maid the lover scarce can chide,
> Whose heart admits an image by her side,
> But smiles well-pleased; — for nigh the day has come,
> When country signifies a larger home;
> And when the strong the weak no more o'erbears,
> But equal rights with Man sweet Woman shares.

> E'en sparkling childhood longs with vague delight
> For broad Esdraelon's flowery pastures bright. (VII, 43–50)

As in his treatment of African subjects, the stereotypical terms Jones uses to describe the oppressed group he champions ('blushing maid', 'the weak', 'sweet Woman') have the effect of slightly undermining his overall message, but even within his own political and intellectual milieu his sentiments can be considered enlightened or even radical. Jones's political maturation after his release from prison saw a growing awareness not just of the plight of women in industrial society, but of the role women might play in the achievement of future political goals. The predominantly masculine voice of his early Chartist poetry begins to give way to a more inclusively humanistic outlook which paradoxically is perhaps closer to Shelley, the poet whose influence on those early works was the strongest. The last lines of the canto are remarkable for their relegation of the divine in relation to the human:

> See Israel then its greatest Temple raise,
> And noblest worship in its Maker's praise;
> Man is the Temple, Truth the corner-stone,
> Freedom the worship, worthy God alone.
> Rent is the veil, Deception's darkling art,
> Holy of holies is the human heart. (VII, 63–68)

God is not rejected but radically re-situated within the sphere of human priority. The insistence that God must be 'worthy' privileges human knowledge above human faith in the divine, and the sanctification of 'the human heart' allies the demystification of religious observance to the political demystification that is the poem's broader theme. Just as in previous sections, this canto ends with a radical achievement which, although situated in a specific location in the future, is transferrable in its essence across historical time and geographical boundaries.

Canto VIII

It is in the eighth and final canto that geographical boundaries actually dissolve and the utopian vision that the whole poem has been moving toward is eventually articulated. What Armstrong has termed Jones's 'non-Anglocentrism' finds full expression in the description of a pan-global society in which borders, national difference, and even linguistic barriers begin to fall away.[54] Perhaps because of a perceived lack of the taint of political history, Jones situates the beginning of the global revolution in Oceania:

> In sunny clime behold an Empire rise,
> Fair as its ocean, glorious as its skies!
> 'Mid seas serene of mild Pacific smiles —
> Republic vast of federated isles.
> Sleepy Tradition, lingering, loves to rest,
> Confiding child, on calm Tahiti's breast;
> But Science gathers, with gigantic arms,
> In one embrace, the South's diffusive charms.
> Nor there alone she rears the bright domain —
> Throughout the world expands her hallowing reign. (VIII, 1–10)

A predicted age of political and social transformation is initially couched in imperialist terms as Jones expresses his vision through a balance of images of the natural bounty of the tropics and the utilization of technology to enhance human experience. The statement that 'Science gathers [...] the South's diffusive charms' would appear to refer to the technological exploitation of natural resources, and 'sleepy Tradition' is swept aside by the ineluctable march for progress. In this new world, capitalized 'Science' is the *primum movens*, and is feminized to suggest reproductive capability. That her 'reign' is 'hallowing' rather than 'hallowed' conveys sanctity on her subjects in a democratizing process which appears to contradict Jones's former association of democracy with the anti-industrial ethos of the Land Plan. Judiciously applied, technology becomes humanity's saviour rather than its enslaver. The next lines celebrate the possibilities of science benefitting humanity by raising the standard of living, chiefly through improvements in locomotion and communication:

> Then, bold aspiring as immortal thought,
> Launched in the boundless, mounts the aeronaut;
> While o'er the earth they drive the cloudy team,
> Electric messenger, and car of steam;
> And guide and govern on innocuous course
> The explosive mineral's propelling force;
> Or, mocking distance, send, on rays of light,
> Love's homeborn smiles to cheer the wanderer's sight. (VIII, 11–18)

This concentration of technological predictions is, unsurprisingly, one of the most quoted passages of Jones's poetry. Before the works of Jules Verne (1828–1905), Edward Bellamy (1850–98), or H. G. Wells (1866–1946) Jones appears to predict fairly accurately some of the major scientific advances of the twentieth century including space travel, powered flight, the internal combustion engine, and televisual technologies (although it must be noted that steam-powered flight never really got off the ground). However, perhaps the most remarkable element of these predictions concerns the social application of technological achievement. The full implications of 'love's homeborn smiles' being sent on 'rays of light' are only being realized in the twenty-first century with the techno-social revolutions associated with the internet, social networking sites, and mobile phone technology. In the finest traditions of a science fiction genre which was yet to flourish, Jones's most telling predictions emphasized not the technologies themselves but their effect on the humans who used them.

Jones presents his vision of the future as a new Enlightenment, with humanity's increasing ability to manipulate the natural world leading not just to substantial health and economic benefits, but to the defeat of superstition and social inequalities based on geographical location:

> Mechanic power then ministers to health,
> And lengthening leisure gladdens greatening wealth:
> Brave alchemy, the baffled hope of old,
> Then forms the diamond and concretes the gold;
> No fevered lands with burning plagues expire,
> But draw the rain as Franklin drew the fire;
> Or far to mountains guide the floating hail,

> And whirl on barren rocks its harmless flail.
> Then the weird magnet, bowed by mightier spell,
> Robbed of its secret, yields its power as well;
> With steely fingers on twin dials placed,
> The thoughts of farthest friends are instant traced. (VIII, 19–30)

Medicine is mechanized, chemistry and meteorology are fully understood and mastered, and a mysterious source of energy is found contained within 'the weird magnet'. To a modern reader the final couplet of the above quotation looks like nothing less than a screenplay direction for Fritz Lang's expressionist science fiction film *Metropolis* (1927). However, reading these lines with the hindsight of over a century of predictive science fiction risks missing the cultural implications of these projected discoveries within their particular historical frame. References to 'alchemy' and Benjamin Franklin's electrical experiments evoke the spirit of the Enlightenment in an attempt to by-pass the historical effects of the industrial applications of the scientific achievements of the eighteenth century. That 'alchemy' is described as 'brave' could be read as nostalgia for purer scientific ambitions than those which led to the creation of large urban centres in Britain formed around the economically-driven technologies of mills and factories. Jones's vision might even be interpreted as a prediction of *post*-industrial society, with technological advances precluding the necessity of the degradation of mass human labour while at the same time enhancing the quality of life for all. The power to use 'mechanic power' in medicine, or to divert weather to where it is most needed, or to communicate with another consciousness via machinery, suggests the application of 'clean' technology. This relates to the modern usage of the term not just in its emphasis on environmental effects, but also in its view of technology as part of a potential shortcut to human happiness. Jones's utopia is a scientific Shangri-La.

As Jones's focus turns to the subject of epistemology, he builds a celebration of human potential from a recognition of humanity's place between two worlds that are coming to be understood — the cosmic and the microcosmic:

> Then shall be known, what fairy-lore mistaught
> When Fancy troubled Truth's instinctive thought,
> Then He who filled with life each rolling wave,
> And denizens to every dewdrop gave,
> Left not this hollow globe's in caverned space
> The only void, unpeopled dwelling-place.
> Then shall the eye, with wide extended sight,
> Translate the starry gospel of the night;
> And not as now, when narrower bounds are set,
> See, but not read the shining alphabet.
> Unheeded knowledge then shall freely scan
> That Mighty world of breathing wonders — man! (VIII, 37–48)

'Fancy' is here viewed negatively in its association with 'fairy-lore'. In this celebration of the rational and empirical world of science, the knowledge of truth is pre-existing ('instinctive thought') but obscured by the obfuscating effects of culture. The association of inevitability with pre-existing potential relates directly to the frequent reference in Jones's Chartist poetry to the demystification of political reality that smooths the path to revolution. It is suggested that the potential for the revolution of the Indian proletariat in the fifth canto is revealed rather than created: 'All wondered 'twas so easy, when 'twas o'er, — | And marvelled it had not been done before' (v, 65–76). This emphasis on revelation is continued as themes of sight and seeing are explored, with the discoveries associated with the microscope and the telescope leading to an eventual focus on humanity itself.

But characteristically for Jones, discussion of humanity leads to discussion of language, and as the focus switches from ocular to oral/aural themes, the prediction of linguistic uniformity as the basis for universal peace is expressed through biblical rather than scientific imagery:

> Those halcyon days shall witness discord cease,
> And one great family abide in peace;
> While ball and bayonet but remain to tell
> That lofty race how low their fathers fell.
> One language then endearingly extends:
> Shall tongues be strangers still, when hearts are friends?
> With Babel's curse war, wrong, and slavery came —
> Their end was shadowed in the cloven flame. (VIII, 55–62)

This identification of linguistic difference with political difference reflects Jones's internationalist proclivities but also relates to Pentecostal ideas of spiritual harmony emanating from the assumption of one shared language. While most would recognize the reference to the Tower of Babel and its association with linguistic dissonance, the phrase 'cloven flame' is a little more obscure. In his article '"In Louring Hindostan"' Paul restricts himself to a technological interpretation when he writes of 'the "cloven flame" of lightning/electricity' but the phrase has much deeper significance with regard to language and is almost certainly derived from the second chapter of Acts:[55]

> And when the day of Pentecost was fully come, they were all with one accord in one place.
>
> And suddenly there came a sound from heaven as of a rushing mighty wind, and it filled all the house where they were sitting.
>
> And there appeared unto them cloven tongues like as of fire, and it sat upon each of them.
>
> And they were all filled with the Holy Ghost, and began to speak with other tongues, as the Spirit gave them utterance.
>
> And there were dwelling at Jerusalem Jews, devout men, out of every nation under heaven.
>
> Now when this was noised abroad, the multitude came together, and were confounded, because that every man heard them speak in his own language.
>
> And they were all amazed and marvelled, saying one to another, Behold, are not all these which speak Galilaeans?
>
> And how hear we every man in our own tongue, wherein we were born? (Acts 2:2–8)

This Biblical account of an event of divinely inspired linguistic unification clearly emphasizes its miraculous quality, but also hints at the awareness of a Chomskyan 'deep structure' underlying all language and suggests a basic human 'oneness'. Jones's reference to this passage and his appropriation of its narrative suggests a similar association of linguistic and political unity, but possibly has its philological roots in the work of nineteenth-century linguistic pioneers including Jakob Grimm (1785–1863), August Schleicher (1821–68), and Wilhelm von Humboldt (1767–1835).

Whether the inspiration for Jones's vision of a unified human speech-system emerged from biblical accounts of miraculous occurrences or the nineteenth-century pre-occupation with the idea of 'Indo-European' as a common source for most European languages, it is worth speculating what form this speech might have taken. That the title of 'The New World' ostensibly conflates through word play the United States with the rest of the globe might suggest that this universal language is English. Although Jones was multi-lingual, and had written poetry in praise of the particular qualities of the German language ('Der Deutsche Sprachschaft'), he can hardly have failed to note the increasing ubiquity of spoken English as the British Empire asserted its linguistic dominance through trade, culture, and colony. His prediction of American political dominance in the early chapters would tend only to continue this philological trend. It is an essential paradox of this canto that, though many of the preceding cantos appear to contain an anti-imperialist critique, its conclusion predicts a future that appears to be dominated by a benign, idealized imperial power. Tucker applies a similar view to the whole of the poem in stronger terms that imply political hypocrisy: 'In default of a genuinely pluralist concept of internationalism, the poem's vantage on world affairs is no less imperially monocular than the system of oppression it decries'.[56] This statement would appear to take Jones's re-reading of British history through an Indian future as a direct contradiction of Armstrong's identification of Jones's 'non-Anglocentrism',[57] or Janowitz's claims for 'the globalism of the poem'.[58] However, with regard to the final canto of the poem it might be suggested that Jones uses a distorted view of the British experience as a template for a radical future world. Given that the most technologically advanced, linguistically unified imperial power at the time of writing was arguably the British Empire, the utopian vision of 'The New World' might be seen as a version of that structure (which in itself resists conclusive definition) perceived through the refractive lens of republican radicalism.

If the final canto of 'The New World' is a celebration of modernity, technology, and a vision of global unity, then it can hardly be unrelated to the cultural behemoth that was the Great Exhibition of 1851. If, as seems likely, Jones did complete his epic poem on his release from prison, and its cantos were composed consecutively, then the eighth canto would have been written during the excitement and controversy surrounding the development of Prince Albert's ambitious project. As a demonstration of capitalist, imperialist, and trade interests, Jones was fundamentally opposed to the exhibition, but his statement of this opposition in *Notes to the People* focused in part on the lack of short term economic benefits, and reveals a grudging admission of the project's aesthetic ambition:

> The Exhibition will prove a failure — however successful it may be as an artistical display and brilliant as a national pomp — yet it will prove a failure as a political and social agent. In anticipation of a glorious season, all the tradesmen of London have overstocked their shops. They think, because London will be

very full, they will have an equal increase in customers. But the fact is, that vast numbers of the resident inhabitants of London are leaving for the continent.[59]

Tellingly, this ultimately inaccurate interpretation appears in the same issue of *Notes to the People* as 'The New World'. Opposition to the Great Exhibition came from across the political spectrum. Jones's ultra-conservative godfather, King Ernst Augustus of Hanover (the erstwhile Duke of Cumberland who was also Queen Victoria's uncle) shared his antipathy towards the project, but his argument centred on popular predictions of public health disasters, workers' revolutions, or the catastrophic collapse of the Crystal Palace under the pressure of such a great weight of humanity. In a letter to Friedrich Wilhelm IV of Prussia he wrote:

> I am not easily given to panicking, but I confess to you that I would not like anyone belonging to me exposed to the imminent perils of these times. Letters from London tell me that the ministers will not allow the Queen and the great originator of this folly, Prince Albert, to be in London while the Exhibition is on.[60]

Of course, history proved the Great Exhibition to be an overwhelming, indeed some might say epoch-defining, success, and it is reasonable to assume that, despite his vocal opposition, some of the build-up to the project's ethos of technical possibility and international co-operation contributed to Jones's vision of a world enhanced by the wonders of science. Jones's embrace of technology as the potential saviour of humanity in 'The New World' reflects not just a shift from his pre-prison ambivalence towards modernity, but an uneasy alignment with patriotic and indeed capitalist celebrations of industrial progress. Jones's imagination was clearly energized by the acceleration of mid-nineteenth-century technical advances: even during his prison term petrol was first refined from crude oil ('explosive mineral's propelling force' — Canto VIII, l.16), the first glider carried a human being ('launched in the boundless' — Canto VIII, l. 12), and, slightly more prosaically, the domestic sewing machine was developed.

As the eighth canto, and the poem, draws to its close Jones's focus returns to meteorological, geographical, and then cosmic imagery in order to present a vision of a benign apocalypse where the divine and the human are melded into one. In this conception of the end of the world, humanity's moral, political, and ultimately spiritual progress is rewarded by a non-violent eschatological event which is perhaps both synchronic and diachronic in its effect:

> Then, as the waifs of sin are swept away,
> Mayhap the world may meet its destined day:
> A day of change and consummation bright,
> After its long Aurora, and old night.
> No millions shrieking in a fiery flood;
> No blasphemies of vengeance and of blood, —
> Making the end of God's great work of joy,
> And of Almighty wisdom — to destroy!
> No kindling comet — and no fading sun:
> But Heaven and Earth uniting melt in one. (VIII, 123–32)

The indeterminacy of this apocalypse is intriguing. If the 'destruction' implied is in fact assimilation between the world of the divine and the world of the human

164   'THE NEW WORLD, A DEMOCRATIC POEM' (1851)

then time ceases to be effectual, and the concept of an 'end' to humanity loses its meaning. Indeed, semantically, it is possible to read 'the end of God's great work of joy' as a reference to divine purpose rather than a conclusive event. The whole poem might be read as a series of interconnected processes of gravitational pulls towards a divine/human centre, rendering this 'end' (conclusion/purpose) as a retrospective description of the whole of human history.

Epilogue

The poem's octet epilogue is a self-reflexive emphasis of the linear nature of the narrative that returns ultimately to a celebration of the old Chartist virtues of steadfast political direction in the face of distraction and opposition. The conclusion of the poem is presented as both an arrival and an acknowledgement of the tension between the perceptions of the nature of human future as pre-ordained or created by conscious action:

> The voyage is o'er. — The adventurous flag is furled.
> The Pilot, Thought, has won the fair NEW WORLD.
> The Sailor's task is done. — The end remains.
> Must he, too, expiate his work in chains?
> But, tho' old Prejudice the path opposed,
> Tho' weeds corrupt around the vessel closed,
> Tho' discord crept among the jealous crew —
> His heart his compass, — and it told him true! (VIII, 133–40)

Although it is the apparently autonomous entity 'the Pilot, Thought' who has achieved this reifying vision of the 'new world', the 'Sailor', especially with regard to the mention of his 'chains', is clearly intended to represent Jones himself, perhaps in reference to Homeric sea-faring narratives. This is his 'voyage', and Jones's stamp on this particular vision of future history represents a unique blend of Chartist, scientific, religious, and prophetic ambition. While the visionary approach of 'The New World' might have emerged from the process of writing poems such as 'The Garden Seat' and 'The Prisoner's Dream' in prison, or the scope of its ambition might have been inspired by Thomas Cooper's *The Purgatory of Suicides*, it remains a text unique both in its statements and in its expression of those statements.

The all-encompassing nature of the narrative of 'The New World' has had the effect of allowing different readerships to see what they want to see in it. On its 1857 republication as *The Revolt of Hindostan: Or The New World*, the *Morning Post*, the conservative newspaper that printed the last of Jones's pre-Chartist poetry, interpreted the work as a message of universal peace which might have belied or indicated a softening of Jones's revolutionary instincts:

> With Mr. Jones's wild politics we have no concern. We are much better pleased to recognise him in his character of a poet, and while we disclaim sympathy with his political opinions, we are not the less willing to acknowledge the grace, beauty and elegance of his writings. Though not free from the leaven of Chartism, his present poem contains many noble sentiments, and bears the impress of a genial, loving nature, which grieves for the sorrows of humanity, and would fain leave the world better and happier than it found it.[61]

From this review we gain very little impression of the 'anti-colonial consciousness' that Paul identifies in the poem,[62] or Armstrong's view of the work as 'a measure of the extent to which the interests of middle-class poetry and poetry committed to specific political programmes and to working-class movements diverged'.[63] Read as a political treatise, 'The New World' perhaps dissolves some of Jones's more unpalatable views into religious or scientific revelation, or embraces a Shelleyan pacifism seemingly at odds with the violent imagery featured in some of his other Chartist poems. This might be related to what Janowitz identifies as the work's aspirations 'to the level of the public poem', or even to Jones's recognition that the Britain that briefly appeared to totter on the brink of revolution when he was imprisoned in the summer of 1848 was a very different place to the more confident, economically buoyant Britain of the early 1850s.[64] Jones increasingly found the need to play a long political game, and he wrote a long political poem reflecting that necessity.

Notes to Chapter 5

1. Ernest Jones, 'The New World, a Democratic Poem', in *NP* (1851), I, 1–15.
2. Gregory Claeys, *Imperial Sceptics: British Critics of Empire 1850–1920* (Cambridge: Cambridge University Press, 2010), p. 25.
3. Janowitz, *Lyric and Love in the Romantic Tradition*, p. 187.
4. Edward Royle, *Chartism* (Harlow: Longman, 1980), p. 120.
5. Mary Ashraf, in her collection, *Political Verse and Song from Britain and Ireland*, publishes three discrete sections of 'The New World' and names them 'The New World', 'Free Speech', and 'The Future'.
6. Janowitz, *Lyric and Love in the Romantic Tradition*, p. 187.
7. Vincent Geoghegan, *Utopianism and Marxism* (London: Methuen, 1987), p. 2.
8. Janowitz, *Lyric and Love in the Romantic Tradition*, p. 187.
9. Armstrong, p. 197.
10. Saville, p. 27.
11. Karl Marx, letter to Friedrich Engels, 4 November 1864, cited in Saville, p. 42.
12. Paul, p. 200.
13. G. D. H. Cole, *Socialist Thought: The Forerunners 1789–1850* (London: Macmillan, 1953), p. 151.
14. Anne Janowitz, 'Ernest Jones: Who Is He? What Has He Done?', *History Workshop Journal*, 57 (Spring 2004), 283–88 (p. 283).
15. Saville, p. 40.
16. Jones, 'The New World', in *NP* (1851), I, 1.
17. Ibid., p. 1.
18. John Newsinger, *The Blood Never Dried: A People's History of the British Empire* (London: Bookmarks, 2006), p. 7.
19. Jones, 'The New World', in *NP* (1851), I, 2.
20. Ibid., p. 1.
21. Ernest Jones, in *NP* (1852), II, 669. Jones published 'Annabel Lee' and 'The Raven' and praised Poe's poetry as 'the pre-eminently most musical of his age' (*NP* (1852), II, 669.
22. The *Red Republican* changed its name to the *Friend of the People* in December 1850.
23. Ernest Jones, 'To the British Democracy', *Friend of the People*, 24 May 1851.
24. Janowitz, *Lyric and Love in the Romantic Tradition*, p. 186.
25. Herbert Tucker, *Epic Britain's Heroic Muse 1790–1910* (Oxford: Oxford University Press, 2008), p. 361.
26. Karl Marx, cited in Simon Dentith, *Epic and Empire in Nineteenth-Century Britain* (Cambridge: Cambridge University Press, 2007), p. 1.

27. Dentith, p. 1.
28. Ernest Jones, 'Britannia', in *NS* 18/7/1846.
29. Randall, p. 186.
30. The term 'slave' or 'slavery' is used forty-four times throughout Jones's *Northern Star* poetry, almost always in obvious reference to Great Britain's working-class population.
31. Paul, p. 202.
32. John Darwin, *The Empire Project: The Rise and Fall of the British World-System, 1830–1970* (Cambridge: Cambridge University Press, 2009), p. 23.
33. Ibid., p. 23.
34. Ibid., p. 23.
35. Ibid., p. 24.
36. Alfred Lord Tennyson, 'The War', in *The Poetical Works of Alfred Tennyson, Poet Laureate* (New York: Harper, 1870), p. 244.
37. Edward M. Spiers notes that 'after Wellington's death, nearly a quarter of a million people filed before his coffin, many of them brought to London in "funeral trains", and a million and a half lined the route to St Paul's on 18 November 1852. [...] Conspicuous in a spectacular funeral was the abundance of heraldic images — pennons, guidons, banners, trophies and banderols — all testifying to the pervasive Victorian interest in chivalry', Edward M. Spiers, 'War', in *The Cambridge Companion to Victorian Culture*, ed. by Francis O'Gorman (Cambridge: Cambridge University Press, 2010), pp. 80–100 (p. 82).
38. Ibid., p. 86.
39. Arthur Wellesley, 1st Duke of Wellington, *Memorandum on Military Governments*, 7 March 1833, cited in Anthony Bruce, *The Purchase System in the British Army, 1660–1871* (London: Royal Historical Society, 1980), p. 65. Interestingly, the 'Iron Duke''s last political assignment was to oversee the defence of London during the widespread Chartist agitation of 1848; therefore it was Wellington — who had commanded the army that included Jones's father at Waterloo (1815) — who was ultimately responsible for Jones's imprisonment.
40. Bruce, p. 75.
41. *The Times*, 23 December 1854.
42. Taylor, pp. 26–27.
43. Ernest Jones, 'The Song of the Starving', in *NS* 25/5/1847.
44. Jones's subsequent support for the principles of British involvement in the Crimean War (see Chapter 6) indicates the complexity of his political positioning in the mid-1850s.
45. *NP* (1851), I, 4.
46. Paul, p. 197.
47. *NP* (1851), I, 135.
48. Ibid., p. 134.
49. Ibid., p. 135.
50. 'From Our Own Correspondent — Meeting of Cavan Landlords', *The Times*, 9 January 1847.
51. James Clarence Mangan, 'Siberia', in *The Collected Works*, III, 158.
52. Shelley, 'The Mask of Anarchy', p. 344.
53. Paul, p. 195.
54. Armstrong, p. 197.
55. Paul, p. 199.
56. Tucker, p. 362.
57. Armstrong, p. 197.
58. Janowitz, *Lyric and Love in the Romantic Tradition*, p. 187.
59. *NP* (1851), I, 15.
60. King Ernst Augustus of Hanover, letter to Friedrich Wilhelm IV of Prussia, cited in Michael Leapman, *The World for a Shilling: How the Great Exhibition of 1851 Shaped a Nation* (London: Headline, 2001), p. 75.
61. *MP* 15/10/1857.
62. Paul, p. 189.
63. Armstrong, p. 197.
64. Janowitz, *Lyric and Love in the Romantic Tradition*, p. 186.

CHAPTER 6

Pseudonymity, Revision, Songs of the Low and High 1851–60

When Jones emerged from prison in July 1850 he found Great Britain a changed place economically, socially, and politically. The potential chaos of 1848 had been replaced by a recovering economy and a growing fascination with the technological advances which the country's industrial dominance was continuing to produce. Correspondingly, membership of the National Charter Association, after reaching a peak of 50,000 in 1842, fell during the years 1848 to 1850 from 5,000 to around 500.[1] Exploring the reasons for Chartism's decline through the 1850s Dorothy Thompson outlines the argument for an economic cause:

> If Chartism was basically a gut reaction to hunger and to the disorganisation caused to traditional industries by the early experience of industrialisation, then clearly the better economic climate, which accompanied and followed the Great Exhibition of 1851, the increasing stability of Britain's major industries in that period and the organisations which these industries allowed to develop among the new industrial workforce are enough to account for its decline and death.[2]

But Thompson recognizes that, as a sophisticated mass political movement, Chartism cannot be dismissed as merely a 'gut reaction', and that while the changing economic climate may have been a contributing factor to the decline of Chartism as a mass platform, 'it would be strange if the long history of conflict within industry were to have ended suddenly with a brief spell of prosperity'.[3] The true picture was of course more complex — the economy prospered unevenly across different industries, and industrial conflict remained, embodied in individual strikes of varying length and severity. A considerable blow to Chartism after the humiliation of the failure of the 1848 Petition was simply the dispersal of political protest through a growing number of reform groups, co-operatives, and trades unions. After ten years of agitation the Charter looked as unlikely as ever to be achieved. Malcolm Chase writes:

> No longer claiming the status of a mass platform agitation, Chartism struggled for primacy of place among a number of competing initiatives. Viewed collectively, Chartists were young in years and not prepared to blunt their considerable energies in pursuit of the unobtainable. This did not mean

that their commitment to the principles embodied in the Charter dissolved: but there was an understandable drift towards the politics of the possible in preference to what increasingly looked like an agitational wilderness.[4]

If it was a chastened and weakened movement to which Jones returned on his emergence from prison, his own enthusiasm for the principles of the Charter were undiminished. Although the celebrations of his release in London were muted, he found a different attitude in the northern industrial heartland: 'Halifax did him proud. If the dank odours of Tothill Fields Prison had dispelled Jones's enthusiasm for Chartism, then "a grand jubilee" in the bracing Pennines' air restored it. He rose to the occasion with an almost messianic sense of purpose'.[5]

Jones's political single-mindedness may have seen him attempt to rally the movement for several years after his release but his poetry responded to the question of how to address a partially mollified, but still disenfranchised, working class by a recognizable diffusion of themes and styles. The relatively direct propaganda pieces of his *Northern Star* poetry were obsolete in a movement that had suffered so resounding a defeat in 1848, whose membership had shrunk accordingly, and that faced questions regarding not only its democratic objectives, but also the nature of the future it envisioned for its representatives. Post-prison poems including 'The Walk Home from Beldagon' and 'The Queen's Bounty' deal directly with an established system of poor relief that Jones saw as designed to prolong the reliance of the working class on the middle class; 'Beldagon Church' and 'Christian Love' were specifically aimed at the perceived hypocrisy of the Anglican Church's role in maintaining the social and political status quo. In the later 1850s, as Jones struggled to hold together a movement that many perceived as having been fatally wounded in 1848, his poetry became even less broadly radical and a return to pre-Chartist styles occurred alongside actual republications of pre-Chartist poetry. *The Battle-Day: And Other Poems* (1855) and *Corayda: A Tale of Faith And Chivalry, and Other Poems* (1860) are collections that rely heavily on re-worked or re-named poems; *The Emperor's Vigil and The Waves and the War* (1856), though comprised of wholly new material, contains poems which harked back in style and theme to the pre-Chartist Jones of the *Morning Post* and the *Court Journal*. Some poems, including Jones's translation of Ühland's 'The Minstrel's Curse', which had been published in the *Court Journal* in 1841 and *Notes to the People* in 1851 and eventually became the ultimate piece of the *Corayda* collection, receive their third iteration in these collections. Even Jones's prison-conceived epic 'The New World, a Democratic Poem', which appeared in the first issue of the *Notes to the People* newspaper in 1851, was republished in 1857 as *The Revolt of Hindostan: Or, The New World* the new title being deliberately suggestive of *The Revolt of Islam*, the alternative title of Shelley's *Queen Mab* (1813), and taking advantage of the poem's apparent prediction of the Indian Uprising of 1857. Jones's poetry of the 1850s is a heterogeneous mix of thematic diffusion, pseudonymous masquerade, stylistic experimentation, and simple regurgitation. What these poems do reveal, however, is the changing nature of Jones's relationship with his readership, as his political shift towards the liberal mainstream is mirrored by an attendant poetic shift from polemic to commentary, and eventually to non-political subjects. They also reveal, as poems are re-worked and republished, similarities between the radical and conservative imaginations that shed further light on the nature of Jones's political journey.

Notes to the People (1851–52)

The first publication vehicle for Jones's post-prison poetry was his own newspaper, *Notes to the People.* In its second issue appeared a relatively long poem titled 'Beldagon Church: A Religious Poem', which is prefaced by a two-page dedication to the Chartists of Halifax. The dedication is a mixture of thanks to the people of Yorkshire for their steadfast support of Chartist principles, their support of Jones's family whilst he was in prison, and more general statements regarding the political situation in Britain and Europe at the time of writing. The dedication does not directly refer to the poem it precedes, but some of its assessments of the contemporary political requirements for democratic progress not just for Great Britain but for the continent of Europe give clues to the directions in which Jones's poetry was moving. The urge to action that characterized much of Jones's pre-prison, *Northern Star* poetry, whether that action consisted of unification or active resistance, is tempered by a recognition that without a coherent philosophical and strategic base, no political organization can achieve its objectives. The date of the disrupted and disappointing Kennington Common meeting that typified the Chartist defeat of 1848 is used to signal a shift in direction for the movement:

> Thence the great distinction between the 10th of April, 1848, and the 10th of April, 1851 — the day of action and the day of thought, and thence the failure of the former day. The misfortune is, that the process was inverted — had the hour of thought occurred in '48, the time of action might have been in '51. But a marshalling of mind is going on in Europe in this year of '51, far mightier than the gathering of force in '48.[6]

There is a recognizably Jonesian evocation of an inexorable, partially covert force here, but implicit within this call for consideration, for an intellectualization of Chartism, is the declaration that Jones himself was the appropriate successor to Feargus O'Connor. And Jones's poetry went a long way towards establishing him as a man of deep thought, intellect, and cultural sophistication. It is in this way that the Romantic aestheticism of Jones's lyrical prison poetry, despite its largely apolitical nature, served a political function. Alongside the geopolitical subjects and philosophical ambition of 'The New World', Jones's prison poetry declared its author to be intellectually worthy of leading the Chartist movement. Between 1846 and 1848, Jones published hardly any poetry that did not have Chartism as its explicit or implicit subject; in prison and after prison, his poetry rediscovered its formerly broad thematic scope. Post-1850, as effective Chartist leader, Jones's poetic persona was able to occasionally detach itself from his political persona, until by the mid-1850s, with the Chartist movement in terminal decline, this detachment shifted in function from a declaration of intellectual worthiness to a strategy of poetic survival.

'Beldagon Church', which is, as its subtitle indicates, a religious poem, can also be read as a political poem in its linking of the Church of England with the dominant ideology.[7] It describes a Sunday service in a fictional Anglican church and compares its opulence, pessimism, and hypocrisy with nature's simplicity, hope, and truth. The poem is by turns sardonic and playful, condemnatory and celebratory. Through a Romantic celebration of nature, natural theology is employed to argue a broadly Nonconformist opposition to the established Church. In the first section, subtitled 'The Walk to the Church', Jones describes the approach to the church as its bells call worshippers to prayer. In familiar language, the English countryside is celebrated through descriptions of 'pebbled runnels' (l. 23) and a 'frolic wind' (l. 26). This idyllic scene is contrasted with the church's 'sepulchral gloom' (l. 33) and 'ghostly statues' (l. 35). Gothic imagery is used to defamiliarize the church environment and the reader is invited to look again at ecclesiastical paraphernalia and iconography and consider its role in what Jones perceives as the established Church's ultimately destructive political function:

> The organ wailed, the echoes rung,
> And thick the painted shadows clung
> Around the panes where, richly wrought,
> Rival Saints and Dragons fought.
> And hovering cherubs smiling eyed
> The contemplated fratricide.
> ('Beldagon Church', ll. 44–49)

This 'contemplated fratricide' may, rather anomalously, refer to the conflict between the saints and the dragons, but more likely concerns Jones's preoccupation with the divide-and-rule policies of the capitalist system. In his preface to the poem he highlights, amongst other sites of conflict, an artificially sustained economic opposition between the agricultural labourer and the urban industrial worker: 'one part of the people has been played off against the other'.[8]

By poetically evoking a negative perception of the site of Beldagon Church, Jones condemns the whole of Anglicanism as a corrupt and hypocritical organization, wallowing in the luxury of 'panelled oak, and silken screen' (l. 63) as much of the population lives in poverty.[9] This is contrasted with the natural world around the church where '[e]very whispering leaf's a preacher' (l. 71), and nature is capable of delivering a 'Revelation straight from God' (l. 74). The poem describing Jones's first encounters with Chartism in 1846, 'The Blackstone Edge Gathering', anticipates this natural theology in its call for 'no cold roof 'twixt God and man' (l. 30). Although no religious denomination is specifically mentioned throughout 'Beldagon Church' this celebration of lay ministry and direct communication with the divine clearly endorses a Nonconformist, disestablishmentarian argument. The political message of the poem is largely indirect, but its satirizing and outright condemnation of Anglicanism is designed to appeal to Jones's often Nonconformist, increasingly northern English constituency.

The demotic ambition of *Notes to the People* largely defines its content, and its poetry should be read within the context of a wider mission to inform and educate. After the grand statements of the relatively long poems, 'The New World', 'Beldagon Church', and 'The Painter of Florence' (see Chapter One), in the first few issues, and the martyrdom calling-cards of the prison poems, the verses scattered through

PSEUDONYMITY, REVISION, SONGS OF THE LOW AND HIGH (1851–60)   171

the remaining issues become less frequent and function as intermezzos, providing relief from the dense prose polemics, fictions, and histories, most of which were also written by Jones. There is a confidence implied by these poems' occasional placement which can be attributed to the fact that Jones, for the first time, truly has his own readership. Although he wrote most of the copy for the *Labourer* newspaper before his imprisonment, he must always have felt the influence of his politically senior co-editor, Feargus O'Connor. The republication within *Notes to the People* of pre-Chartist poems at this point represents a desire for copy rather than a conscious attempt to recover a former poetic voice. However, some of the shorter poems seem to have been written specifically for publication within this newspaper, and make their only appearance here. 'The Slave Ship', for instance, is uncredited but very much in Jones's style and consists of seventeen six-line stanzas detailing the death from heat and starvation of almost all of the crew and prisoners on a Spanish slave ship caught in the doldrums.[10] The ship finally sinks in a storm off Senegambia with only one former slave alive on board as witness, rejoicing that he will not die in a 'christian realm':

> He touched not the sail nor the driving helm;
>   But he looked on the raging sea,
> And he gazed — for the waves that would overwhelm,
>   Would leave his spirit free;
> And he prayed that the ship to no christian realm,
>   Before the storm might flee. ('The Slave Ship', ll. 91–96)

Alongside the common destruction of the slaves and the slavers representing a moral condemnation of the whole business of slavery, Jones's de-familiarization of Christianity as the immoral agent in this narrative is in keeping with the kind of radical inversion which characterizes many of the statements made either in prose or in poetry within *Notes to the People*. Prose accounts of the radical history of Britain and poems including 'The New World' and 'Beldagon Church' share a primary function in attempting to invert traditionally-held conceptions of the nature of British history, society, and imperialism.

Although the popularity of Chartism as a mass platform was in steep decline even by the early 1850s, Jones wrote his most popular poem, 'Song of the Low' (see Chapter One), during this period. He also wrote 'Christian Love', whose premise rests on a fundamental philosophical inversion which has real political implications: it is arguably his most explicit poetic advocacy of violent political action. Like 'The Slave Ship', 'Christian Love' makes its only appearance in this newspaper, in the seventeenth issue, and is a vitriolic twenty-two-line lyric that bears the mark of political frustration, both with the social effects of industrial capitalism, and with less extreme reformers whom Jones perceives as holding back the march of political progress.[11] The four verse sections alternate five and six lines and the increasing repetition of a triple rhyme and then a quadruple rhyme in the ABAAB CDCCCD scheme brings a crescendo of emphasis:

> Oh! Christian Love is a thing divine,
>   And Charity saveth tenfold; —
> But a Christian HATE is a thing as sublime —

The hatred of sin and the idol's shrine,
   Where Mammon is worshipped in gold.

The hatred of murder, and craft, and deceit, —
   That upholdeth the money-lord's sway:
Oh! if British hearts had a manful beat,
Tho' the tyrants stood thick as the stones in the street,
I'd trample them down like the dust at my feet,
   In the light of a single day!

('Christian Love', ll. 1–11)

Jones's unequivocal embrace of hatred as an emotion to be utilized for moral advancement is a striking poetic conceit. The elevation of 'HUMAN LOVE' to the status of highest divine achievement in the second section of 'Beldagon Church' (l. 191) seems in contradiction to the contention that 'Christian HATE', with its even more emphatic double capitalization, could be 'a thing as sublime'. And yet Jones's anger could be interpreted as taking its inspiration from Christ's outburst at the moneychangers in the temple as recounted in Matthew 21:12; indeed, the reference to 'Mammon', the New Testament personification of pecuniary greed, would seem to support this. The focus of the poem is the necessity for physical action to overcome tyrannical opposition, but in a shift from the protagonists that tended to feature in Jones's *Northern Star* poetry, the active agents here are not 'them and us', but 'them and me'. Although the trigger for action is the familiar recovery of masculinity by 'British hearts', it is the poetic 'I' who will gain power from this transformation, and 'trample them down like the dust at my feet'. The egocentric nature of this declaration of leadership (which, in a democratic organization, would probably only be possible couched in poetic terms) appears to go much further than convening or organizing meetings or even directing policy; it might be thought of as several steps on from Jones's youthful statement that he was 'forming the tone of the mighty mind'. Jones's poetic persona appears to have taken on the collective responsibility for the working class overcoming its oppressors, establishing itself as a conduit for the conversion of mass desire into action.

Accompanying the shift in agency the work appears to imply, the second half of the poem culminates in an explicitly stated justification for violent action:

Oh! War, they say, is a sinful thing,
   And a blessing is peace, they say —
And obedience and patience their guerdon shall bring:
But well they may preach to the suffering —
   When none are the gainers but they!

They may shrink in horror from bloodshed and fight,
   And the words that they speak may be true:
But there is such a thing as the Wrong and the Right,
And there is such a thing as tyrannical might:
And the tears of the many are worse in my sight,
   Aye! e'en than the blood of the few. (ll. 12–22)

In this poem Jones seems to have found the ultimate expression of his particular brand of moral absolutism, and to have settled, after many attempts, on an effective

PSEUDONYMITY, REVISION, SONGS OF THE LOW AND HIGH (1851–60)   173

variation on Shelley's oppositional relationship between the 'many' and the 'few' in 'The Mask of Anarchy' (1819). The implication of the poem is that policies enforced by 'tyrannical might' which inflict suffering on the majority are sufficient cause for revolution, and that there is a moral equivalence between widespread low- or medium-level suffering ('tears') and the specifically targeted high-level suffering implied by the term 'blood'. The italicization of the last line's provocative statement emphasizes the condensation of what appears to be a justification of, or even a call for, violent revolution. Significantly, though, the political specificity of this poem ends with the term 'British'; there is no mention of Chartism as an organization, and the piece's protagonists and antagonists are couched in mythic or archetypal terms. The focus of an oppressed people's agency through a single speaker gives the poem, in spite of its emphasis on action, the feel of an exercise in dreamlike wish-fulfilment.

While the expression of personalized desire in 'Christian Love' might highlight Jones's increasing isolation as a political leader in a shrinking organization, there is still an immense confidence represented by the poem's directness of message, its untrammelled radical ambition. However, given the subsequent direction of Jones's political, and poetic, career, it is not surprising that this poem was never republished or included in a collection. In many ways it represents the apotheosis of Jones's radical voice, and while some of Jones's Chartist poetry could be repackaged as generally democratic in a European sense (see discussion of 'The Cry of the Russian Serf to the Czar' and 'The Italian Exile to his Countrymen' in the *Battle-Day* collection below), or regarded as nostalgic reminders of the pre-1848 Chartist struggle, 'Christian Love' is far too unequivocal in its approach. The ephemeral literary status of 'Christian Love' is indicative of the wider fate of Jones's radical energies in the early 1850s. After having been energized by the heightened prestige conferred on him by his time in prison, the gradual realization that Chartism was still a diminishing influence in British politics, despite his best efforts, led Jones to attempt to re-establish his poetic career in new ways, and to not only redefine his relationship with his existing readership, but to seek new readerships.

Rhymes on the Times (1852)

At the same time that Jones was working on *Notes to the People*, he embarked on a poetic project which, whatever its political implications, shows evidence of enormous poetic confidence. Although *Notes to the People* contained several examples of original and new poetry, it also contained works which had been published previously, either during the two years of political activism leading up to Jones's imprisonment, or from the 'conservative' years before this. Jones appeared to wish to consolidate his poetic reputation with a prolific output, and to broaden his appeal with the publication of some poetry which, like much of his prison-composed work, did not have politics as its main focus. Thus, works including translations of Arndt's 'The Stars' and Ühland's 'The Minstrel's Curse', and the original poem 'To Her', all of which had been published in the conservative *Court Journal* in the early 1840s, appeared ten years later in a radical newspaper. Between 1846 and 1848 Jones had republished 'The Cornfield and the Factory' as a broadly anti-industrial poem,

174 PSEUDONYMITY, REVISION, SONGS OF THE LOW AND HIGH (1851–60)

and re-worked 'To Louis Philippe'/'To Byron'/'The Poet's Mission' for publication in the *Northern Star*, but the desire for copy that necessitated the republication of poems in *Notes to the People* began a trend of republication that persisted and intensified through the 1850s. Jones produced seven books or pamphlets of poetry during this period: *Rhymes on the Times* (1852), *The Battle-Day: And Other Poems* (1855), *Emperor's Vigil and The Waves and the War* (1856), *Poetic Thoughts of E. C. J.* (1856), *Songs of Democracy* (1857), *The Revolt of Hindostan: Or, The New World* (1857), and *Corayda: A Tale of Faith and Chivalry, and Other Poems* (1860). Of these only *Rhymes on the Times*, *Emperor's Vigil*, *The Poetic Thoughts of E. C. J.*, and *Corayda* contained predominantly original poetry; and of these four volumes, the title poem of *Corayda* had been composed fifteen years earlier, and *Rhymes on the Times* and *The Poetic Thoughts of E. C. J.* were published pseudonymously.

Rhymes on the Times was published in February 1852 by T. Brettell of Haymarket under the initials 'E. C. J.', a pseudonym whose necessity becomes apparent when the political colour of the poems it contains is considered. Jones had only used the initials E. C. J. once before, when he published his first poem in a British publication, 'To Her', in the *Court Journal* in 1840. Thereafter, his *Court Journal* work was signed 'Karl'. The *Rhymes on the Times* pamphlet contains seven poems which, as Miles Taylor has noted, are 'doggerel satire and recognisably Jones's own work'.[12] Further evidence in support of the identification of Jones as the author is contained in the copy currently held in the British Library which was bequeathed by the estate of the author John Fowles (1926–2005). Although the volume is listed as Jones's work by the British Library, Fowles's copy contains a librarian's note that reads, '? Ernest Charles Jones (1819–69): chartist, barrister, advocate of land reform and communalism', suggesting uncertainty regarding authorship, but Fowles's copy also carries a handwritten presentation inscription from the author that reads, 'Mrs Joseph Maudslay, with the Authors [*sic*] affectionate love'.[13] The handwriting is unmistakeably that of Jones and confirms the volume as an extraordinary, pseudonymous poetic aside from a writer whose radical sympathies were simultaneously being expounded in the *Notes to the People* newspaper.

All seven of the poems contained in *Rhymes on the Times* are on the subject of contemporary politics, and where political allegiance is revealed it is decidedly Tory. Whilst two of the poems, 'The Invasion' and 'Victory of Lagos', concern the effects of international politics on Great Britain, the other five, 'The Quack', 'Reform', 'The Farmer's Last New Song', 'Lord Palmerston's Song', and 'Lord Derby', focus on parliamentary politics and particularly the troubles of the Whig government led by Prime Minister Lord John Russell (1792–1878), which eventually collapsed in the same month as the volume's publication. The pamphlet reads as a collection of political sketches in song form, satirically attacking Whig policies and encouraging the return of a Tory government under the Prime Ministership of Lord Derby. In stark contrast to Jones's post-1846 political pronouncements up to this point and beyond, the opinions expressed are isolationist, anti-reform, and racist, professing support for low taxes, governmental assistance for farmers and landowners, and the restoration of Conservative Party political dominance to 'prop the Church and Throne'.[14]

PSEUDONYMITY, REVISION, SONGS OF THE LOW AND HIGH (1851–60)   175

The opening poem, 'The Invasion', introduces the isolationist, patriotic register of the pamphlet by criticizing the British Army's Commander-in-Chief, Sir Charles Napier (1782–1853) for allegedly fomenting panic with regard to the possibility of a French invasion following the 1851 *coup d'état* of Napoleon III.[15] The poem employs similar nationalistic aggrandizing of the British people to that seen in Chartist poems including 'A Chartist March' and 'The Patriot's Test', but this time for a wholly different end:[16]

> One can't believe that in this land
>   Of freedom and of joys,
> We don't possess a noble stock
>   Of British sailor boys,
>
> Who'd arm and fight with loyal hearts,
>   And every danger brave,
> To guard their homes, and spurn the thought
>   Of being Frenchmen's slaves.
>
> Why every Special, with his staff,
>   Would gladly keep the law,
> And love the chance of turning out,
>   The dirty French to floor.
>
> Then don't despair if Frenchmen come,
>   We've forces here in plenty;
> One British arm is stronger much
>   Than '*foreigneerers*' twenty!
>
> ('The Invasion', ll. 29–44)

The message of this poem is that Great Britain's military dominance is so complete it negates the necessity for the drilling of naval forces or domestic militia in order to fend off 'the little Gallic Cock' (l. 52). Although the poem is presented entirely without irony in its register, the ironies present when considering the identity of its author are manifold. Jones's championing of the 'Specials' is particularly paradoxical given that members of this volunteer constabulary force, sworn enemies of Chartists in many of their demonstrations, were ultimately responsible for his arrest in 1848. The description of Great Britain as a 'land | Of freedom and of joys' is about as far from Jones's Chartist political pronouncements regarding the state of the nation as it is possible to get. The poem ends with a celebration of the reassuring figure of the Duke of Wellington, the 'Iron Duke', in the role of national protector should the French prove a real threat. Jones's father had served under Wellington at the Battle of Waterloo, but the elderly duke had also been responsible for co-ordinating the 1848 anti-Chartist crackdown that led to Jones's arrest. The final stanza represents something of a non sequitur as discussion of the putative French invasion is abandoned and praise for Wellington ('Hero of a Hundred Fights', l. 61, 'Old England's pride', l. 68) gathers momentum:

> All hail! Good Duke, may you be spared
>   For many a year to come,
> To reap the glory and renown
>   Of noble deeds you've done. (ll. 77–80)

PSEUDONYMITY, REVISION, SONGS OF THE LOW AND HIGH (1851–60)

In fact, Wellington died in September of that year.

The *Northern Star* Chartist poems 'Britannia' and 'England's Greatness' are anti-imperialist diatribes highly critical of British foreign policy, but although the third poem in *Rhymes on the Times*, 'Victory of Lagos', is similarly anti-interventionist, its means of expression belongs more to the 'Little Englander' school of politics than to the vaunted internationalism of Jones's work under his own name.[17] British forces had captured Lagos in 1851, ostensibly to prevent its further use as a centre for the slave trade. In doing so they installed Akintoye as king or *Oba*, ousting his slave-dealing predecessor, Kosoko. The poem begins by arguing that the weight of existing domestic and international pressures on the British does not justify another foreign intervention:

> Are not our dangers sad enough,
>   By railways and by mine explosions?
> Don't halfpenny boats sometimes blow up,
>   Through rotten boilers and corrosions?
>
> Don't Amazons at sea take fire,
>   And make one tremble at such horrors,
> And raise a well-deserved ire
>   At slothful Admiralty jobbers?
>
> Don't Caffre wars and Afric's clime
>   Now decimate our armies brave?
> Don't lots of foul, dark, Irish crime
>   Send landlords to untimely graves?
>
> ('Victory of Lagos', ll. 1–12)

It need hardly be stated that Jones's siding with landlords here against their Irish tenants is in complete contradiction to his writings under his own name, whether in prose or verse. The opinions expressed in this poem and in the wider volume are almost parodic in the closeness of their alignment with grassroots Tory attitudes of the mid-nineteenth century. They are the poetic equivalent of an angry letter to *The Times*. The amplitude of expression is itself perhaps a slight undermining of the pamphlet's messages. Two stanzas in particular employ racist epithets which are difficult to read in the twenty-first century, and even more difficult to associate with the man who composed 'The New World' just a year or two before:

> Why should our rulers deem it wise
>   To side with any dirty Black;
> Why did they heed Akitoye's cries,
>   For whom we do not care a rap?
> [...]
> Then up ye Lords and Commons great,
>   And ask the meaning of such wars;
> Dismiss the Secretary of State
>   For meddling in this Nigger cause. (ll. 33–36, 53–36)

The occasional use of skin colour as an imagistic intensifier in 'The New World' owes more to Victorian orientalism than the kind of outright racism the above statements appear to represent. Even taking into account the 'of their time' argument which must always be considered when reading historical texts, the use of language in these stanzas is deliberately offensive. The speaker uses racial difference to amplify national difference and to argue for a laissez-faire international policy.

'The Quack' and 'Reform' both attack Lord John Russell's attempts to reform Parliament and the electoral system, the latter in a relatively straightforward manner, the former using a medical metaphor for satirical purposes:[18]

> Dr. Russell he thought that John Bull was ill,
>> So he straightway prescribed him a wonderful Pill,
> His Physic he shaped, in the newest form,
>> And the name of his nostrum he called *Reform!*
> ('The Quack', ll. 1–4)

The commonplace personification of Great Britain (or, more properly, England) as 'John Bull' allows Jones to characterize Russell as a quack doctor whose medication does more harm than good. After a punning allusion to the Corn Laws unsubtly flagged by italicization ('Some aching about *his poor old corn*', l. 14) and an anti-Semitic reference to a 'jolly, fat rollicking City Jew' (l. 24) to represent financial mismanagement, 'John Bull' dismisses 'Dr. Russell', and the solution is found in a change of doctor: 'Dr. Derby was sent for — John soon got about | Whilst Dr. Russell was at once kicked out' (ll. 41–42). This is one of four poems from a total of seven which concludes with a celebration of the installation of a Tory government.

'Reform' contains more specific statements regarding electoral reform, and its third stanza perhaps provides a clue to Jones's possible motivation for publishing the volume as a whole:[19]

> 'Twould be better by far, to preserve the Ten Pounders,
>> And try a reform in a moderate way;
> 'Twas clear that Lord John had given up 'Rounders,'
>> And 'Fives' was the radical game he would play.
> ('Reform', ll. 9–12)

'Ten Pounders' and 'Fives' refer to the amount of money in pounds a man's property must be worth before he was deemed eligible to vote. The 1832 Reform Act had lowered the amount to ten pounds, but Russell was proposing to balance democratic representation between rural and urban districts by lowering the eligible property values in towns to five pounds. In opposing the 1852 Reform Bill, Jones is demonstrating one of the areas where Tory and radical political ambitions intersect. As Robert Saunders has noted, 'The Bill which Russell introduced in February 1852 was little to the radicals' taste, and was buried in the general wreck of his government before it was even properly debated'.[20] Tories wanted no reform at all, while radicals considered Russell's proposals to be obstructively piecemeal. The lack of movement on reform in the twenty years since the 1832 Reform Act indicated that a similar hiatus might follow any successful contemporary Reform Act, however unsatisfactory to most parties. It was perhaps this prospect that drove Jones to produce *Rhymes on the Times*. The collapse of the Whig administration led to a minority Tory government, but its instability was such that it lasted only until a no-confidence vote in December 1852, when a Whig-Peelite coalition was formed under Lord Aberdeen. *Rhymes on the Times* appears to be Jones's attempt to destabilize the Whig government and shore up the fragile Tory administration of Lord Derby in the month that it gained power; to 'pour the tide of his song' and 'form the tone' of an entirely different 'mighty mind'.

The extent of the influence or popularity of *Rhymes on the Times* is not known. Shorn of association with its famous author, the pamphlet was only briefly mentioned in (fittingly) the *John Bull* newspaper of 4 September 1852, which described the volume as 'clever and spirited'. Jones's association with it renders it an intriguing piece of literary ephemera, but any attempt to ascertain his reasons for publishing it must remain supposition. Its unswerving alignment to Tory policy may simply relate to the old adage that 'my enemy's enemy is my friend'. Or, Jones's assumption of a Tory voice (it is worth considering that the title of the volume may be a reference to the venerable Tory newspaper) might represent an attempt to become a literary Chartist 'double agent' within the ranks of Toryism — it is certainly the case that a static Tory government was a more preferable opponent for Chartists than a reforming Whig one which might undermine them with a 'little Charter'. The Chartists and the Tories occasionally found common ground in their hatred of the Whigs; in 1841 Feargus O'Connor urged fellow Chartists to vote tactically for the Tory party 'not in the hope of establishing a Chartist-Tory alliance, but mainly with the idea of punishing the Whigs for their anti-working-class measures'.[21] Following his former mentor's lead Jones wrote an article for *Notes to the People* in 1851 arguing against Chartist support for the kind of partial reform Russell was proposing, entitled 'The Middle-Class Franchise — Why Will It Injure the Democratic Cause?' The possibility that Jones was actually revealing his true political colours here is highly unlikely — the extreme contradiction with his openly professed opinions is surely too marked. He had only relatively recently been released from prison for his democratic idealism and after attempting to re-ignite interest in the Charter he eventually shifted towards the Reform League whose direct genesis was in the very Bill that *Rhymes on the Times* was so opposed to. But whether Jones was playing a complicated political game here, or merely attempting to exercise an amoral political influence through his verse, he appears to be enjoying himself. There is exhilaration evident in the volume that is perhaps derived from the brief wearing of a political mask; the thrill of being, however briefly, a pseudonymous agent provocateur. The occasional slip in metrical regularity (which is uncharacteristic of Jones, who would usually rather distort syntax than lose rhythm) suggests, in keeping with their status as 'sketches', that the poems were composed rapidly in response to the on-going development of the political events they cover.

The Battle-Day: And Other Poems (1855)

Although the publication of *The Battle-Day: And Other Poems* took advantage of public interest in the Crimean War it would not be accurate to suggest that its contents were composed in response to that event. However, Jones's decision to publish a collection whose title poem appeared to reflect themes arising from the conflict marks a shift away from his identification with predominantly radical

PSEUDONYMITY, REVISION, SONGS OF THE LOW AND HIGH (1851–60)   179

material towards a new ambition to reach a much wider cross-section of the poetry-reading British public. Jones had been editing the nominally radical Chartist weekly newspaper, the *People's Paper*, since the demise of *Notes to the People* in 1852, and would continue to do so until 1858, but as Taylor notes, the content of the publication steadily became less radical and more salaciously populist as time went on.[22] Early issues of the paper saw some republication of Jones's Chartist poetry, but this became less frequent and eventually vanished altogether. *The Battle-Day* saw the first airing of Jones's poetry for two years, and signals the beginning of not only a different type of double address to that employed by his pre-prison Chartist poetry, but a conscious effort to recycle earlier material to a much greater extent. Indeed, *The Battle-Day* might be described as a collection that was not so much composed by Jones in 1855, but edited.

Whether or not there is something deceitful in the wholesale repackaging of earlier material, Jones's practice during the latter half of the 1850s of republishing, revising, and re-titling his poetry has confounded several modern commentators. Taylor claims that the *Battle-Day* collection 'included only two new verses', and, in a footnote, identifies these as 'The Cry of the Russian Serf to the Czar' and 'The Italian Exile to his Countrymen'.[23] Isobel Armstrong praises Jones's internationalism, but identifies its expression in the same two poems when she claims that 'True to his non-Anglocentric vision, Jones wrote on Russia and Italy in "The Cry of the Russian Serf to the Czar" and "The Italian Exile to his Countrymen"'.[24] In fact, these two short poems from the 1855 *Battle-Day* collection are revised and re-titled Chartist poems published in the *Northern Star* nine years earlier under the titles 'Our Destiny' and 'Our Cheer' — they also appeared in the *Chartist Lyrics and Fugitive Pieces* pamphlet of 1846. Jones's re-titling changes the speaker of each poem to reflect current European political concerns — the poems seem occasional, but are in fact commodities given, in modern commercial parlance, a 'rebranding'. The distance between the speaker and the subjects in 'Our Cheer' discussed in Chapter Three adapts particularly well to a poem that could have been read by contemporaries as a representation of the voice of the Italian politician and activist Giuseppe Mazzini (1805–72), whose extended exiles and sojourns in London made him a focus of pan-European ideas of nationalism and democracy:

> My countrymen! why languish
>   Like outcasts of the earth,
> And drown in tears of anguish
>   The glory of your birth?
> Ye were a free-born people
>   And heroes were your race:
> The dead, *they* are our freemen,
>   The living — our disgrace!
>   ('The Italian Exile to His Countrymen', ll. 1–8)[25]

The revision in the case of both of these poems is minor (for example, in the above work, 'Briton' and 'British' are changed to 'Roman'), but the lack of specificity inherent in Jones's use of mythic archetypes and literary tropes in his poetry enabled certain works to be re-used and re-read in sometimes wholly different contexts.

Armstrong reads the *Battle-Day* collection's title poem as a reflection on the failure of the Chartist leadership and its implications for the organization as a mass movement. In 1855, this would have been an appropriate subject for discourse: 'Jones is clearly meditating the collapse of revolutionary energy in Chartism and the disintegration of its leadership'.[26] However, 'The Battle-Day; Or, The Lost Army' began life as a narrative poem called 'Lord Lindsay' which, according to Taylor was composed in the spring of 1845 and was 'eventually published in the *Labourer* towards the end of 1847 and by MacGowan in 1848 (and republished as *The Battle Day* in 1855)'.[27] The tale of a titled warrior whose habitual indecision and loss of nerve eventually causes the downfall of a whole army might seem to allegorize the political events of the late 1840s or early 1850s, but was actually composed some years before, when Jones's interest in politics, as far as anyone knows, did not extend to Chartism.

Jones's status as an important political figure but a minor poet has, quite naturally, led critics to cherry-pick examples of his prolific writings in order to illustrate points which are often about other, more demonstrably canonical, writers.[28] But in Jones's case, this approach is fraught with difficulties; his poetry frequently rewards the consideration of contextual information due to its often explicitly political nature, but it is also a body of work that responds to a holistic strategy of engagement. The apparent, or original, topics of many of Jones's poems are often subject to a fluidity that tends to offend the modern reader's desire for a stable aesthetic in poetry. The immediacy of message that Jones is often reaching for, rather than relying on an historical specificity, is predicated on a perception of emotional truth. Jones uses the indeterminacy of poetic language to approach political issues through the generalized emotional themes of loyalty, pride, steadfastness, revenge, or outrage; and as the occasions for these themes re-occur the poetry which treats them can be revived. The politics of the day was often of the highest priority to Jones, and therefore political expediency authorized a policy of the use and re-use of poetry which, for those of a more aesthetically refined sensibility, might appear opportunistic or even mercenary. Jones's attitude to the production and publication of his work was often a long way from John Stuart Mill's ideal of 'overheard' poetry.

It is possible that Jones's embrace of thematic or aesthetic transposition also took its inspiration from practices already common in Chartist and indeed wider culture. The discovery of the *National Chartist Hymn Book* in Todmorden, West Yorkshire, in 2009 — the only known existing copy of any Chartist hymn book (although there are plenty of references to such publications in the *Northern Star* and other Chartist organs) — reveals that Chartist hymns were, in common with most hymns in the mid-nineteenth century, sung to different tunes in different locations and at different times.[29] The decision to attach a particular melody to a particular hymn was often based on local tradition, and each hymn was assigned a code denoting its metre which corresponded to a pre-existing bank of known melodies. Mike Sanders, who has carried out extensive analysis of the *National Chartist Hymn Book* since its discovery, gives an indication of how a commonly accepted code indicates a systematic process by which two distinct artefacts might be melded into one apparently unified whole:

PSEUDONYMITY, REVISION, SONGS OF THE LOW AND HIGH (1851–60)   181

For example, C. M. indicates common meter (86.86) — the numbers refer to the number of syllables in each line of each quatrain. S. M. indicates short meter (66.86) and L. M. indicates long meter (88.88). In addition the *National Chartist Hymn Book* deploys a number of less familiar meters such as '6 8's' (indicating a six-line stanza with eight syllables per line), '7's' (quatrains of seven syllables per line), and '4 8's & 2 6's' (four lines of eight syllables followed by two lines of six syllables). The fifteenth hymn is marked P. M. or particular meter (in this case a six-line stanza arranged 878747).[30]

This elaborate vocabulary of transposition, common wherever hymns are sung, points to a culture that does not see artistic objects as fixed, determinate entities but as pliable materials to be adapted at will. However, at least in Chartist congregations, this 'tremendous flexibility and variety' is not arbitrarily applied; Sanders notes that 'the moral (and thus political) confidence engendered by the Chartist lyric might well be strengthened by the use of a well-known hymn tune.'[31] Jones's involvement with the products and practices of the culture of Chartist hymnody is indicated by his use of the term to describe some of his works ('Hymn for Ascension-Day', 'Easter Hymn', 'Hymn for Lammas-Day'), and it is reasonable to assume that the broader hymnological acceptance of an interchangeable approach to hymn lyrics might have influenced or 'authorized' his decisions to re-use work when he saw fit.

Despite the *Battle-Day* collection consisting of wholly recycled material, it was one of Jones's most well-received publications, especially in the mainstream press, where the relatively apolitical subject of its title poem allowed for an aesthetic appreciation of Jones's talent uncomplicated by the expression of radical political opinions. The reviewer in the *John Bull* of 29 September 1855 referred to this separation of the politician from the poet:

> We have no predilection for the prose of Mr. Ernest Jones; but we are bound to say that in verse he makes a more creditable appearance. When he escapes from the low realities of his political entourage to the heights of Parnassus, his style and spirit seem to undergo a process of purification, and those who would scout the Chartist's company, may yet be pleased to spend an hour with the poet.[32]

The even more avowedly conservative *Spectator* magazine found equal cause to celebrate the apparently newfound eclecticism of Jones's poetic interests:

> Those who happen to be acquainted with the poetical productions of Ernest Jones must allow that they possess clearness and force, a genial perception of nature, a vigorous imagination, and a vivid poetical spirit. Persons who expect that the great Chartist leader will infuse low Radical ideas in low Radical fashion into his verses will find themselves mistaken.[33]

It is worth considering that the connotations of the term 'low' in this Tory magazine will have included issues of class as much as issues of politics. The implication might be that this review was in some measure welcoming a prodigal gentleman, or at least the artistic side of him, back into the fold. Neither publication noted the preponderance of republished material in this volume but instead treated it as a new and welcome direction for a writer whose poetic abilities could be admired while his political sensibilities were deplored. However, it was clearly acceptable to conservative British readers for Russian serfs to be represented as threatening their royal oppressors in terms including, 'we will share your heaven — or ye shall share our hell' (The final words of 'The Cry of the Russian Serf to the Czar'/'Our Cheer'), while the same words would not have been tolerated in the context of the British industrial/class relations for which they were originally composed.

Unusually, the title poem of the *Battle-Day* collection is not the longest work in the volume. Almost twice the length is the first poem, 'The Cost of Glory', which is actually a slightly altered version of 'The Painter of Florence' (see Chapter One), which was published in the third issue of *Notes to the People* in 1851. The poem is now divided into four discrete sections, 'I — The Country House', 'II — The Visit', 'III — The Pictures', and 'IV — The Painter of Florence', but in many respects remains identical to its previous incarnation. However, the concluding thirty-six lines, which bemoan the hoarding of Britain's artistic heritage by the aristocratic classes, are omitted from the republished version. This is an attempt by Jones to depoliticize his work in a similar manner to the political diffusion achieved by the re-titling of Chartist material in the case of 'The Cry of the Russian Serf to the Czar' and 'The Italian Exile to his Countrymen'. The original version of the poem ended with the following quatrain:

> Go! stranger! Rouse the sons of thought!
> Go! tell them far and near!
> And take me! Take me to the world!
> Or make the world come here!
> ('The Painter of Florence', ll. 702–05)[34]

Mild as this might seem compared with some of Jones's more violent lyrics, the exclamatory and messianic register of this stanza would clearly have counted, in the eyes of the *Spectator* magazine, as 'low Radical ideas expressed in low Radical fashion', as would the condemnation of the aristocracy's retention of artistic national treasures. It seems that Jones recognized this possibility and truncated his poem accordingly, which would indicate that he put together this collection with an eye on its probable reception by the mainstream readership and press.

The title poem itself, 'The Battle-Day: Or, The Lost Army' is a chivalric tale whose setting and themes align with the allegorical medievalism of 'The Minstrel's Curse' and 'The Monarch's Death-Prayer', which Jones translated from the original German of Ludwig Ühland for the *Court Journal* in 1841.[35] The poem's protagonist, Lord Lindsay (whose name provides the title of the poem's original publication), suffers throughout his life from phases of crippling doubt which work against the advantages conferred upon him by his noble birth. Doubt and jealousy ruin his marriage and doubt leads to the indecision in leadership which causes his army to fail at the crucial moment in the climactic battle scene of the poem. The final stanza of the poem serves as an epigraph for its main character, and as an affirmation that faith, both religious and secular, is the basis of life's, and the afterlife's, achievements:

> His useless life so wildly passed! —
> So many deeds and none to last! —
> A sigh of regret for his parting breath;
> Of all that seed but one fruit — Death!

PSEUDONYMITY, REVISION, SONGS OF THE LOW AND HIGH (1851–60)   183

> And the Beyond? To him unknown:
> A tear — a knell — a prayer — a stone!
> A sod wrapped round a soulless clay,
> And a keyless gate to a trackless way!
> For Death, to him all light without,
> Was worse than agony — was *Doubt*.
> So high a heart — so sad a fate!
> Wanting but faith to have been great.
> ('The Battle-Day', ll. 457–68)

The poem ends on the theme of the loss of spiritual and historical immortality after having considered consecutively the destructive effects of doubt in the domestic sphere and the military sphere, thus creating a thematic crescendo around its central premise. Like so many of Jones's pre-Chartist works, the poem follows the Aristotelian template for tragedy by detailing the fall of a high-born protagonist.

Jones's republication, renaming, and choice of the poem as the title work undoubtedly reflects an attempt to engage with the public fascination for the events of the Crimean War, and with the growing criticism of the quality of leadership of Britain's armed forces; Tennyson's 'Charge of the Light Brigade' had been published to instant acclaim in the *Examiner* the year before. However, as a poem written in 1845, long before the war but just prior to Jones's direct involvement with politics, 'Lord Lindsay'/'The Battle-Day' concerns themes of leadership, faith, and the capacity of individual agency to influence the wider community which are recurrent throughout his poetry from its early days. For Roy Vickers, these themes are grounded in Jones's sense of both religious and political calling which are inextricably bound up with each other, once Jones 'converts' to the Chartist cause. They also provide the basis of a double address to the working classes and the privileged classes which becomes an increasing feature of Jones's poetry through the 1850s and which the republication of *The Battle-Day* collection and much of the poetry it contains fortuitously consolidates:

> To Jones, Christianity was a righteous cause around which the personal and collective political activism of the working classes could be represented and mobilised; it also demonstrated to the privileged classes that the Chartists were worthy of the franchise. [...] As a symbolic language and a means of political expression, Jones's Christian discourses not only relate the workings of his personal conscience to the collective realm of political activism; they demonstrate his principled stance to the privileged classes as well.[36]

As a poem composed on the cusp of Jones's plunge into 'low Radical' politics, 'The Battle-Day' can be read as an expression of a phase in the development of its author's reconciliation of personal and political modes of thinking. However, the allegorical nature of its setting means that its 1855 republication presents a discourse around the nature of leadership and faith that operates both at an international and historical level, and at the level of domestic Chartist politics. Perhaps more importantly in terms of the development at this stage of Jones's poetic voice, the double address which in *Northern Star* poetry used to consist of elevation of the working class and threat toward the privileged classes now decreases in its polarity as the subject matter becomes more ideologically mainstream. Radicalism is diffused by generalized support for the overthrow of tyrannical foreign governments in poems including 'The Cry of the Russian Serf to the Czar' and 'The Italian Exile to his Countrymen'. The appearance of these poems in a subsection entitled 'Cries of the Nations', alongside other former Chartist lyrics including 'Onward and Upward' and 'The Coming Day', which importantly do not specify Great Britain as the site of conflict, internationalizes their voice of protest and implicitly defines tyranny as a 'foreign' problem. By these means, Chartist lyrics, with their titles or their framing contexts tweaked, can be read approvingly by middle-class or even conservative readerships. At the same time, the title poem can be read as a broadly patriotic commentary on recent events in the Crimean War.

The rest of the collection consists of poems which have largely been re-titled or re-grouped. For example, 'The Garden Seat', which was written by Jones in prison and first published in *Notes to the People* in 1851, becomes 'The Poet's Invitation', in a subsection entitled 'The Poet'. The same subsection contains 'To Chateaubriand', which was published in the *Morning Post* in 1843, now re-titled 'The Poet's Death', and the Shelleyan 'The Poet's Prayer to the Evening Wind', which is discussed in Chapter One. Of course, there is nothing dishonourable about publishing in a collection poems which have previously only appeared in newspapers, but Jones's retitling of many of these works, alongside his renaming and republishing of 'Lord Lindsay'/'The Battle-Day', suggests a furtiveness that attempts to conceal the recycling of his work. At the very end of the collection, even this pretence is largely dropped as the introduction and first part (amounting to a substantial nineteen pages) of *My Life* is reprinted wholesale with its original 1845 pseudonym ('Percy Vere') as its new title.

If the *Battle-Day* collection seems to represent an ideological and poetic shift toward the centre ground then it should be seen in the context of the political reality of the day for Jones. Although his post-prison efforts had seen membership of the National Charter Association rise from five hundred to nearly two thousand,[37] this was a long way from the days when the association could muster more than a million signatures for a petition to present to Parliament, and it could barely be said to represent a national movement any more. Although Jones continues to refer to himself as a Chartist, and is referred to as such by the conservative newspapers who review his poetry, faction and disintegration in reality take Chartism back to the status of just an idea. Indeed, two authoritative works on the history of Chartism end their narratives long before the mid-1850s: Chase's *Chartism: A New History* ends in 1852, while Thompson's *The Chartists: Popular Politics in the Industrial Revolution* ends in 1850. Jones's political and therefore poetic identity, especially after his imprisonment, is bound up with Chartism, and the *Battle-Day* collection perhaps represents an attempt by him to establish a mainstream poetic identity whilst retaining democratic credentials with non-specific reformist/radical poems including 'Onward and Upward' and 'The Coming Day'. Interestingly, two formerly major voices in Chartist poetry effected significant transformations in the nature of their radicalism at around this time: William James Linton abandoned his newspaper the *English Republic* in 1855 due to poor sales, whilst in 1856 Thomas

Cooper renounced his former free-thinking philosophy and embarked upon a lecture tour devoted to practical applications of Christian morality. Both men went on to establish post-Chartist literary reputations without significant accusations of apostasy, and the *Battle-Day* collection is the beginning of Jones's attempt at a similar process. The problem for Jones was that, unlike Linton or Cooper, he had placed himself at the very heart of the movement at the beginning of its decline.

The Emperor's Vigil, and The Waves and the War (1856)

The Emperor's Vigil, and The Waves and the War is a collection that builds upon the good reviews received by *The Battle-Day: And Other Poems* by once again proving relevant to the events of the Crimean War, but this time more directly and with poetry composed specifically for the occasion. In another gently dislocating shift away from the themes of Chartism, democracy is a feature of the poetry, but it is British or European democracy contrasted favourably with the tyranny of feudal Russia. In the broadly patriotic register of the volume, this democracy (the nature of which, in the case of Great Britain, Jones had been protesting against for ten years) is not even presented as the lesser of two evils. Jones is able to court a British conservative readership by transposing his radical voice onto a safely foreign stage.

The collection is divided into two halves — 'The Waves and the War' and 'Waifs'. The former consists of eight pieces making up a poeticized narrative account of the Baltic theatre of the Crimean War, while the latter consists of six individual poems which nevertheless all deal with the subject of war and Britain's place in the world. It is possible that the Crimean War proves a useful distraction for Jones from the failures of his ambitions in domestic politics, or even that Great Britain's involvement in the conflict might cause it to re-assess the nature of its own political make-up. In either case the war is depicted as a struggle between West and East; between 'the triumph of human right' and 'the tyrant of nations'.[38]

One of the most striking aspects of *The Emperor's Vigil* is the consistency of its register; unlike much of Jones's post-prison output there is a real sense of continuity between the pieces in the collection. As one might expect, many of the figures featured in the poetry, whether geographical, meteorological, or human, are mythologized, and the whole is shot through with medieval literary tropes. The first section of 'The Waves and the War' is titled 'The Baltic Fleet' and gives an account of the British Navy (under the command of Sir Charles Napier, the target of 'The Invasion' in *Rhymes on the Times* four years earlier), embarking for the Baltic, cheered by crowds of onlookers and accompanied part way by a flotilla of smaller civilian craft. From the beginning the responsibility for the vast military mobilization is laid at the feet of the Russian Czar:

> He would not let them rest
> On the waters of the West,
> Where they slumbered in their bays — those sons of England's might —
> With their great white shadowy shrouds
> Folded calm as brooding clouds,
> Dreaming of old victories in the drowsy summer-light.

He would not let them rest,
Those war-ships of the West,
The Czar of sullen Muscovy in drunkenness of pride;
And they gather now and throng,
The beautiful and strong,
Like a fairy pageant floating for a pastime on the tide.

They toy and they play
With the waters on their way;
They tack and they veer, as if in sport upon the sea;
But evermore they write
In those furrows creamy-white,
Our messages of ruin to thine empire and to thee.

The gentle ocean laughed
To the countless pleasure-craft,
That with music and with joyousness came dancing in delight;
And, as though 'twere a caress,
Round the mighty ships they press,
As you cheer a gallant charger ere it rushes to the fight.

('The Baltic Fleet', ll. 1–24)

This beginning of the poem, with its light imagery ('drowsy summer-light', 'gentle ocean') and medieval terms ('pageant', 'gallant charger') might be read as an idealization of contemporary political events, but even as Jones recognizes and celebrates the idealism of the Allies' cause, he does not shy away from the complicated results of modern warfare. Whilst the Baltic theatre and the rebuffed attacks on the Russian port of Kronstadt did not present the public with the outright carnage associated with the Siege of Sevastopol (1854–55) or the Battle of Balaclava (1854), the naval stalemate which occurred, despite the successful bombardment of Bomarsund (1854), was a severe test of the Allies' nerve. This was the first major war to be fought since the invention of the telegraph, effective photography, the steamship, and a complex railway system, and the rapidity of its events, combined with the rapidity of those events being relayed to the public through the media, created a different perception of the idea of war. This was not a distant war fought on foreign soil but a subject of 'live' reporting as newspaper correspondents telegraphed their reports instantaneously to newsrooms across Europe. Such public engagement with geopolitical events was unprecedented.

The subject of 'The Waves and the War' is as much the public perception of the Crimean War (or its Baltic campaigns) as the war itself. The second section, 'The Baltic', imagistically transforms the geography of the region into a vast medieval tournament field, emphasizing not the battles themselves, but their observation by the wider world:

And all within through a circle wide
The azure tides are sleeping;
A gallant field for a tournay's pride,
Where monarchs the lists are keeping.

The mountains hoar on the girdling land,
That rise in their vast gradations,

PSEUDONYMITY, REVISION, SONGS OF THE LOW AND HIGH (1851–60)   187

> The mighty seats of that theatre grand,
>   Are crowded with watching nations.
>
> The Heralds that open and close the lists,
>   Are the cloudy children of heaven:
> They come in the spring in a robe of mists,
>   In cars by the West Wind driven. (ll. 9–20)

Once more Jones returns to the figures of Shelley's 'Ode to the West Wind', associating political change with the weather in order to imply the inevitability of the action being taken. This is the same historical determinism that lies behind many of the prophetic statements contained in the Chartist poetry published in the *Northern Star*. The sanctioned, officiated competitive structure of the medieval tournament that Jones uses as an extended metaphor for the campaign might also suggest an attempt at containment or enclosure of a potentially unpredictable political situation — a poetic attempt to inscribe a history that could have gone either way. However, the suggested simplification of the campaign, alongside the apparent triumphalism of the first section's account of the departure of the British fleet, should be contrasted with the political pragmatism of the poem's concluding sections, where the speaker attempts to convey the nature of the political achievement of a military conflict which gained Britain no new territory and diverted only an indirect threat. Before this, the fifth and longest section of the poem, 'The Emperor's Vigil', after which the collection is named, gives an account of the conflict from Czar Nicholas I's perspective.

'The Emperor's Vigil' presents the Czar as a lonely and isolated figure, and its account of the Emperor of Russia surveying his realm and his eventual death (Nicholas I died in February 1855, before the end of the Crimean War) bears similarities to Jones's translation of Ludwig Ühland's 'The Monarch's Death-Prayer' (see Chapter One). It begins in a very similar manner to the poem Jones had published in the *Court Journal* in 1841:

> At Cronstadt in his granite palace
>   Walked the despot to and fro;
> Gazing through the seaward windows,
>   Asking tidings of the foe.
>
> Redly had the sun descended
>   On the sea-line cold and clear;
> Barren wastes of tumbling waters
>   Spread before him far and near.
>
>   ('The Emperor's Vigil', ll. 1–8)

Perhaps because of his childhood associations with the Duke of Cumberland, who would become King Ernst of Hanover, Jones seems continually fascinated by the pressures and dilemmas of kingship, portraying them through poems including 'The Monarch's Death-Prayer', 'The Minstrel's Curse', 'The New World', 'Corayda', and the prose tale 'The Confessions of a King'. Although Czar Nicholas is portrayed in an unsympathetic light, it is interesting that Jones devotes the greater part of his long poem to this 'despot's' perspective of the conflict. When the emperor retreats to his tower as Kronstadt is bombarded by the Allies he is wracked by dream-visions of the ghostly revenge of the multitudes who have died under his reign:

> Ha! they mount from mine and dungeon!
>   Ha! they break from shroud and chain!
> All the heroes he has murdered
>   All the martyrs he has slain.
>
> Trampling up the murky zenith,
>   Still they climb the horizon's rim,
> All their shadowy footsteps speeding
>   Over half the world to him. (ll. 97–104)

Here the poem departs from its function as historic chronicle and shifts into the realm of the dream-vision that characterizes much of 'The New World': historical progression and political balance are achieved in an imagined alternate world where tyrannical wrong-doing is repaid with karmic retribution. Both poetically and politically, the themes of Jones's Chartist imagery are transposed wholesale onto contemporary Russia.

After its dramatic or novelistic excursion into an account of the Crimean War, and particularly its Baltic theatre, from the perspective of Nicholas I, 'The Waves and the War' confronts the realities of the Allies' achievements through the voice of British soldiers and sailors returning home and defining their mission to a confused and questioning public. The seventh section of the poem, 'The Return', represents Jones's attempt to articulate the complex reasons for, and achievement of, a pan-European conflict whose *casus belli* proved scant justification for the suffering caused in the eyes of a significant proportion of the British public:

> We return — but not down-hearted;
>   Not a warrior vails his brow:
> Proud and joyous we departed,
>   And as proud return we now.
>
> Do you ask for our achievements —
>   What the cities we laid low?
> Greater 'tis to save a kinsman,
>   Greater than to smite a foe.
>
> And your eyes, to mete our service,
>   Need not wander o'er the flood:
> See in England — not in Russia —
>   What we did for England's good.
>
> England's shores were in our keeping,
>   England's commerce in our trust:
> Are your widowed mothers weeping?
>   Are your stately mansions dust?
>
> ('The Return', ll. 1–16)

Although the aim of the Crimean War is associated in a wider sense with democracy in Jones's poetic conception of it, the poem is also broadly patriotic, and might even be read as being in favour of British imperial interests. The ideological relationship

PSEUDONYMITY, REVISION, SONGS OF THE LOW AND HIGH (1851–60)   189

between the ethos of this poem and Jones's more avowedly radical works is complex, and is indicative of the different political approaches Jones negotiated in the years after his release from prison. While 'The Waves and the War' in one sense represents the kind of geopolitical observation that characterized Jones's poetic account of the bombardment of Mogador, 'Peace to Earth' (see Chapter One), his political stance in the later poem is more defined, and his engagement with the issues raised is deeper. However, by this point in his career, the political baggage that Jones carries is considerable, and it is difficult now, as reviews proved it was difficult then, to read any of his post-1850 poetry without relating it to Chartism or radical politics.

'The Waves and the War' ends with its eighth and final section, 'Prayer for Peace', taking the form of an invocation to the 'God of Battles' to 'give us peace!' (l. 1). This apparently paradoxical request condenses the conflicted voices implicit within the collection which negotiate the ideological lacunae between conceptions of domestic radicalism and international justice, partial democracy and outright tyranny, and patriotism and internationalism. The 'Waifs' which follow 'The Waves and the War' are individual poems linked by the broad theme of history and war, and vary between the patriotic 'Signs of Glory', which celebrates the English sense of honour in war, and 'The Fountains of History' which uses godlike Shelleyan personifications to interpret the contemporary geopolitical landscape. Whilst the latter, with its image of workers 'creeping to labour with faint bleeding feet' (l. 21) seems to some extent in keeping with the kind of visionary radicalism which produced 'The New World', the former, with its claim that 'An Englishman fights not for idle dross | But for honour, and glory, and right' (ll. 3–4), would seem to contradict the anti-imperialist harangues of 'England's Greatness', 'Britannia', and indeed 'The New World'. In its examination of the aims and achievements of the Crimean War, the *Emperor's Vigil* collection sets domestic politics, class conflict, and anti-imperialism aside for the greater good in order to bolster patriotic support for British intervention in world affairs.

Poetic Thoughts of E. C. J. (1856)

As far as an artistic production can be described as such, the collection *Poetic Thoughts of E. C. J.* is apolitical in nature — its few elements of social commentary shy away from statements which might identify its writer's political leanings. Probably because of the effectively pseudonymous initials of the title, the poems contained in the volume have never been written about, nor has the volume been referred to by critics as a Jones collection, although the British Library lists it as such in its catalogue. In fact, Jones's 1856 return to the nom de plume of E. C. J. is even more appropriate for this collection than in the case of *Rhymes on the Times*, due to the politically neutral, Romantic nature of the poetry contained within. The volume reads as a continuation of the poetic career of the Jones who published 'To Her' under the name 'E. C. J.' in the *Court Journal* in 1840, with a smattering of satire and social commentary amongst a preponderance of love poetry and medieval tropes. Published simultaneously in both Paris and London, the volume may represent an attempt by Jones to make money from a particular branch of his poetic output whilst retaining the choice of deniability should critical appreciation turn against him. Whether Jones made any money from the volume is not known, but there is no evidence that the collection was reviewed by the periodicals which tended to take note of Jones's work under his own name including *John Bull*, the *Morning Post*, or the *Spectator*.

The Paris publisher was Gustav Gratiot of Rue Mazarine, whose publications included illustrated French translations of Plutarch's *Parallel Lives* (*Vie des Hommes*, 1853), but given the pseudonymous nature of the project, Jones's choice of London publisher is interesting. Darton & Co. was a Quaker publishing house founded to produce children's literature and morally instructive works in 1787. The continued involvement of various Darton family members ensured the company retained its reputation for wholesome, 'polite' literature until its eventual closure in 1876. *Poetic Thoughts* is certainly inoffensive enough (with one possible exception) in its style of poetry and language, and it also contains moments of piety and moral instruction. There is nothing of the political firebrand of *Notes to the People*, and Chartism seems a very long way from this poetically conservative volume. Perhaps it is significant that Jones chose a publishing house largely known for its children's books as a vehicle for a return to something like his youthful poetic style.

Formally, *Poetic Thoughts* reflects the general poetic eclecticism of Jones's mid-1850s output and covers styles as disparate as short lyrics, verse dramas, verse narratives, dramatic monologues, sea shanties, and single stanza epigrams. Most of the rhyme schemes are couplets or alternating rhymes and there is no evidence of the formal experimentation of 'The Prisoner's Dream' or parts of 'Beldagon Church'. Thematically, the poems deal variously with love and yearning, religious devotion, loss and mourning, medieval allegory, social satire, and social commentary. The collection opens with 'Give me that faded flower', a lyric considering the emotional value attached to objects in contrast to their transient worth or intrinsic potential:[39]

> Give me that faded flow'r,
>   'Tis far more dear to me
> Than when in summer bow'r
>   It grew so fair and free;
> For then it had but pow'r
>   Like roses of its kind;
> It bloom'd its little hour,
>   Then vanished with the wind.
>   ('Give Me that Faded Flower', ll. 1–8)

Though framed as a love lyric, the real subject of this poem is the rose itself, and the status conferred upon it by the attentions of the speaker's lover. The association of human emotions attached to the dried flower transcends not just the meaning of its brief life but death and decay themselves, as the blossom achieves a form of immortality through the stimulation of the speaker's imagined senses:

> And now 'twill ne'er know death,
>   Its sweetness must remain,

PSEUDONYMITY, REVISION, SONGS OF THE LOW AND HIGH (1851–60)   191

> And nourish'd by thy breath,
>   The rose will bloom again.
> Its leaves have felt thy sigh,
>   Its buds have caught thy tear;
> Then say what flow'r could I
>   Find half so sweet or dear?
> Then give me that faded flow'r,
>   So worthless in thine eyes,
> And till my dying hour
>   The treasure I shall prize. (ll. 13–24)

Despite the flower, and especially the rose, being such an overused commonplace in the love poetry of the Victorian period and indeed preceding periods, this poem's evocation of themes of memory and mortality acts as a perfect introduction to a volume that includes a remarkable number of poems whose principal subject is death and loss. Of thirty-nine poems in the collection, eighteen deal explicitly with the theme of death, and several others concern loss of one form or another. If the poems contained in the volume were composed in the period immediately preceding its publication, and there is no evidence to the contrary, then it may be significant that Jones's wife, Jane Atherley, was suffering from a long period of sickness which would culminate in her death at the age of thirty-eight in 1857.

A poem that combines the theme of death with a typically Jonesian chivalric setting is 'The Stranger Knight' whose title shares its medieval trope with the subtitle of 'To Chateaubriand: A Voice from England to the Stranger Bard', which eventually became 'The Poet's Death' in the *Battle-Day* collection. The term 'stranger knight' refers to foreign monarchs who are given membership of the Order of the Garter, but is also the title of an 1814 Gothic tale by George Soanes (1790–1860). Soanes shared with Jones the distinction of being a translator of German Romantic literature. In Jones's brief, forty-line narrative poem the 'stranger knight' shadows a 'gallant young knight' through battle, appearing to protect the latter while not actually engaging the enemy; but when the stranger knight is struck down by an arrow his identity is revealed as the lover of the gallant young knight, who has followed him to war in armoured disguise. The poem's celebration of a passive feminine heroism might be read as a commentary on Jane Atherley's considerable sacrifice for her husband's political ideals, particularly the financial penury she suffered during his imprisonment. However, such a reading might also note that the words Jones gives the dying stranger knight, 'Weep not for me! | Too happy to die in thus saving thee' (ll. 33–34), could represent poetic wish-fulfilment on Jones's part, given his wife's recorded misgivings regarding many of his political actions.[40]

At the other end of the thematic spectrum is a comic verse drama called 'Miss Twad, and the Marquis de Sansterre', which details a romance between its presumably contemporary elderly characters.[41] Miss Twad is described as 'a Bath old maid' while the Marquis is a stereotypical penniless foreign aristocrat on the make whose name translates unsubtly as 'without land'. It is entirely possible that Jones is also having fun with the surname 'Twad', which is suspiciously similar to the vulgar term 'twat'. It may be that this is a literary in-joke referring to Robert Browning's

192   PSEUDONYMITY, REVISION, SONGS OF THE LOW AND HIGH (1851–60)

unintentional use of the term in his own dramatic verse of 1841, *Pippa Passes*, when he mistakenly assumed the word meant a particular type of nun's headgear. Jones's occasional formal shadowing of Browning with his dramatic monologues, and known familiarity with his works, supports this theory.

However, clearer intertextual links are apparent between Jones's poem and both 'The Lady's Dressing Room' (1732) and 'A Beautiful Young Nymph Going to Bed, Written for the Honour of the Fair Sex' (1734) by Jonathan Swift, particularly in its opening lines which feature Miss Twad instructing her '*femme de chambre*' in the construction of her '*toilette*' before a visit from her elderly beau:

> 'Julia, Julia, — do make haste,
> Give me the red cosmetic paste.
> I know not what my lord will say
> I'm such a horrid fright to-day.
> Now the Bambarra Dye prepare,
> And quickly come and tint my hair;
> There, hold the mirror in the sun,
> I must examine how 'tis done.
> Was ever such a figure seen?
> You've tinged one part a purplish green.
> While patches all about my head,
> Appear to me a fiery red.'
> ('Miss Twad, and the Marquis de Sansterre', ll. 1–12)

Apart from a general satirical swipe at female artifice and cosmetics, Jones's poem shares with Swift's works a contempt for the old attempting to appear young. All three poems are written in iambic tetrameter rhyming couplets and it is conceivable that Jones's opening words, 'Julia, Julia', echo the rhythm of one of the most famously scatological lines in eighteenth-century poetry: 'Oh! *Celia, Celia, Celia* shits!' ('The Lady's Dressing Room' l. 117).[42] While Jones balances the misogyny of his piece with an equally mean-spirited description of the Marquis's appearance, his rendering of the old gentleman's accent is pure Anglo–centric music hall: 'And tink I mean de stuff I say' (l. 49), 'Wat fun I vil have afterwards' (l. 55).

While 'Miss Twad, and the Marquis de Sansterre' represents a broadly comic example of social satire, the collection as a whole has a serious, even sombre, register. Many of its poems are lyrical expressions of romantic yearning or loss, and one piece, 'The Jacksons', echoes themes of some of Jones's prose fiction works in its treatment of the issue of domestic abuse.[43] Even 'On Hearing of the Fall of Sebastopol', which begins with the joyous news of the famous Crimean War victory being spread through a city's streets, ends with a study of a widowed mother's grief over the death of her soldier son.[44] Tellingly, however, this comparison between private grief and public celebration is not politicized. *Poetic Thoughts*, as its title suggests, is Jones's most intensely personal collection, and might represent an attempt to ascertain if his poems stand alone as aesthetic artefacts without the association of his name and political baggage. As an experiment in pseudonymity, *Poetic Thoughts* differs greatly from *Rhymes on the Times*, not just in ambition, but in the nature of its subjects. The earlier volume is entirely outward-looking — the opinions of the author are only apparent in relation to events in the outside world;

PSEUDONYMITY, REVISION, SONGS OF THE LOW AND HIGH (1851–60)   193

Poetic Thoughts is largely self-absorbed, Romantic, and insular, even its satires and narratives are small in scope. In keeping with its explicitly introspective title, it represents an ambition to achieve what Northrop Frye identifies as the centripetal tendency in some poetry, or even what John Stuart Mill identifies as poetry which is composed to be 'overheard'.[45] Unfortunately for Jones, despite his attempts to broaden his poetic readership, his *Poetic Thoughts* appear to have been barely heard at all.

Corayda: A Tale of Faith and Chivalry, and Other Poems (1860)

Although *Songs of Democracy* was published in 1857 and *The Revolt of Hindostan: Or, The New World* appeared in the same year, both of these collections consisted of largely recycled material; the former a pamphlet of Chartist songs including 'The Song of the Low' renamed as 'The Song of the Lower Classes' (by which it is sometimes still known), the latter a revised republication of Jones's prison-conceived epic. It might be the case that part of the raison d'être of *Songs of Democracy* was to publicize *The Revolt of Hindostan*. It is significant that Jones's re-naming of his epic not only took advantage of its apparent prediction of the Indian Uprising, but potentially shifted its political focus away from British domestic politics. *Corayda: A Tale of Faith and Chivalry, and Other Poems*, published in 1860, contained the first substantially new material since *Poetic Thoughts*, although, as noted above, its title poem had actually been composed in 1845. *Corayda* was Jones's final poetic publication; and at two hundred pages, it is also his longest. The title poem is a hundred and eleven pages long and consists of twenty-nine short sections, sixteen in Part One and thirteen in Part Two. The rest of the collection is made up of twenty 'Scatterings' — short lyric poems largely recycled from earlier publications including 'To Her' from the *Court Journal*, and 'Earth's Burdens' and 'The Sea Shell on the Desert' from *Notes to the People*;[46] another section of 'Percy Vere' amounting to twelve pages; and a group of poems labelled 'Transmarine', all of which are translations of the works of European writers including Freiligrath, Schiller, Dupont, and Ühland.

The collection is dedicated, with permission, to Sir Edward Bulwer-Lytton MP (1803–73), with whom Jones had been acquainted since 1840.[47] Although their association was literary, and Jones makes much of this in his dedication, the very fact that this volume is dedicated to a famous author who is also a Tory politician is an important statement regarding the apolitical ambition of the book. Jones appears to be attempting to forge a literary reputation that excludes his former politico-poetic associations, responding to praise from reviewers in conservative newspapers who admired his verse while deploring his radicalism. In his dedication he defines the two planes as entirely, and justifiably, separate:

> In permitting me to inscribe this work to yourself you have shown, by one additional and valuable example, that the Republic of Letters is beyond and above the political differences of the passing day. History bears witness to this fact. The politics of a Milton or a Dryden, diverse though they be, perish like their lives: their poems are immortal as their souls.
> It is well that we should be reminded of this truth. It is well we should have a common ground, far from the field of party and passion, where we can meet

amid the higher attributes of our humanity. It is well, when there is so much of the sordid and degrading in the political arena of the age, that men of widely different politics should say: 'There is something truer and nobler than all this — a calm and holy sanctuary of thought, wherein at least, if nowhere else, all men are brethren, and all brethren are friends'.[48]

This conception of the literary sphere as a 'holy sanctuary of thought' is a long way from the attitude to literature and its potential agency for change, and its responsibility to employ that agency, which led to Jones condemning Browning and Tennyson for their lack of literary/democratic credentials in the *Labourer* in 1847 (see Chapter Two). Jones may have maintained personal relationships with figures of varied political colour throughout his radical years, and the nature of his pseudonymous publications might complicate the conception of the apparent interdependence of his literary and political sensibilities, but this explicitly separatist statement employs an aesthetic philosophy to request that his work be judged entirely on its own merits.

The fact that more than half of this substantial volume consists of an epic poem written before Jones's direct involvement with politics obviously assists the attempt to depoliticize its literary reception. The first stanza of 'Corayda' describes the homeland of its eponymous hero in terms which emphasize not just the poem's medievalist, mythic approach to narrative subject, but specifically its distinctness from modern reality:

> 'Twas in an ancient kingdom
> In the old world far away,
> In those ages dim and grey,
> Where 'mid the lonely mountains
> A pastoral province lay. ('Corayda, Part I, I', ll. 1–5)[49]

The concentration of terms in this stanza serving to distance this world from contemporary, rapidly industrializing nineteenth-century Britain is remarkable: '*ancient* kingdom', '*old* world', '*far* away', 'ages *dim and grey*', '*lonely* mountains', '*pastoral* province'. If Jones's dedication wishes to escape the 'sordid and degrading' realities of Victorian Britain then 'Corayda' provides a means to do so and endows its protagonist with the simple virtues of faith, honesty, and loyalty. The narrative is something of a *Bildungsroman* which plots Corayda's development from boy to man as he leaves his remote family cottage, becomes involved in battles and courtly intrigue, and is finally crowned king of his nation in the peculiarly meritocratic manner with which only fairy tales view the institution of monarchy. Some of the short sections making up the piece — which vary in form and metre in keeping with Jones's characteristic virtuosity — step outside of the narrative and act as chants or commentaries in the style of a Greek chorus or the repetitions included in some Scandinavian verse cycles such as the *Kalevala*. Perhaps through the influence of Jones's steeping in Germanic myth, the second section, 'The Spirits' Call', echoes the form of North European myths as it uses an invocation of animal spirits to celebrate and introduce its hero:

> The stag-hound pants for the bugle call,
> The steed strikes the ground as he waits in the stall,

The eagle looks up when the thunder is nigh,
And brooks not to rest though his eyrie be high,
                                    Corayda!

The falcon will dart from his hood to the skies,
As the fire of his heart overflows through his eyes;
All are straining — attaining — or seeking a goal:
The soulless are stirring — why slumbers thy soul,
                                    Corayda?

('Corayda, Part I, II', ll. 1–10)[50]

The narrative unfolds across the two parts of the poem, with the break coming as Corayda is banished from the kingdom after being falsely accused of treachery. Familiar tropes and themes emerge from different sections of the poem: section V of Part II, 'The King's Vigil' echoes (or prefigures) 'The Emperor's Vigil' and the 'The Monarch's Death-Prayer' — 'Within his chamber lone the king | Listed his empire's death knell ring' (ll. 9–10).[51] Section XI of Part II, 'The Nightly Halt', with its lively narrative of ambush and battle, covers much of the same poetic ground as 'The Battle-Day' or even sections of 'The New World'. Indeed, with the inclusion of short narrative translations of Schiller's 'The Diver' and Ühland's 'The Minstrel's Curse', the theme of lowly individuals engaging with monarchs becomes a substantial feature of the collection as a whole. That the latter poem concludes the collection gives a curiously circular ring to Jones's poetic career, given that its first publication was almost twenty years earlier in the *Court Journal*.

As though aware that *Corayda* would be Jones's last poetry publication, the review in the *Morning Chronicle* of 18 February 1860 is fittingly elegiac in its register. And the process of welcoming a prodigal gentleman back to the fold which is apparent in several conservative reviews of his works seems almost complete:

> Were a Walhalla to be erected among us, we think that posterity would grant Mr. Ernest Jones a niche as the most favourable representative of the minor minstrels of the nineteenth century. His whole life through he appears to have obeyed poetic impulses, and fostered theories which can only be accounted for on that assumption. There has been something truly chivalrous in the way that Mr. Ernest Jones has fought against the most savage opposition, but never besmirched his name by one questionable deed. Through good and evil report he has remained true to himself, and instead of regarding him with aversion, we ought to feel thankful that the masses have been championed by a sweet-blooded gentleman, who has ever taught them that their only hope of victory will be found in fair argument and persuasion.
>
> For the present, Mr. Jones's political occupation is gone; there is positively nothing on which the people require enlightenment; and, laying aside social topics, Mr. Jones has recently been disporting in the magic realms of poesy. Many of our readers will remember the previous volumes of poetry Mr. Jones produced, and the surprise created by the true ring of metal they gave out; we had recognised among us a really popular poet, who laid bare his heart's agony, and won sympathy from even his most virulent opponents.[52]

In contrast to Jones's separation of poetry and politics in his dedication to the volume, the reviewer here seems to attribute Jones's political waywardness to his poetic sensibility: his 'poetic impulses' have led him down politically erroneous, though well-meaning tracks. The affection for Jones here seems evident, but it might partly be attributed to a conservative impulse to appropriate ideologically Jones's political reputation in order to neutralize its potential for influence. Indeed, the term 'sweet-blooded', while it could be interpreted as referring to Jones's aristocratic connections, could also be read as patronizing or even infantilizing; in which case Jones is not so much being neutralized as neutered. In any case, the publication of *Corayda* in 1860 coincided with something of a withdrawal from active politics for Jones, though he was to return with a substantial role in the liberal Reform League movement later in the decade. At the time of the publication of his last poetry collection the Chartist movement was no more, and Jones was working as a barrister, though his tendency to champion politically contentious or radical causes was a constant reminder of his radical past.

It is impossible to assess Ernest Jones's post-prison poetic career without considering shifting grounds of identity and readership. If Jones's mission in 1846 was to charge his poetry with an engagement with the 'mighty mind' of the people, then the story of his poetry through the 1850s is one of a redefinition of that mind, and his relationship with it. With his confidence and status within the diminished Chartist movement at a high during the two years he published *Notes to the People*, his relationship with his readership became more sophisticated, and the poetry published within that newspaper shows evidence of a heightened awareness of the heterogeneity of this readership. There is a broader range of form and register to the poetry than in the pre-prison years, and works like 'Beldagon Church' and 'The New World' lay some claim to being 'public' poems in a more general sense than in a merely Chartist context. But while Jones had some initial success revitalizing Chartism, its slow decline was inevitable in the face of radicalism changing, being dispersed into protest and activism on more specific issues than fundamental reform of the franchise (as discussed at the beginning of this chapter). Eventually, rather than follow radical poetry into an arena such as gender politics in the manner of Hugh Arthur Clough or Elizabeth Barrett Browning, Jones shifted the public engagement of his poetry to the middle ground, attempting to catch the mood of the nation with *The Battle-Day* and *The Emperor's Vigil*, collections which reflected and confronted issues raised by the Crimean War.

Jones was employed throughout the 1850s as the editor of a series of radical newspapers (*Notes to the People*, 1851–52; *The People's Paper*, 1852–58; *Cabinet Newspaper*, 1858–60), and part of his strategy of republishing pre-existing or already published work can be attributed simply to the fact that he was often too busy to compose original material. It is probably significant that the relative flurry of poetic activity between 1855 and 1857, which saw the publication of *The Battle-Day: And Other Poems, The Emperor's Vigil* and *The Waves and the War, Poetic Thoughts of E. C. J., Songs of Democracy*, and *The Revolt of Hindostan: Or, The New World*, occurred when Jones was fully established as the editor of the *People's Paper*, and its circulation was stable enough for him occasionally to write or edit his own creative output.

The nature of that output was often a return to the kinds of mythological narratives absorbed during Jones's German upbringing which nevertheless chimed with mid-nineteenth-century British medievalism. Situated somewhere between Ludwig Ühland's chivalric themes and Robert Browning's dramatic forms, poems including *My Life/Percy Vere*, 'Lord Lindsay'/'The Battle-Day', *Corayda*, and many lesser works exploit the mid-nineteenth-century preoccupation with the moral simplicity of a mythically evoked past. The fact that 'The Battle-Day' can, and has, been interpreted as an allegorical treatment of the events of Chartism despite being composed before Jones's involvement with the movement attests to the universality of its narrative and themes. The same could be said of 'Corayda', whose young protagonist's journey from a rural idyll to a land of intrigue where he is courageous in battle, favoured, betrayed, and banished before a triumphant return to ascendancy could easily be read as an allegory of Jones's own progress through the Chartist movement.

Whilst *Rhymes on the Times*, which makes no claims to poetic depth or complexity, can be characterized as a political experiment, *Poetic Thoughts* is very much an experiment of a poetic nature. It is an expression of Jones's desire for recognition as an aesthetically sensitive poet at a time when his radical readership had diminished to almost nothing, and his reviews in the mainstream press read all of his poetry in relation to his political identity. The positive nature of some of these reviews must have allowed him to believe that through the de-politicization of his poetry and his poetic voice, he could achieve a renegotiation with his readership which allowed him a return to some of the middle-class values and poetic subjects of his pre-Chartist days, while at the same time retaining the in-built status and admiration which political leadership and sacrifice had afforded him. The pseudonymous publication of *Poetic Thoughts*, with its conscious casting off of a politically saturated identity, tested the strength of the former without reliance on the latter.

But in reality, what often sets Jones's poetry apart is the distinctiveness of the poetic conceit of inversion which is recognizable through much of his radical work. The loss of this quality robs Jones of the basis for much of his strongest voice. At the same time, as the *Corayda* collection amply demonstrates, Jones is often at his most comfortable when expressing the desires, troubles, and lives of high-born or socially aspirational subjects. The conflict between these poetic modes can be seen to operate through much of Jones's poetic career, but especially in these later years. It is noticeable that throughout his career, Jones's individual poetic speaking voices, or his most distinctly drawn poetic characters, are almost always privileged subjects, whilst his expression of the working-class voice is almost always collective. Jones could sing the song of the low, but his speaking voice would always tend toward the high. In the years between 1851 and 1860, the changing nature of politics and the pressures of editorial responsibility meant that Jones's poetic career followed this tendency toward its natural end.

Notes to Chapter 6

1. Chase, pp. 316 & 333.
2. Thompson, p. 330.
3. Ibid., p. 330.

4. Chase, p. 333.

5. Ibid., p. 337.

6. Ernest Jones, Dedication for 'Beldagon Church: A Religious Poem', in *NP* (1851), I, 21.

7. Ernest Jones, 'Beldagon Church: A Religious Poem', in *NP* (1851), I, 21–27.

8. *NP* (1851), I, 22.

9. Note Jones's use of silk yet again in a negative context. See Chapter Two.

10. Ernest Jones, 'The Slave Ship', in *NP* (1851), I, 488.

11. Ernest Jones, 'Christian Love', in *NP* (1851), I, 337 (in Kovalev, pp. 170–71).

12. Taylor, p. 166.

13. Joseph Maudslay (1801–61) was the son of Isambard Kingdom Brunel's engineering associate Henry Maudslay (1771–1831). Joseph was himself an engineer who invented the oscillating marine engine. The 1851 census confirms that he lived in Lambeth with his wife Anna and their seven children. Jones's connection to Maudslay or his wife has not been documented.

14. Ernest Jones, 'The Farmer's Last New Song', in *Rhymes on the Times by E. C. J.* (London: Brettell, 1852), pp. 12–13 (l. 28). Hereafter *Rhymes on the Times* is referred to as *RT*.

15. Ernest Jones as 'E. C. J.', 'The Invasion', in *RT*, pp. 3–5.

16. Ernest Jones, 'A Chartist March', *NS* 13/6/1846, and 'The Patriot's Test', *NS* 29/1/1848.

17. Ernest Jones as 'E. C. J.', 'Victory of Lagos', in *RT*, pp. 8–10.

18. Ernest Jones as 'E. C. J.', 'The Quack', in *RT*, pp. 6–7.

19. Ernest Jones as 'E. C. J.', 'Reform', in *RT*, p. 11.

20. Robert Saunders, 'Lord John Russell and Parliamentary Reform, 1848–67', *English Historical Review*, 120 (December 2005), 1289–1315 (p. 1290).

21. Thompson, p. 262.

22. Taylor, pp. 160–63.

23. Ibid., p. 177.

24. Armstrong, p. 197.

25. Ernest Jones, 'The Italian Exile to his Countrymen', in *BD*, pp. 51–52.

26. Armstrong, p. 198.

27. Taylor, pp. 70–71.

28. Armstrong's discussion of 'The Battle-Day' in *Victorian Poetry: Poetry, Poetics and Politics*, especially for a work published in 1993, is relatively substantial at a page long, but it is framed within a discussion of Chartist poetry more generally, which in itself falls within a chapter entitled 'The Radical in Crisis: Clough'.

29. A copy of the *National Chartist Hymn Book* can be viewed at the Working Class Movement Library in Salford.

30. Mike Sanders, '"God is our guide! our cause is just!": The *National Chartist Hymn Book* and Victorian Hymnody', *Victorian Studies*, 54, 4 (Summer 2012), 679–705 (p. 684).

31. Ibid., p. 685.

32. Review of *The Battle-Day: And Other Poems* by Ernest Jones, *John Bull*, 29 September 1855.

33. Review of *The Battle-Day: And Other Poems* by Ernest Jones, *Spectator*, 11 August 1855.

34. Jones, 'The Painter of Florence', in *NP* (1851), I, 47.

35. Ernest Jones, 'The Battle-Day: Or, The Lost Army', in *BD*, pp. 20–32.

36. Vickers, p. 75.

37. Chase, p. 338.

38. Ernest Jones, 'The Waves and the War IV: The Words of the West', in *The Emperor's Vigil and The Waves and the War* (London: Routledge, 1856), pp. 16–19.

39. Ernest Jones, 'Give Me that Faded Flower', in *Poetic Thoughts of E. C. J.* (London: Darton & Co, Paris: G. Gratiot, 1856), pp. 1–2 (p. 1). Hereafter *Poetic Thoughts of E. C. J.* is referred to as *PT*.

40. Taylor notes several instances of Jane Atherly's concern about the familial consequences of Jones's political actions in letters to relatives and indeed to Jones himself.

41. Ernest Jones, 'Miss Twad, and the Marquis de Sansterre', in *PT*, pp. 52–59.

42. Jonathan Swift, 'The Lady's Dressing Room', in *British Literature 1640–1789: An Anthology*, ed. by Robert Demaria Jr. (Oxford: Blackwell, 1996), pp. 430–33 (p. 431, l. 117).

43. Ernest Jones, 'The Jacksons', in *PT*, pp. 15–24.

44. Ernest Jones, 'On Hearing of the Fall of Sebastopol', in *PT*, pp. 50–52.

PSEUDONYMITY, REVISION, SONGS OF THE LOW AND HIGH (1851–60)   199

45. John Stuart Mill, 'Thoughts on Poetry and its Varieties', in *Dissertations and Discussions Political, Philosophical and Historical*, 2 vols (London: John W. Parker & Son, 1859–75), I, 71.
46. Ernest Jones, 'Earth's Burdens', in *NP* (1851), I, 66, and 'The Sea Shell on the Desert', in *NP* (1851), I, 130.
47. Taylor speculates that it was Bulwer-Lytton who gave Jones (or 'E. C. J.', or 'Karl') his introduction to the *Court Journal* (p. 50). If this is true then this distinguished literary and political figure would appear curiously to have bookended Jones's twenty-year-long British poetic career.
48. Ernest Jones, 'Dedication to the Right Honourable Edward Bulwer Lytton, Bart. M. P.', in *Corayda: A Tale of Faith and Chivalry, and Other Poems* (London: W. Kent, 1860), p. v. Hereafter *Corayda: A Tale of Faith and Chivalry* is referred to as *CTFC*.
49. Ernest Jones, 'Corayda, Part I, I. The Childhood Home', in *CTFC*, p. I.
50. Ernest Jones, 'Corayda, Part I, II. The Spirits' Call', in *CTFC*, p. 3.
51. Ernest Jones, 'Corayda, Part II, v. The King's Vigil', in *CTFC*, p. 67.
52. Review of *Corayda: A Tale of Faith and Chivalry, and Other Poems*, *Morning Chronicle*, 18 February 1860.

CONCLUSION

In the second chapter of this study I suggested that the ideological distance between Jones's conservative and radical identities was always greater than the corresponding poetic distance. In this regard it might be recalled that Jones's first anti-industrial poem, 'The Cornfield and the Factory', was published in the conservative *Morning Post* newspaper in January 1844, two years before his involvement with Chartism. Throughout Jones's poetic career, the malleable, allusive, and indeterminate nature of poetic language served to bridge social, cultural, and ideological gaps. Jones's initial dislocation as a British subject raised in the German states was partially addressed by an early engagement with English literature, the translation of German poems into English, and the composition of German language poetry whose themes concerned communication: 'Licht und Sprache' ('Light and Speech'); 'Der Deutsche Sprachschatz' ('The German Vocabulary'); 'Politisches' ('On Politics'). Through Jones's attempts in his early poetry to address issues including Ireland, rural unrest, and international conflict, we can trace a young man's political development up to the point where he is radicalized, and his poetry finds an audience receptive to his declarative style.

In personal terms, the cause(s) of this radicalization will never be known, and speculation will remain just that; but analysis of the poetry from either side of this ideological divide at least provides more information about the contextual framework surrounding this famous act of political apostasy, and questions the nature of the divide itself. Jones's appropriation and adaptation of conservative mythic tropes and themes for Chartist poetry tells us much about the nature of the radical and conservative imaginations, but also about the proximities between them. It might seem perverse to doubt the democratic instinct of a man who spent time in prison for that cause and subsequently spent the rest of his life striving towards that end in one way or another, but the concept of benevolent monarchy in a medieval setting is rarely far from Jones's poetic imagination. Much of his poetry, conservative or radical, is a reaction to industrialization, but in his embrace of the Land Plan and mythic interpretation of its bucolic promise, modernity is rejected wholesale. Indeed, it is remarkable how much of Jones's poetry, pre- or post-1846, can be considered both conservative *and* radical. 'The New World', which declares itself a democratic poem and concludes with a world transformed by superior technology, fails to identify the industrial circumstances in which this technology is produced, and its most sympathetic character is a well-meaning king. However Jones's political ambitions might have changed following his Chartist engagement, his poetic imagination reveals his underlying ideological approaches to contemporary issues, and their mythic consistency.

That Jones used his poetry as a means to introduce himself to his fellow Chartists and to define his relationship with them is indisputable, but the extent of his poetry's influence on Chartism will always be open to question. Jones may have poured the tide of his songs over England, but to what degree he formed the tone of the 'mighty mind' of the people is not merely a question of amplitude, but of the precise nature of this 'tone', and this 'mighty mind'. Given our own cultural and historical dislocation from the relevant issues, we can only approach these questions through the imperfect means of attempting to inhabit the Chartist reader's imagination — but in this way we can at least consider the factors and parameters. At the very least, through sustained close analysis of a body of work which has only been approached through discrete samples before, this study has established the validity of the opinion that Chartist poetry was an important medium of political discourse. There is scope for much more study in this area but I would also hope that my exploratory research into the links between the Chartist and Irish nationalist poetic traditions would yield critical fruit in the future.

The poetry that Jones produced while in prison is significant on many levels. The lyrical works provide an insight into what happens to Jones's poetic imagination when it is separated from day-to-day life and politics, and reveal the extent to which romanticism pervades his poetic method. Shorn of its political imperative, at this point his poetry appears to recover its aesthetic ambition, and we hear an independently mature voice for the first time. Despite the poem's overarching political theme, it is this voice that produces his epic work, 'The New World'. Although many of the errors committed by critics in terms of Jones's poetry have been down to the chronological complications caused by republication, it is the chronological structure of 'The New World' which many have failed to grasp. Should future observers disagree with my analysis of the poem's detailed approach to historical progression and imperialist critique, I would hope they would still find useful the canto-by-canto structural breakdown I have provided for this significant work.

In terms of poetic production, the theme that most completely pervades this study is that of republication and revision. Some poems, including 'The Cornfield and the Factory' and 'The Minstrel's Curse', were republished with little or no revision despite the very different contexts of their subsequent appearances. But Jones also re-worked formerly conservative poems for radical (re)publication ('The Farmer'/'The Peasant'), toned down the radical message of poems for more mainstream publication ('The Painter of Florence'/'The Cost of Glory'), and re-named previously published poems to give them contemporary relevance ('To Chateaubriand'/'The Poet's Death', 'Our Destiny'/'The Cry of the Russian Serf to the Czar' and 'Our Cheer'/'The Italian Exile to his Countrymen'). While these acts of poetic regeneration (an admittedly charitable phrase) tell us much about Jones's attitude to poetic production, and about the mobility, and occasionally surprising proximity, of poetic subjects, they also inform our understanding of the act of reading, and the nature of readership. Indeed, because of the particular social definition of the relationship between the Chartist poet and the Chartist reader, the figure of the Reader has loomed larger in this study than would have been the case had its subject written with less direct intent. Jones's cultural distance from much of his radical audience, attributable to both his German upbringing and his social status, provides us with a uniquely formed, but no less valuable, perspective on the nature of this readership. Equally, analysis of radical and conservative reactions to Jones's poetry provides a distinctive contribution to discussion regarding the nature of the relationship between politics and aesthetics. Consideration of this continually pertinent subject can only be enriched by a historical snapshot of a sometimes very different cultural attitude to this relationship.

Poetry which has evaded contemporaneous and modern critical reaction is contained in Jones's two pseudonymous collections, *Rhymes on the Times* and *Poetic Thoughts of E. C. J.*. The latter volume fleshes out a particular poetic identity seen in its immature form in Jones's *Court Journal* poems and hinted at in some of his lyrical prison poetry. Here, Romantic solitude and introspection take the place of moral certitude and social engagement, and the type of poetry offered appears to emerge from a middle-class aesthetic largely divorced from contemporary political realities. *Rhymes on the Times* could not be more different. This pamphlet shares with Jones's Chartist poetry a certainty and purpose which directs the reader to conclusions whose moral simplicity disguises a political complexity, but it imparts a wholly different message. Just as we will never know the real reasons for Jones's immersion in Chartist politics, we will probably never know the reasons for the political duplicity represented by this volume. But examination of these and many other issues raised by a detailed engagement with Jones's poetry illuminates perennially relevant discussion regarding the relationship between politics and poetry, both in its production and reception. Jones's extraordinary life and the often extraordinary poetry it produced continue to both ask and answer questions which transcend their historical relevance.

Jones the Manchester barrister, mid-1860s
(reproduced with kind permission of Gerald-Massey.org)

BIBLIOGRAPHY

Works by Ernest Jones

The Battle-Day: And Other Poems (London: Routledge, 1855)
Corayda: A Tale of Faith and Chivalry, and Other Poems (London: W. Kent, 1860)
Diary, Manchester County Record Office, MS. f281.89 J5/30
The Emperor's Vigil and The Waves and the War (London: Routledge, 1856)
Manuscript Poems, Manchester County Record Office, MS. f281.89. J5/30
My Life (London: T. C. Newby, 1845)
Notes to the People, 2 vols (London: Merlin Press, 1967)
Poetic Thoughts of E. C. J. (London: Darton & Co, Paris: G. Gratiot, 1856)
Rhymes on the Times by E. C. J. (London: Brettell, 1852)
Songs of Democracy (London: John Lowry, 1856)
The Wood Spirit: A Novel (London: Boone & Co., 1841)

Individual Poems

'A Chartist Chorus', *Northern Star*, 6 June 1846 (in Kovalev, p. 136)
'A Chartist March', *Northern Star*, 13 June 1846
'A Prisoner's Night-Thought', in *Notes to the People*, 1, 63
'A Song for the People', *Northern Star*, 4 March 1848 (in Kovalev, pp. 151–52)
'The Age of Peace', *Northern Star*, 4 December 1847
'The Battle-Day: Or, The Lost Army', in *The Battle-Day: And Other Poems*, pp. 20–32
'Beldagon Church: A Religious Poem', *in Notes to the People* (1851), 1, 21–27
'The Better Hope', *Northern Star*, 5 September 1846
'The Blackstone Edge Gathering', *Northern Star*, 22 August 1846 (in Kovalev, pp. 140–41)
'The Boy's Mountain Song', *Court Journal*, 18 October 1841
'Britannia', *Northern Star*, 18 July 1846
'Christian Love', in *Notes to the People* (1851), 1, 337 (in Kovalev, pp. 170–71)
'The Coming Day', in *The Battle-Day: And Other Poems*, pp. 54–55
'The Cornfield and the Factory', *Morning Post*, 20 January 1844
'The Cost of Glory', in *The Battle-Day: And Other Poems*, pp. 1–19
'The Cry of the Russian Serf to the Czar', in *The Battle-Day: And Other Poems*, p. 50
'Das Lebens-Ziel', *Court Journal*, 2 July 1842
'Der Deutscher Sprachschaft', *Deutsche Londoner Zeitung*, 25 April 1845
'Earth's Burdens', in *Notes to the People* (1851), 1, 66
'Echoes No. I: The Golden Harp', *Morning Post*, 19 January 1844
'Echoes No. II: The Cornfield and the Factory', *Morning Post*, 20 January 1844
'Echoes No. III: The Farmer', *Morning Post*, 6 February 1844
'England', *Northern Star*, 23 January 1847
'England's Greatness', *Northern Star*, 4 July 1846
'The Factory Town', *Northern Star*, 13 February 1847 (in Kovalev, pp. 141–45)
'The Farmer's Last New Song', in *Rhymes on the Times*, pp. 12–13
'The Fountains of History', in *The Emperor's Vigil and The Waves and the War*, pp. 69–72
'The Garden Seat', in *Notes to the People* (1851), 1, 66
'Geister-Ahnung', *Court Journal*, 5 March 1842

'The German Boy's Song', *Court Journal*, [undated]
'Give Me that Faded Flower', in *Poetic Thoughts of E. C. J.*, pp. 1–2
'The Goodwin Sands', *Court Journal*, 2 October 1841
'Hymn for Lammas-Day', in *Notes to the People* (1851), I, 70 (in Kovalev, pp. 164–65)
'The Insurrections of the Working Classes', *Labourer*, I (1847), 11–18
'The Invasion', in *Rhymes on the Times*, pp. 3–5
'The Italian Exile to his Countrymen', in *The Battle-Day: And Other Poems*, pp. 51–52.
'The Jacksons', in *Poetic Thoughts of E. C. J.*, pp. 15–24
'Lines on the Brocken', *Court Journal*, 22 May 1841
'Literary Review', *Labourer*, II (1847), 94–96
'The March of Freedom', *Northern Star*, 18 March1848 (in Kovalev, pp. 152–57)
'The Minstrel's Curse', *Court Journal*, 4 December 1841
'Miss Twad, and the Marquis de Sansterre', in *Poetic Thoughts of E. C. J.*, pp. 52–59
'The Monarch's Death-Prayer', *Court Journal*, 25 December 1841
'The New World, a Democratic Poem', in *Notes to the People*, I, 1–15
'The New Year's Song of Our Exile', *Northern Star*, 16 January 1847
'On Hearing of the Fall of Sebastopol', in *Poetic Thoughts of E. C. J.*, pp. 50–52
'Onward', *Labourer*, I (1847), 234 (in Kovalev, p. 150)
'Onward and Upward', in *The Battle-Day: And Other Poems*, p. 53
'Our Cheer', *Northern Star*, 8 August 1846
'Our Destiny', *Northern Star*, 11 July 1846 (in Kovalev, p. 137)
'Our Summons', *Northern Star*, 16 May 1846 (in Kovalev, pp. 135–36)
'Our Trust', *Northern Star*, 27 May 1848
'Our Warning', *Northern Star*, 1 August 1846
'The Painter of Florence: A Domestic Poem', in *Notes to the People*, I, 41–47
'The Patriot's Test', *Northern Star*, 29 January 1848
'Peace to Earth', *Morning Post*, 26 September 1844
'The Peasant', in *The Battle-Day: And Other Poems*, pp. 47–49
'The Poet's Death', in *The Battle-Day: And Other Poems*, p. 66 (in Kovalev, pp. 178–79)
'The Poet's Invitation', in *The Battle-Day: And Other Poems*, pp. 63–64
'The Poet's Mission', *Northern Star*, 17 October 1846 (in Kovalev, p. 179)
'The Poet's Prayer to the Evening Wind', in *The Battle-Day: And Other Poems*, pp. 61–62
'Poland's Hope', *Northern Star*, 27 February 1847
'Politisches', *Deutsche Londoner Zeitung*, 25 April 1845
'Prison Bars', in *Notes to the People* (1851), I, 64 (in Kovalev, p. 162)
'The Prisoner's Dream', in *Notes to the People* (1851), I, 67–68
'The Quack', in *Rhymes on the Times*, pp. 6–7
'St. Coutt's', in *Notes to the People* (1851), I, 69
'The Sea Shell on the Desert', in *Notes to the People* (1851), I, 130
'Signs of Glory', in *The Emperor's Vigil and The Waves and the War*, pp. 57–58
'The Silent Cell', in *Notes to the People* (1851), I, 66–67 (in Kovalev, pp. 163–64)
'The Slave Ship', in *Notes to the People* (1851), I, 488
'Soldier and Citizen: to the Oppressed of Either Class', *Northern Star*, 1 April 1848
'The Song of the Low', in *Notes to the People* (1852), II, 953 (in Kovalev, pp. 174–76)
'The Song of the Starving', *Northern Star*, 25 May 1847
'The Stars', *Court Journal*, 9 October 1841
'The Stranger Knight', in *Poetic Thoughts of E. C. J.*, pp. 2–4
'To Chateaubriand: A Voice from England to the Stranger Bard', *Morning Post*, 13 December 1843
'To Her', *Court Journal*, 8 November 1842
'To the British Democracy', *Friend of the People*, 24 May 1851

206 BIBLIOGRAPHY

'To the Men of Ireland', in Saville, pp. 216–18
'To Wordsworth', in *Notes to the People*, I, 69
'The Two Races', *Northern Star*, 12 September 1846
'Victory of Lagos', in *Rhymes on the Times*, pp. 8–10
'The Working-Man's Song', *Northern Star*, 1 May 1847

Other Works

ABBÉ, DEREK VAN, *Goethe: New Perspectives on a Writer and his Times* (London: Allen and Unwin, 1972)

ANDERSON, BENEDICT, *Imagined Communities: Reflections on the Origins and Spread of Nationalism* (London: Verso, 1983)

ARMSTRONG, ISOBEL, *Victorian Poetry: Poetry, Poetics and Politics* (London: Routledge, 1993)

ASHRAF, MARY (ed.), *Political Verse and Song from Britain and Ireland* (London: Lawrence & Wishart, 1975)

ASHTON, OWEN, ROBERT FRYSON, and STEPHEN ROBERTS (eds.), *The Chartist Legacy* (Rendlesham: Merlin Press, 1999)

BENNETT, ANDREW, *Romantic Poets and the Culture of Posterity* (Cambridge: Cambridge University Press, 1999)

BREUILLY, JOHN, GOTTFRIED NIEDHART, and ANTONY TAYLOR (eds.), *The Era of the Reform League: English Labour and Radical Politics 1857–1872* (Mannheim: Palatium, 1995)

BRISTOW, JOSEPH (ed.), *The Cambridge Companion to Victorian Poetry* (Cambridge: Cambridge University Press, 2000)

BRONTË, EMILY, *The Poems of Emily Brontë*, ed. by Derek Roper and Edward Chitham (Oxford: Clarendon, 1995)

BROWNING, ELIZABETH BARRETT, *The Works of Elizabeth Barrett Browning*, ed. by Sara Donaldson and others, 5 vols (London: Pickering & Chatto, 2010)

BRUCE, ANTHONY, *The Purchase System in the British Army, 1660–1871* (London: Royal Historical Society, 1980)

BURKE, KENNETH, *A Rhetoric of Motives* (New York: Prentice Hall, 1950)

——*Language as Symbolic Action: Essays on Life, Literature and Method* (Berkeley: University of California Press, 1968)

BYRON, GEORGE GORDON (Baron), *Don Juan*, ed. by Truman Guy Steffan and Willis W. Pratt, 4 vols (Austin: University of Texas Press, 1957)

CHASE, MALCOLM, *Chartism: A New History* (Manchester: Manchester University Press, 2007)

CLAEYS, GREGORY, *Imperial Sceptics: British Critics of Empire 1850–1920* (Cambridge: Cambridge University Press, 2010)

COLE, CHARLES, 'The Strength of Tyranny', *Northern Star*, 9 May 1846

COLE, G. D. H., *Socialist Thought: The Forerunners 1789–1850* (London: Macmillan, 1953)

COLERIDGE, SAMUEL TAYLOR, *Biographia Literaria: Or, Biographical Sketches of My Literary Life and Opinions*, 2 vols (New York: Putnam, 1848)

——*Coleridge: Selected Poems*, ed. by Richard Holmes (London: HarperCollins, 1996)

DAMES, NICHOLAS, *Amnesiac Selves: Nostalgia, Forgetting, and British Fiction, 1810–1870* (Oxford: Oxford University Press, 2001)

DARWIN, JOHN, *The Empire Project: The Rise and Fall of the British World-System, 1830–1970* (Cambridge: Cambridge University Press, 2009)

DAVENPORT, ALLEN, 'Ireland in Chains', *Northern Star*, 25 April 1846

DAVIES, IOAN, *Writers in Prison* (Oxford: Blackwell, 1990)

DEMARIA JR., ROBERT (ed.), *British Literature 1640–1789: An Anthology* (Oxford: Blackwell, 1996)

DENTITH, SIMON, *Epic and Empire in Nineteenth-Century Britain* (Cambridge: Cambridge University Press, 2007)

DONAGHY, HENRY J., *James Clarence Mangan* (New York: Twayne, 1974)

ELIADE, MIRCEA, *Myth and Reality*, trans. by Willard R. Trask (New York: Harper & Row, 1968)

ENGELS, FRIEDRICH, *The Condition of the Working Class in England*, ed. and trans. by W. O. Henderson and W. H. Chaloner (Oxford: Blackwell, 1958)

FRANTA, ANDREW, *Romanticism and the Rise of the Mass Public* (Cambridge: Cambridge University Press, 2007)

FEGAN, MELISSA, *Literature and the Irish Famine 1845–1919* (Oxford: Clarendon Press, 2002)

FOUCAULT, MICHEL, *Discipline and Punish: The Birth of the Prison*, trans. by Alan Sheridan (London: Penguin, 1991)

FRAZER, JOHN DE JEAN, 'A Word to the People', in *Political Verse and Song from Britain and Ireland*, ed. by Mary Ashraf (London: Lawrence & Wishart, 1975), p. 190

——'Harvest Pledge', *Nation*, 8 July 1848

FROST, THOMAS, 'Scott, Byron, and Shelley', *Northern Star*, 2 January 1847

FRYE, NORTHROP, *Fables of Identity: Studies in Poetic Mythology* (New York: Harcourt Brace, 1991)

GAMMAGE, R. G., *History of the Chartist Movement 1837–1854* [1854] (London: Merlin Press, 1969)

GEOGHEGAN, VINCENT, *Utopianism and Marxism* (London: Methuen, 1987)

GOTTFRIED, LEON, *Matthew Arnold and the Romantics* (London: Routledge & Keegan Paul, 1963)

GRAMSCI, ANTONIO, *Letters from Prison* (London: Jonathan Cape: 1975)

GRAY, PETER, *Famine, Land and Politics: British Government and Irish Society* (Dublin: Irish Academic Press, 1999)

HARRISON, ANTHONY H., *Victorian Poets and the Politics of Culture: Discourse and Ideology* (Charlottesville: University of Virginia, 1998)

HESS, SCOTT, 'William Wordsworth and Photographic Subjectivity', *Nineteenth-Century Literature*, 63, 3 (December 2008), 283–320

HILL, CHRISTOPHER, *A Turbulent, Seditious, and Factious People: John Bunyan and his Church* (Oxford: Oxford University Press, 1988)

HÖLDERLIN, FRIEDRICH, *Friedrich Hölderlin: Poems and Fragments*, trans. by Michael Hamburger (London: Routledge, 1966)

HOLYOAKE, G. J., *Sixty Years of an Agitator's Life*, 2 vols (London: Fisher Unwin, 1892)

JANOWITZ, ANNE, 'Ernest Jones: Who Is He? What Has He Done?', *History Workshop Journal*, 57 (Spring 2004), 283–88

—— *Lyric and Labour in the Romantic Tradition* (Cambridge: Cambridge University Press, 1998)

KLABES, GUNTER, 'Political Reality and Poetic Mission: Hölderlin's and Shelley's Heterocosm', in *English and German Romanticism: Cross-Currents and Controversies*, ed. by James Pipkin (Heidelberg: Winter, 1985), pp. 301–21

KOVALEV, Y. V., and A. A. ELISTRATOVA (eds.), *Antologiya Chartistskoi Literaturui (An Anthology of Chartist Literature)* (Moscow: Foreign Languages Publishing House, 1956)

KOHL, NORBERT, *Oscar Wilde: The Works of a Conformist Rebel*, trans. by David Henry Wilson (Cambridge: Cambridge University Press, 1989)

KUDUK, STEPHANIE, 'Sedition, Chartism, and Epic Poetry in Thomas Cooper's The Purgatory of Suicides', *Victorian Poetry*, 39, II (Summer 2001), 165–86

LANGFORD, JOHN ALFRED, *Prison Books and Their Authors* (London: Tegg, 1861)

LAWNER, LYNNE, 'Introduction', in Antonio Gramsci, *Letters from Prison* (London: Jonathan Cape, 1975)

LEAPMAN, MICHAEL, *The World for a Shilling: How the Great Exhibition of 1851 Shaped a Nation* (London: Headline, 2001)

208   BIBLIOGRAPHY

LEIGH HUNT, THORNTON (ed.), *The Correspondence of Leigh Hunt*, 2 vols (London: Smith, Elder & Co., 1862)

LINTON, WILLIAM JAMES, 'Irish Harvest Song', in Kovalev, p. 201

LLOYD, DAVID, *Nationalism and Minor Literature: James Clarence Mangan and the Emergence of Irish Cultural Nationalism* (Berkeley: University of California Press, 1987)

LOOTENS, TRICIA, 'Victorian Poetry and Patriotism', in *The Cambridge Companion to Victorian Poetry*, ed. by Joseph Bristow (Cambridge: Cambridge University Press, 2000), pp. 256–59

MAGNUSON, PAUL, 'The "Conversation" Poems', in *The Cambridge Companion to Coleridge*, ed. by Lucy Newlyn (Cambridge: Cambridge University Press, 2002), pp. 32–44

MAIDMENT, BRIAN, *The Poorhouse Fugitives: Self-taught Poets and Poetry in Victorian Britain* (Manchester: Carcanet, 1987)

MANGAN, JAMES CLARENCE, *The Collected Works of James Clarence Mangan*, ed. by Jacques Chuto and others, 4 vols (Dublin: Irish Academic Press, 1996–99)

MILL, JOHN STUART, 'Thoughts on Poetry and its Varieties', in *Dissertations and Discussions Political, Philosophical and Historical*, 2 vols (London: John W. Parker & Son, 1859–75), I

NEWLYN, LUCY (ed.), *The Cambridge Companion to Coleridge* (Cambridge: Cambridge University Press, 2002)

NEWSINGER, JOHN, *The Blood Never Dried: A People's History of the British Empire* (London: Bookmarks, 2006)

O'CONNOR, FEARGUS, and ERNEST JONES (eds.), *The Labourer: A Monthly Magazine of Politics, Literature, Poetry*, 4 vols (London: M'Gowan and Co., 1847–48)

O'GORMAN, FRANCIS (ed.), *The Cambridge Companion to Victorian Culture* (Cambridge: Cambridge University Press, 2010)

O'GORMAN, FRANCIS, 'Matthew Arnold and Rereading', *Cambridge Quarterly*, 41, 2 (2012), 245–61

O'GORMAN, FRANCIS, and KATHERINE TURNER (eds.), *The Victorians and the Eighteenth Century: Reassessing the Tradition* (Aldershot: Ashgate, 2004)

PAUL, RONALD, '"In Louring Hindostan": Chartism and Empire in Ernest Jones's *The New World, a Democratic Poem*', *Victorian Poetry*, 39.2 (Summer 2001), 189–204

PICKERING, PAUL A., '"Repeal and the Suffrage": Feargus O'Connor's Irish "Mission", 1849–50', in *The Chartist Legacy*, ed. by Owen Ashton, Robert Fryson, and Stephen Roberts (Rendlesham: Merlin Press, 1999), pp. 119–46

PIPKIN, JAMES (ed.), *English and German Romanticism: Cross-Currents and Controversies* (Heidelberg: Winter, 1985)

POULET, GEORGE, 'Phenomenology of Reading', *New Literary History*, I, (1969), 53–68

PRESCOTT, FREDERICK CLARKE, *Poetry and Myth* (New York: Macmillan, 1927)

PUGIN, A. W. N., *Contrasts: Or, a Parallel Between the Noble Edifices of the Middle Ages, and Similar Buildings of the Present Day* (London: [self-published], 1836)

RADFORD, ANDREW, and MARK SANDY (eds.), *Romantic Echoes in the Victorian Era* (Aldershot: Ashgate, 2008)

RANDALL, TIMOTHY, 'Chartist Poetry and Song', in *The Chartist Legacy*, ed. by Owen Ashton, Robert Fryson, and Stephen Roberts (Rendlesham: Merlin Press, 1999), pp. 171–95

READ, DONALD, and ERIC GLASGOW, *Feargus O'Connor: Irishman and Chartist* (London: Edward Arnold Ltd. 1961)

REYNOLDS, MATTHEW, *The Realms of Verse 1830–1870: English Poetry in a Time of Nation-Building* (Oxford: Oxford University Press, 2001)

ROBERTS, STEPHEN, *The Chartist Prisoners: The Radical Lives of Thomas Cooper (1805–1892) and Arthur O'Neill (1819–1896)* (Oxford: Lang, 2008)

ROBINSON, JEFFREY C., *Unfettering Poetry: Fancy in British Romanticism* (Basingstoke: Palgrave, 2006)

BIBLIOGRAPHY   209

ROYLE, EDWARD, *Chartism* (Harlow: Longman, 1980)
SALVESEN, CHRISTOPHER, *The Landscape of Memory: A Study of Wordsworth's Poetry* (London: Edward Arnold, 1965)
SANDERS, MIKE, ' "God is our guide! our cause is just!": The *National Chartist Hymn Book* and Victorian Hymnody', *Victorian Studies*, 54, 4 (Summer 2012), 679–705
—— *The Poetry of Chartism: Aesthetics, Politics, History,* Cambridge Studies in Nineteenth-Century Literature and Culture (Cambridge: Cambridge University Press, 2009)
SAUNDERS, ROBERT, 'Lord John Russell and Parliamentary Reform, 1848–67', *English Historical Review*, 120 (December 2005), 1289–1315
SAVILLE, JOHN (ed.), *Ernest Jones: Chartist* (London: Lawrence & Wishart, 1952)
SHELLEY, PERCY BYSSHE, *The Letters of Percy Bysshe Shelley*, ed. by Frederick L. Jones, 2 vols (Oxford: Clarendon, 1964)
—— *Shelley: Poetical Works,* ed. by Thomas Hutchinson (London: Oxford University Press, 1967)
SPIERS, EDWARD M., 'War', in *The Cambridge Companion to Victorian Culture*, ed. by Francis O'Gorman (Cambridge: Cambridge University Press, 2010), pp. 80–100
TAPPAN, EVA MARCH (ed.), *The World's Story: A History of the World in Story, Song and Art,* 14 vols (Boston: Houghton Mifflin, 1914), VII
TAYLOR, MILES, *Ernest Jones, Chartism, and the Romance of Politics 1819–69* (Oxford: Oxford University Press, 2003)
TENNYSON, ALFRED LORD, *The Poetical Works of Alfred Tennyson, Poet Laureate* (New York: Harper, 1870)
THOMPSON, DOROTHY, *The Chartists: Popular Politics in the Industrial Revolution* (New York: Pantheon Books, 1984)
TUCKER, HERBERT, *Epic Britain's Heroic Muse 1790–1910* (Oxford: Oxford University Press, 2008)
ÜHLAND, LUDWIG, *The Poems of Ludwig Ühland*, trans. by William Collett Sandars (London: Ridgway, 1869)
—— *Poems of Ühland*, ed. by Waterman T. Hewett (London: Macmillan, 1904)
VICKERS, ROY, 'Christian Election, Holy Communion and Psalmic Language in Ernest Jones's Chartist Poetry', *Journal of Victorian Culture*, 11, 1 (Spring 2006), 59–83
WELLESLEY, ARTHUR, 1st Duke of Wellington, *Memorandum on Military Governments*, 7 March 1833
C. WESTRAY, 'To the Chartists', *Northern Star*, 20 February 1841
WILLIAM S. VILLIERS SANKEY, 'Ode', in Kovalev, p. 76.
WILDE, OSCAR, *De Profundis*, ed. by Robert Ross (London: Methuen & Co., 1919)
WILLIAMSON, GEORGE S., *The Longing for Myth in Germany: Religion and Aesthetic Culture from Romanticism to Nietzsche* (Chicago: University of Chicago Press, 2004)

Newspapers

Court Journal, London, 2 May 1829–25 December 1925
★Daily News, London, 21 January 1846–11 May 1912
Deutsche Londoner Zeitung: Blätter für Politik, Literatur und Kunst, London, 4 April 1845–14 February 1851
John Bull, London, 11 December 1820–28 June 1964
★Morning Post, London, 12 February 1772–1 October 1937
Nation, Dublin, 15 October 1842–28 July 1848
★Northern Star and National Trades' Journal, Leeds, 18 November 1837–27 November 1852

★ Accessed via <http://gale.cengage.co.uk/product-highlights/history/19th-century-british-library-newspapers.aspx> [accessed 20 April 2011]

INDEX

Note: individual poems are listed by the titles under which they are substantially discussed within the relevant pages. Revised or republished pieces have the original titles placed in brackets after them.

Aberdeen, Lord 178
Akintoye, King 176
Anderson, Benedict 98–99
Armstrong, Isobel, *Victorian Poetry: Poetry, Poetics and Politics* 2, 128, 158, 162, 165, 179, 180, 198 n. 28
Arndt, Ernst Moritz 3, 19, 22–24, 55, 76
Arnold, Matthew 33
Ashraf, Mary, *Political Verse and Song from Britain and Ireland* 2, 165 n. 5
Ashton, Owen 3

Bellamy, Edward 159
Bennett, Andrew 88 n. 12
Bright, John 136
Brontë, Emily 110–11
Browning, Elizabeth Barrett 80–81, 196
Browning, Robert 8, 12, 44, 60, 191–92, 194
Bruce, Anthony 138
Bulwer-Lytton, Sir Edward 193–94, 199 n. 47
Bunyan, John 107, 124 n. 45
Burke, Kenneth 63, 77
Byron, Lord 3, 12, 22, 25, 134
    influence on Jones 12–14

Carlyle, Thomas 19, 29, 66
'Charge of the Light Brigade' 137
Chartism
    history 7–8, 157, 167–68, 184
        Land Plan 3, 8, 29, 38, 45, 49–58, 81, 148, 159, 200
Chartist Circular 69
Chase, Malcolm, *Chartism: A New History* 2, 5, 55, 123 n. 4, 167–68, 184
Chateaubriand, François René de 34
Chomsky, Noam 161
Christian Socialist Journal 118–19, 125 n. 61
Claeys, Gregory 126
Clough, Arthur Hugh 83, 196
Cobbett, William 60, 93
Cobden, Richard 136
Cole, G. D. H. 129
Coleridge, Samuel Taylor 7, 19, 105–06, 109, 111, 113
Cooper, Thomas 12, 22, 88 n. 2, 89 n. 36, 93–94, 104, 127, 164, 184–85

Court Journal 6, 19, 25, 31–34, 67, 168, 173, 182, 187, 189, 195
Crimean War 4, 136–38, 142, 166 n. 44, 183, 184, 185–89
Cumberland, Duke of (King Ernst of Hanover) 5, 34, 138, 163, 187

'D. C.' 22
Daguerre, Louis 103
Dames, Nicholas 62
Darwin, John 134
Davenport, Allen 45, 56, 61, 88 n. 2
Davies, Ioan 117
Defoe, Daniel 32
Dentith, Simon 131–32
Derby, Lord 174, 177
Deutsche Londoner Zeitung 6, 30–31, 128
Disraeli, Benjamin 46
Donaghy, Henry J. 54
Dublin University Magazine 54
Dupont, Pierre 193

Eliade, Mircea 61, 63
Eliot, George 19
Engels, Friedrich 80, 83, 126, 128
    The Condition of the Working Class in England 17
English Civil War 144–45
English Republic 184
English Restoration 146
Examiner 183

Farnham, Lord 150
Fegan, Melissa 58
Ferguson, Niall 130
First Anglo-Sikh War 140
First Reform Act (1832) 177
Foucault, Michel 96, 99, 149
Fourier, Charles 127
Fowles, John 174
Franklin, Benjamin 160
Franta, Andrew 68–69
Frazer, John de Jean 57
Freiligrath, Ferdinand 193
Friend of the People 131

INDEX   211

Frost, Thomas 12
Frye, Northrop 63, 193

Gammage, R. G., *History of the Chartist Movement 1837–54*: 4, 46, 122 n. 3
Geoghegan, Vincent 127
German Romanticism 19–31, 55, 63, 191
Gibbon, Edward 129
Glorious Revolution 146
Goethe, Johann Wolfgang von 29, 60, 98
Gottfried, Leon 12
Gramsci, Antonio 107
Gray, Peter, 42 n. 55
Great Exhibition 162–63
Grimm, Jakob 162

Harney, George Julian 70, 88 n.14, 131
Harrison, Anthony H. 66–67
Heine, Heinrich 32
Hemans, Dorothea Felicia 83
Hess, Scott 103
Hill, Christopher 106
Holyoake, G. J. 46
Hölderlin, Friedrich 24–25
Homer 132, 164
Horace 3, 65 n. 33
Humboldt, Wilhelm von 162
Hunt, James Leigh 17, 93, 127–28

Indian Uprising (Rebellion) 41 n. 8, 126, 136, 168
Irish Famine 54–57, 149, 150
Irish Nationalism 3, 53–59, 152, 201

Jameson, Fredric 134
Janowitz, Anne 129
    Lyric and Labour in the Romantic Tradition 2, 51, 61, 86, 90, 109, 126, 128, 165
John Bull 178, 181
Jones, Ebenezer 45, 75
Jones, Ernest Charles:
    life:
        arrest and imprisonment 6, 91–96, 123 n. 7
        birth 5
        Chartist 'conversion' 6, 11, 21, 40–41, 44–45, 71
        Chartist leadership 6, 74, 144, 172, 197
        death 7
        father, Captain Charles Jones 5, 28, 34, 138
        internationalism 81–83, 128–29, 162, 176, 179, 189
        schooling 5, 19, 98
        wife, Jane Atherley 6, 191
    poems:
        'The Age of Peace' 84–87
        'The Battle-Day; Or, The Lost Army' ('Lord Lindsay') 179, 182
        'Beldagon Church: A Religious Poem' 168, 169–70, 190

'The Better Hope' 28–29, 33–34, 68, 81, 121
'The Blackstone Edge Gathering' 2, 9, 9 n. 1, 28, 77–81, 170
'The Boy's Mountain Song' (trans. from Ühland) 25, 27–28
'Britannia' 132, 176, 189
'A Chartist Chorus' 65 n. 42
'A Chartist March' 175
'Christian Love' 9, 168, 171–73
'The Coming Day' 184
'Corayda' 187, 194–95
'The Cornfield and the Factory' 14, 32, 35, 38–39, 43 n. 57, 44–45, 52, 104, 132, 173, 200
'The Cost of Glory' ('The Painter of Florence') 182
'The Cry of the Russian Serf to the Czar' ('Our Destiny') 173, 179, 181–82, 184
'Der Deutsche Sprachschatz' 30, 162, 200
'The Diver' (trans. from Schiller) 195
'Earth's Burdens' 193
'Easter Hymn' 120, 181
'England' 62–63, 84
'England's Greatness' 65 n. 42, 71, 132, 139, 176, 189
'The Factory Town' 49–53, 65 n. 42, 139
'The Farmer' ('The Peasant') 14, 35, 39–40
'The Farmer's Last New Song' 174
'The Fountains of History' 189
'The Garden Seat' 101–07, 110, 112, 117, 122, 164, 184
'Geister-Ahnung' 33–34
'The German Boy's Song' (trans. from Stolberg') 28
'Give me that faded flower' 190–91
'Der Glocken-ruf' 33
'The Golden Harp' 35, 37–38
'The Goodwin Sands' 32–33
'Hymn for Ascension Day' 120, 181
'Hymn for Lammas-Day' 120–22, 181
'The Invasion' 174, 175–76, 185
'The Italian Exile to his Countrymen' ('Our Cheer') 173, 179, 184
'The Jacksons' 192
'Das Lebens-Ziel' 33
'Licht und Sprachte' 30, 200
'Lines on the Brocken' 32
'Lines on Lady Stepney's New Work' 31–32
'Lines on Miss Adelaide Kemble' 31–32
'Lord Derby' 174
'Lord Palmerston's Song' 174
'The March of Freedom' 56–57, 87–88, 121, 140
'The Minstrel's Curse' (trans. from Ühland) 25–26, 168, 173, 182, 187
'Miss Twad, and the Marquis de Sansterre' 191–92
'The Monarch's Death-Prayer' (trans. from Ühland) 25, 26, 182, 187, 195

'The New World, a Democratic Poem' 4, 6, 8, 9, 14, 15, 95, 107, 126–66, 168, 169, 176, 187, 189, 201
'The New Year's Song of Our Exile' 84
'On Hearing of the Fall of Sebastopol' 192
'Onward' 18, 64 n. 7, 90
'Our Cheer' 49, 51, 71, 76–77, 121
'Our Destiny' 71, 72–74
'Our Summons' 71, 72, 139
'Our Trust' 64 n. 7
'Our Warning' 71, 74–75
'The Painter of Florence: A Domestic Poem' 13, 14, 170
'The Patriot's Test' 175
'Peace to Earth' 35–37, 189
'The Peasant' 38, 39–40
'Percy Vere' (*My Life*) 184, 193
'The Poet's Death' ('To Chateaubriand') 34–35, 184, 191
'The Poet's Invitation' ('The Garden Seat') 184
'The Poet's Mission' ('To Louis Philippe'/'To Byron') 20–25, 174
'The Poet's Prayer to the Evening Wind' 15, 184
'Poland's Hope' 84
'Politische' 30–31, 200
'Prison Bars' 100, 117, 122
'The Prisoner's Dream' 110–17, 122, 164, 190
'A Prisoner's Night-Thought' 98–100, 101, 117, 122
'The Quack' 174, 177
'The Queen's Bounty' 168
'The Rainbow of Hope' 32
'Reform' 174, 177–78
'St Coutts's' 117–20
'The Sea Shell on the Desert' 193
'Signs of Glory' 189
'The Silent Cell' 107–10, 116, 122
'The Slave Ship' 171
'The Song of the Low' 2, 9 n. 1, 15–16, 77, 90, 171
'The Song of the Starving' 139
'A Song for the People' 57
'The Stars' (trans. from Arndt) 32, 173
'The Stranger Knight' 191
'The Sun' 32
'To Chateaubriand: A Voice from England to the Stranger Bard' 34–35, 184
'To Her' 31, 173, 189, 193
'To Wordsworth' 14
'The Two Races' 46–49, 71, 144, 147
'Victory of Lagos' 174, 176–77
'The Walk Home from Beldgaon' 168
'The Waves and the War' 185–89
'The Working-Man's Song' 81–83, 90, 120, 121
publications:
  Battle-Day: And Other Poems 16, 34, 168, 174, 178–85

  Cabinet Newspaper 196
  Chartist Lyrics and Fugitive Pieces 71, 179
  Corayda: A Tale of Faith and Chivalry, and Other Poems 4, 168, 174
  The Emperor's Vigil and The Waves and the War 168, 174, 185–89
  Infantine Effusions 5
  Labourer 6, 58, 131, 180, 194
  My Life 6, 44
  Notes to the People 4, 13, 96–173, 184
  People's Paper 179, 196
  Poetic Thoughts of E. C. J. 4, 174, 189–93, 202
  The Revolt of Hindostan (see also 'The New World') 4, 15, 41 n. 8, 126, 164, 174. 193
  Rhymes on the Times 4, 173–78, 185, 202
  Songs of Democracy 193
  The Wood Spirit 6

Kalevala 194
Keats, John 12, 31, 132
Klabes, Gunter 25
Kohl, Norbert 99
Kosoko, King 176
Kovalev, Y. V., *An Anthology of Chartist Literature* 2, 22
Kuduk, Stephanie 94
Kydd, Samuel 70, 88 n. 14

Lamb, Charles 105
Landar, William Collett 25
Landon, Letitia Elizabeth 155
Lang, Fritz 160
Langford, John Alfred 123 n. 16
Lawner, Lynne 107
Leibniz, Gottfried 78
Linton, William James 12, 22, 45, 56, 75, 184
Lloyd, David 55
London Working Man's Association 7
Longfellow, Henry Wadsworth 131

Maclise, Daniel 54
Magnuson, Paul 105
Maidment, Brian
  The Poorhouse Fugitives: Self-taught Poets and Poetry in Victorian Britain 2, 48, 61, 67–68, 75
Mangan, James Clarence 53–55, 150–51
Martineau, Harriet 58
Marx, Karl 32, 80, 83, 89 n. 32, 126, 128–29, 146
Massey, Gerald 62–63
Maudsley, Joseph 198 n. 13
Mazzini, Giuseppe 179
McDouall, Peter Murray 70, 88 n. 14
medievalism 3, 8, 58–63, 101, 194
Miani, Battle of 140
Mill, John Stuart 180, 193
Milton, John 120
Mitchell, John 91, 123 n. 8
Mogador, Bombardment of 35–36

Moore, Thomas 28
Morning Chronicle 195–96
Morning Post 6, 34–40, 55, 164–65, 168, 184, 200
mythopoeia 3, 8, 44–65, 82

Napier, Sir Charles 140, 174, 185
Napoleon III 176
Nation 37, 54, 57
natural theology 75–76
New Quarterly Review 44
Newport Rising 7
Newsinger, John 130
Northern Star 2, 6, 8, 12, 19, 20, 41, 44–89, 90, 117,
  131, 132, 133, 137, 139, 166 n. 30, 174, 180,
  183–84, 187

O'Connell, Daniel 37, 55
O'Connor, Feargus 7, 8, 29, 38, 45, 58, 93, 97, 169,
  171, 178
O'Gorman, Francis 41 n. 5, 68, 166 n. 37
O'Neill, Arthur 93–94
Owen, Robert 127

Park, Mungo 155
Paul, Ronald, "In louring Hindostan': Chartism and
  Empire in Ernest Jones's *The New World, A
  Democratic Poem*' 2, 90, 96, 129, 146, 161, 165
Peterloo Massacre 5, 15
phenomenology 3, 67–71
Philippe, Louis 21, 34
Pickering, Paul A. 55
Poe, Edgar Allan 131, 165 n. 21
Pope, Alexander 132
Poulet, George 67, 70–71
Prescott, Frederick Clarke 63
Pugin, Augustus W. N. 45

Radford, Andrew, and Mark Sandy, *Romantic Echoes in
  the Victorian Era* 12
Randall, Timothy 3, 132
Red Republican 131
Reform League 7, 95, 123 n. 20, 178, 196
Repeal Association 37, 55, 91
Retreat from Kabul 136–37
Reynolds, Matthew 71
Roberts, Stephen 93–94
Robinson, Jeffrey C. 111
Royle, Edward 126
Rückert, Friedrich 3, 19, 55
Ruskin, John 66
Russell, Lord John 174, 177, 178

Saint-Simon, Henri 127
Salvesen, Chistopher 115–16
Sanders, Mike 180–81
  The Poetry of Chartism: Aesthetics, Politics, History 2,
    8, 12, 57, 62–63, 70, 75

Sankey, William S. Villiers 17
Saunders, Robert 177
Saville, John, *Ernest Jones: Chartist* 2, 5, 21, 74, 94–95, 128
Schiller, Friedrich 3, 19, 193
Schleicher, August 162
Scott, Sir Walter 60
Second Punic War 143
Second Reform Act (1967 Representation of the
  People Act) 7
Shakespeare, William 108
Shelley, Mary 75
Shelley, Percy Bysshe 3, 6, 12, 21, 25, 40, 49, 51,
  68–69, 73, 75, 132, 134, 147, 151, 168
  influence on Jones 14–18
Smith, Charlotte 33
Soanes, George 191
Southey, Robert 12, 14, 134
Spectator 181
Spiers, Edward M. 136
Stepney, Lady Catherine 32
Stolberg, Friedrich Leopold von 3, 19, 28, 55
Stott, Benjamin 66, 88 n. 2
Swift, Jonathan 192

Talbot, William Henry Fox 103
Taylor, Miles, *Ernest Jones, Chartism, and the Romance of
  Politics 1819–69:* 2, 4, 5, 6, 43 n. 57, 59–60, 74, 92,
  95–96, 174, 179, 180, 199 n. 47
Tennyson, Alfred Lord 8, 12, 44, 60, 71, 135–36, 183,
  194
Thompson, Dorothy, *The Chartists: Popular Politics in the
  Industrial Revolution* 2, 5, 55, 58–59, 167, 184
Times 91, 100, 138, 150, 176
Tucker, Herbert 131, 162

Ühland, Ludwig 3, 19, 24, 76, 168, 182, 187, 193
  influence on Jones 25–28

Verne, Jules 159
Vickers, Roy, 'Christian Election, Holy Communion,
  and Psalmic Language in Ernest Jones's Chartist
  Poetry' 2, 183
Voltaire 78

Wagner, Richard 20
Walcott, Derek 132
Waterloo, Battle of 138, 176
Wellesley, Arthur, 1st Duke of Wellington 136, 138,
  166 n. 37, 166 n. 39, 175–76
Wells, H. G. 159
Wilde, Oscar 99–100, 115
Williamson, George S. 20
Wordsworth, William 3, 12, 19, 115
  influence on Jones 14

Young, Edward 98
Young Ireland Movement 55, 91